Presidential Debates

Presidential Debates

FORTY YEARS OF HIGH-RISK TV

Alan Schroeder

Columbia University Press   New York

COLUMBIA UNIVERSITY PRESS
Publishers Since 1893
New York   Chichester, West Sussex

Copyright © 2000 Columbia University Press

Library of Congress Cataloging-in-Publication Data

Schroeder, Alan, 1954–
Presidential debates : forty years of high-risk TV /
Alan Schroeder.
p. cm.
Includes bibliographical references and index.
ISBN 0–231–11400–1 (alk. paper)
1. Campaign debates—United States.
2. Television in politics—United States.
3. Presidents—United States—Election.
I. Title: Forty years of high-risk TV. II. Title.

JF2112.D43 S37 2000
324.7'3'0973—dc21   00–035831

Printed in the United States of America
Designed by Audrey Smith

c 10 9 8 7 6 5 4 3 2 1

THIS BOOK IS DEDICATED TO

Carl, Jennifer, and Kirsten Schroeder,
and Dan Hammons

Contents

ACKNOWLEDGMENTS ix

Introduction: The First Presidential Debate 1

Part I: PREPRODUCTION
Chapter One: The Predebate Debate 13
Chapter Two: Strategy and Preparation 38
Chapter Three: Predebate News Coverage 65

Part II: PRODUCTION
Chapter Four: The Debaters 95
Chapter Five: The Questioners 124
Chapter Six: The Productions 148

Part III: POSTPRODUCTION
Chapter Seven: Postdebate News Coverage   173
Chapter Eight: The Audience   200

Conclusion: The Future of Presidential Debates   215

NOTES   223

REFERENCES   253

SCHEDULE OF TELEVISED PRESIDENTIAL
AND VICE PRESIDENTIAL DEBATES: 1960–1996   259

INDEX   263

Acknowledgments

The author would like to acknowledge the many individuals who have made this book possible. Particular thanks are owed to those whose contributions went beyond the call of duty and whose guidance put me on a path to other valuable sources: Bob Asman, Bob Barnett, Rick Berke, David Broder, Janet Brown, Marty Brownstein, Hal Bruno, Diana Carlin, Steve Chaggaris, Steve Doocy, Ed Fouhy, Bob Goodwin, James Hoge, Mickey Kantor, Joshua King, Jim Lehrer, Richard C. Leone, Barry Paris, Marty Plissner, Sam Popkin, Adam Rosman, Kevin Sauter, Carole Simpson, Margaret Warner, Brady Williamson, and Judy Woodruff. I also thank Claire Denzler and Hank Price at WBBM in Chicago, Roma Hare at WETA in Washington, D.C., and Erin O'Connor at NBC New York.

I am indebted to Gary Orren and Marvin Kalb, my professors at the John F. Kennedy School of Government, as well as Pippa Norris of the *Harvard International Journal of Press/Politics*, for their encouragement.

Thanks, too, to the staffs of the various libraries and archives used in my research, especially John Lynch at the Vanderbilt Television News Archives; Bruce Dumont at the Chicago Museum of Broadcasting; Jim Cidrone of the John F. Kennedy Library; Susan Naulty of the Richard Nixon Library; Bob Bohannon and David Stanhope at the Jimmy Carter Library; Geir Gundersen of the Gerald R. Ford Library; Mike Dugan of the Ronald Reagan Library; Linda L. Schuler of the Ronald Reagan Center for Public Affairs; Debbie Carter of the George Bush Library; and others on the efficient and helpful staffs at the Kennedy, Nixon, Ford, Carter, Reagan, and Bush libraries, as well as the Library of Congress.

My grateful appreciation goes to Ann Miller of Columbia University Press for her confidence and direction during the writing process. I also thank Liz Hartman, Anne McCoy, and Ron Harris of Columbia University Press and Rita Bernhard for her invaluable editorial suggestions.

Finally, I would like to thank my colleagues at Northeastern University in Boston. This project was generously supported by a research and development grant from the Office of the Provost and by faculty development stipends from the School of Journalism. Thanks to Dean James Stellar and associate deans Malcolm Hill and Kay Onan in the College of Arts and Sciences, and, most particularly, my compatriots in the School of Journalism: Belle Adler, Nicholas Daniloff, Charles Fountain, William Kirtz, Laurel Leff, Gladys McKie, and James Ross. Your support and friendship are deeply appreciated.

Presidential Debates

Introduction

THE FIRST PRESIDENTIAL DEBATE

*I should say the most important thing about the business of govern-
ment and politics is not to bore the people.*
  —*Richard Nixon to Jack Paar on the Tonight Show, 25 August 1960*

26 September 1960. At exactly 7:30 P.M., a shiny Oldsmobile
carrying Vice President Richard M. Nixon pulled into an interior drive at
the CBS broadcast facility in downtown Chicago. As with other details surrounding the first presidential debate in history, the timing of Nixon's
arrival at this skating rink–turned-TV station had been meticulously plot-
ted. Like dueling divas, Nixon and his opponent, John F. Kennedy, would
reach the studio a comfortable quarter hour apart.

For Richard Nixon, the evening began almost as unpromisingly as it
would end. Stepping out of the backseat of the car, he banged his knee
sharply and painfully against the door; bystanders waiting to greet him saw
the color drain from his face. Just two weeks earlier, the vice president had
concluded twelve days of hospitalization for a knee infection caused by a
similar mishap with a car door. Almost immediately after his release, Nixon
had bounded back onto the campaign trail, hoping to make up for lost time
with an intensive schedule of cross-country travel. Now, heading into the

most critical media event of his life, he looked exhausted, underweight, and wan—"better suited for going to a funeral, perhaps his own, than to a debate," in the view of journalist David Halberstam.[1]

At the WBBM loading dock, Nixon quickly composed himself and started through a high-power receiving line. Gathered to greet this first of the star debaters were the titans of American broadcasting: fierce competitors like William Paley of CBS, Robert Sarnoff of NBC, and Leonard Goldenson of ABC, momentarily allied in their patronage of the 1960 debates. Working the line, Nixon came to Oliver Treyz, the president of ABC News, who greeted the candidate by asking what no one else had dared: "How do you feel?"

At a dinner commemorating the debate twenty-five years later, Treyz would recall the moment: "I asked the question because he looked ill. And he said, 'Not so well. I have a temperature of a hundred and two degrees.'" When Nixon pulled from his pocket the bottle of Terramycin he was taking, Treyz asked if he wished to cancel. Nixon declined, saying he did not want to be seen as a coward.[2]

Poor physical health and a freshly injured knee were only the beginning of Richard Nixon's troubles. For weeks, a more vexing problem had been brewing: a lack of appreciation by campaign decision makers for the momentousness of the occasion. "Nixon knew the power of television very well," said Ted Rogers, Nixon's TV adviser, "but I don't think the people around him did." According to Rogers, Kennedy's staff handled their candidate as a thoroughbred, while Nixon's treated theirs like a mule, "working him to death."[3] Nixon had turned down an invitation from debate producer-director Don Hewitt for a preproduction meeting; Kennedy used his session to grill the director about staging details. As Hewitt saw it, for Nixon the debate was "just another campaign appearance."[4]

To prepare for the broadcast, Vice President Nixon studied briefing books alone, dismissing suggestions that he rehearse with aides. Senator Kennedy, by contrast, brought an entourage to Chicago two days ahead of schedule and spent much of the weekend holed up in a hotel suite practicing his responses out loud. In the hours immediately before broadcast, members of Kennedy's campaign team were still lobbing questions at him.

Fifteen minutes after Nixon's arrival at WBBM, the network executives reassembled to greet the man who would emerge as the evening's undisputed champion. Unlike his Republican counterpart, John F. Kennedy arrived fit, rested, and ready. Weeks of open-air campaigning around the country had left Kennedy bronzed and glowing. Journalist Howard K. Smith, who moderated the first debate, would compare JFK to an "athlete come to receive his wreath of laurel." Said Nixon adviser Rogers, "When he came in the studio I thought he was Cochise, he was so tan."[5]

As Kennedy strode down the long corridor linking the driveway to Studio One, Nixon was already on the debate set, posing for cameramen with an air of jocularity that would quickly evaporate. "Have you ever had a picture printed yet?" Nixon teased one of the photographers, getting a laugh from the group. "You're always taking them, I never see them printed." Kennedy's entrance into the studio a few moments later immediately siphoned attention away from Nixon. "I assume you two guys know each other," Hewitt cracked, as the rivals extended their hands in greeting. The cameramen clamored for shots of the pair shaking hands; over and over they obliged, their chit-chat muffled by the sound of flashbulbs.

"You get that tan the way I do?" Nixon asked Kennedy, prefiguring post-debate interest in the candidates' appearance. "Riding around in open cars? It's the wind, you know, not the sun." Though Kennedy's answer is not recorded, it is apparent from the question that the vice president was struck by how well his opponent looked. Did Nixon sense that his own posthospital pallor was no match for Kennedy's summer glow? For weeks, TV consultant Rogers had urged Nixon to use a sunlamp. Like most of Rogers's advice, the recommendation went unheeded.

After shooing away the photographers, Don Hewitt ushered Kennedy and Nixon to their seats on the debate set for a quick orientation. Footage of this meeting shows Nixon casting his glance at a monitor off-screen, uncomfortably shifting positions in his chair, seeming to pass in and out of a daze. Kennedy, who does not deign to look at Nixon, occupies his side of the studio set with the casual presumption of a lion in his den.

To both debaters Hewitt offered the services of CBS's top makeup artist, imported from New York for the occasion. When Kennedy said no, Nixon quickly followed suit, in a show of machismo that proved to be a serious tactical blunder. "What I tried to explain to Dick," Rogers later recalled, "was he has a certain characteristic of his skin where it's almost transparent. And it was a very nice thought to say 'I don't want any makeup,' but he really needed it in order to have what we would call even an acceptable television picture."[6]

Nixon himself knew this. Two weeks before the first debate, he spoke of the cosmetic peculiarities of his skin in a TV interview with Walter Cronkite: "I can shave within thirty seconds before I go on television and still have a beard, unless we put some powder on, as we have done today."[7] Instead of a proper predebate makeup job, an aide slathered Nixon's face with an over-the-counter cosmetic called "Lazy Shave," the same product the vice president had worn in his "kitchen debate" with Nikita Khrushchev a year earlier. Meanwhile, unknown to Nixon, Kennedy got a touch-up from his own people.

In the technical checks that followed, each debater took a final opportunity to sit before the lens for last-minute adjustments. Kennedy advisers examined the shade of their man's dark suit to make sure an appropriate contrast would be achieved on camera, and a staff person was dispatched back to the hotel for a blue shirt, which the senator donned for the broadcast. Another handler had brought along a pair of long socks, in case regular socks looked too short when the candidates were shown sitting on the set.

If JFK's tech check was obsessive, the other side's was fatalistic. Alarmed by Nixon's on-screen appearance, Hewitt asked Ted Rogers if he approved of the way his debater looked. Although Rogers pronounced himself "satisfied"[8]—"resigned" might have been a better word—Hewitt felt concerned enough to press the matter with his CBS boss, Frank Stanton. Stanton again asked Rogers if the shots of Nixon were acceptable, and again Rogers said yes.

Exacerbating his misfortune, Nixon had selected a light gray suit which, according to CBS News president Sig Mickelson, "blended into the background and, if anything, exaggerated his pale appearance."[9] At the Republicans' insistence, stagehands repainted the gray backdrop several times in the hours before the debate, but each new coat dried lighter than Nixon's people had anticipated. As air time approached, the backdrop was still moist from the latest application.

With less than half an hour to go, both candidates retired to their dressing rooms.

In Hyannis Port, Massachusetts, Jacqueline Kennedy, six-months pregnant with her second child, was hosting a debate-watching party. About thirty people had gathered in the Kennedys' summer home on Nantucket Sound, where the guest list included Jackie's sister, Lee Radziwill; Professor and Mrs. Archibald Cox; Professor and Mrs. Arthur Schlesinger Jr.; Democratic committeewomen from around New England; and, last but not least, about a dozen journalists.

The Kennedy "Listening Party," as the newspapers would anachronistically term it, offers further evidence of how differently the two political camps regarded the debate. While the wife of the Democratic candidate used the occasion for public relations, Patricia Nixon spent a quiet evening watching at home with her two daughters in Washington, out of sight of reporters until the next day, when she would be enlisted for damage control.

The Boston press breathlessly reported every detail of Jacqueline Kennedy's party on this cool Cape Cod evening: the coffee and pastries in the dining room; the lemon-yellow couch where the hostess perched next to Professor Cox; two-and-a-half-year-old Caroline sleeping upstairs; Jackie's pearl necklace and coral-colored, silk maternity dress. Sensitive to recent press reports about her expensive wardrobe, Mrs. Kennedy assured reporters that the outfit had been sewn by a local seamstress.

Jacqueline Kennedy had rented a sixteen-inch portable television set for the debate. "I own one in Washington," she told her guests, "but we don't have one here. I guess I'll have to break down and buy one." A *Boston Globe* photo showed the TV set incongruously situated atop a piece of antique furniture identified as an "early American Governor Winthrop desk."[10]

As the program drew nearer, Jacqueline confessed to being nervous. "I'm not apprehensive," she said in the debutante voice the whole country would soon recognize. "But I'm always nervous before he speaks. I must say I have no reason to be." With partygoers scattered around the room in chairs and on the floor, the moment approached. Mrs. Kennedy herself clicked on the set, took a deep breath, and sat down to watch.

"The candidates need no introduction," began moderator Howard K. Smith. And for the next hour the country's first televised presidential debate unfolded, attracting the largest audience that had ever assembled for a political event. An estimated seventy million Americans watched on TV, while several million more listened on radio.[11]

The issues Kennedy and Nixon addressed were familiar to anyone following the news in 1960: communism and national security; labor and farm problems; the candidates' leadership experience. Though the substance of their remarks would account for most of the ink in the next day's papers, it was the debaters' personal characteristics that resonated most strongly with the viewers. "Within hours," wrote David Halberstam, "no one could recall anything that was said, only what they looked like, what they felt like."[12]

In his landmark book *The Making of the President*, campaign chronicler Theodore White famously limned the contrast between performers:

Kennedy "calm and nerveless in appearance," Nixon "tense, almost fright-ened, at turns glowering and, occasionally, haggard-looking to the point of sickness." For Richard Nixon, White concluded, "everything that could have gone wrong that night went wrong."[13] Media historian Erik Barnouw noted that Kennedy's "air of confidence" came across not only in his statements and gestures but more crucially during the cutaway reaction shots: "A glimpse of the listening Kennedy showed him attentive, alert, with a sugges-tion of a smile on his lips. A Nixon glimpse showed him haggard; the lines on his face seemed like gashes and gave a fearful look."[14]

What viewers at home could not know was that these same images were igniting a parallel debate in the control room of WBBM-TV, where the issue was not public policy but visual aesthetics. Candidate cutaways had been a flashpoint in the lengthy and contentious predebate negotiations between the campaigns and the networks, but no firm guidelines emerged as to how the program would be shot. By prior agreement, the candidates' television representatives sat in the control room during the program: Ted Rogers for Nixon and, for Kennedy, a former WBBM producer named Bill Wilson. With the debate under way, Wilson chided Hewitt that he "owed" Kennedy more reaction shots.

"What do you mean?" Hewitt asked. "I've cut away from Kennedy more than I've cut away from Nixon."

But the reaction shots Wilson wanted were of Nixon. The two advisers got into a heated argument with each other and with Hewitt, each side demanding more reactions of the other's candidate, each keeping a running count of the cutaways. Hewitt was hollering at them both to stop interfer-ing with his work, which, as he saw it, was to serve as a surrogate for people watching in their living rooms. "I didn't try to catch the candidates in a gri-mace," Hewitt later explained. "I listened to the comments and tried to anticipate the public—to switch to a reaction shot when I thought viewers would expect one."[15] Although Nixon's close-up cutaways would loom larg-er in the national perception than Kennedy's, postdebate tallies showed eleven reactions of Kennedy running a total of 118 seconds, compared to nine of Nixon totalling 85 seconds.

The potency of these images may unintentionally have been enhanced by improvements in TV technology. The day before the debate, CBS engineers outfitted the studio cameras with new tubes that delivered a sharper than normal picture. "This was unfortunate for Nixon," CBS's Mickelson con-cluded. "The cameras exaggerated his paleness and heavy beard, but it was a break for Kennedy, who looked robust and healthy. As the cameras had exaggerated Nixon's apparent ill health, they likewise enhanced Kennedy's rugged vitality."[16] An additional visual factor must be considered: as black and white broadcasts, the debates exuded a documentary crispness that verged on the hyperreal. Especially when compared to debates from later, color-TV years, the 1960 debates offer the clarity and punch of a *Life* magazine photo essay come to life.

Beyond production considerations, an eleventh-hour phone call from running mate Henry Cabot Lodge apparently helped steer Nixon onto the wrong tactical course. Lodge, who had debated Kennedy in their senatorial race in 1952, advised Nixon to take the high road and "erase the assassin image" that had dogged him throughout his political career.[17] And so it was that Richard Nixon adopted a posture of conciliation, even deference, to his fellow debater. "The things that Senator Kennedy has said many of us can agree with," Nixon declared in his opening statement. "I can subscribe completely to the spirit that Senator Kennedy has expressed tonight."[18] At one point, the Republican nominee chose to forgo a response altogether, passing up the opportunity to rebut his opponent's remarks.

"Thank you, gentlemen. This hour has gone by all too quickly." With this coda from Howard K. Smith, the historic encounter drew to a close. In Texas, Henry Cabot Lodge, the running mate who had counseled gentility in his predebate phone call to Nixon, was heard to say, "That son of a bitch just cost us the election."[19]

Before leaving the studio, Kennedy and Nixon posed for a final round of photographs, making small talk about travel schedules and weather as the shutters clicked away. Afterward, JFK told an aide that whenever a photographer prepared to snap, Nixon "would put a stern expression on his face and start jabbing his finger into my chest, so he would look as if he was laying down the law to me about foreign policy or communism. Nice fellow."[20]

Outside the TV station, a crowd of twenty-five hundred political enthusiasts had gathered in the street. Asked by a reporter to estimate the ratio of Democrats to Republicans, a Chicago police officer quipped, "I'd say it's about twenty-five hundred to zero."[21] As Nixon slipped out the back, Kennedy triumphantly emerged at the main entrance of the building to greet his supporters. "When it was all over," Don Hewitt said, "a man walked out of this studio president of the United States. He didn't have to wait til election day."[22]

In what history records as the first example of postdebate spin, Jacqueline Kennedy turned to her guests at program's end and exclaimed, "I think my husband was brilliant."

For most of the hour, Mrs. Kennedy had watched the debate "almost immobile," as one observer put it, though she did get up several times to adjust the picture on the temperamental TV set. Others in the highly partisan Kennedy living room broke into laughter when Nixon misspoke and declared, "It's our responsibility that we get rid of the farmer," before correcting himself and saying, "the surpluses." The hostess concealed her reaction to this verbal slip behind a "Mona Lisa–kind of smile."[23]

Fifteen minutes after the debate ended, the phone rang at the Kennedy home in Hyannis Port: The senator was on the line. Jacqueline took the call upstairs, away from the guests, and reappeared a few minutes later. Her husband had asked about the listening party, she said; otherwise their conversation remained private. One of the reporters present wrote that after the call Mrs. Kennedy was "as flushed with happiness and suppressed excitement as a schoolgirl."[24]

Richard Nixon's first indication that the debate had not gone his way came from long-time secretary Rose Mary Woods, a woman he counted among his most honest critics. Shortly after the broadcast, Woods got a call from her parents in Ohio, who asked if the vice president was feeling well. When the debate aired in California, Nixon's own mother phoned with the same question. And so the reaction went. "I recognized the basic mistake I had made," Nixon would write in *Six Crises*. "I had concentrated too much on substance and not enough on appearance. I should have remembered that 'a picture is worth a thousand words.' "[25]

Indeed. In the days that followed, the thousands of words printed about the first Kennedy-Nixon debate would be no match for the pictures that had seared themselves into the nation's consciousness. Patricia Nixon, flying to her husband's side the next day, gamely told a reporter, "He looked wonderful on my TV set." Nixon himself assured interviewers that, despite a weight loss, he felt fine. Press secretary Herbert Klein lamented that "the fault obviously was television," while other Republicans voiced public displeasure with their candidate's kid-gloves approach to his opponent.[26]

JFK, on the other hand, reaped an immediate windfall. Theodore White described the change in the crowds that turned out for Kennedy the next day in northern Ohio: "Overnight, they seethed with enthusiasm and multiplied in numbers, as if the sight of him, in their homes on the video box, had given him a 'star quality' reserved only for television and movie idols." *Time* magazine wrote that before the debate reporters had amused themselves by counting "jumpers" in the crowds—women who hopped up and down to get a better look at Kennedy. "Now they noted 'double jumpers' (jumpers with babies in their arms). By week's end they even spotted a few 'leapers' who reached prodigious heights."[27]

Although the mythology surrounding the first Kennedy-Nixon broadcast would greatly amplify in the years to follow, the moral of the story has never varied: presidential debates are best apprehended as *television shows*, governed not by the rules of rhetoric or politics but by the demands of their host medium. The values of debates are the values of television: celebrity, visuals, conflict, and hype. On every level, Kennedy and his team perceived this, while Nixon and his did not.

After Chicago, campaigns would have no choice but to school themselves in the subtleties of the small screen; eagerly have they taken to the task. "It didn't matter whether the televised debate had been decisive in Kennedy's victory," wrote social critic Todd Gitlin. "What mattered was that the management of television was one factor that candidates believed they could control. The time of the professional media consultant had arrived."[28]

Today, with the merger of politics and television complete, presidential debates operate as a wholly owned subsidiary of the campaigns. Candidates and their handlers dominate every step of the process, from make-or-break issues like participation, schedule, and format to such arcana as podium placement, camera angles, and which star gets which dressing room. Nothing is unnegotiated, nothing left to chance.

Still, when the red light blinks on to signal the start of the program, the steamroller nature of live TV supersedes the campaigns' stewardship. Spontaneity is the overriding determinant of presidential debates, and a major reason, perhaps *the* major reason, audiences continue to watch in such staggering numbers. "Modern debates are the political version of the Indianapolis Speedway," says political scientist Nelson Polsby. "What we're all there for—the journalist, the political pundits, the public—is to see somebody crack up in flames."[29]

Presidential Debates: Forty Years of High-Risk TV will take the reader on a backstage tour through the fractious world of presidential debates, where the perils are enormous and the precautions illusory. We will meet the cast of characters in the behind-the-scenes drama: the candidate-stars, who perform under unimaginable pressure before the largest audiences of their careers; the advisers, who strive to protect them by whatever means necessary; the journalists, who narrate, and reinterpret, their story; the moderators and questioners, who serve as supporting players; the debate sponsors and production crews, who navigate a minefield of politics and egos to bring the programs to air; and the viewers, the ostensible beneficiaries of the exercise, who have been accurately labeled the "forgotten participants."[30]

We will approach presidential debates as their producers do, traveling along a chronology of preproduction, production, and postproduction, the standard time line by which all television shows are staged. By definition, the live telecast overshadows all else; but as the experience of 1960 shows, debates are also profoundly influenced by what happens before and after the fact—in the campaign, in the media, in the body politic. Thus our exploration begins with the predebate period, when rules are hammered out, candidates prepped, and press expectations set, and ends in the postdebate aftermath, when media interpretations and viewer reactions finally wrest control of the event away from the politicians.

The images of John F. Kennedy and Richard M. Nixon that filled the air waves on 26 September 1960 can be read as harbingers of change. A revolutionary programming genre burst forth that night in Chicago, one that fundamentally realigned both politics and the media in America. In the forty years since Kennedy-Nixon, televised debates have lost none of their fascination for the press and the public, and none of their terror for candidates. Choreographed and unscripted, contrived and authentic, debates straddle the fault line between artifice and reality—like everything else on TV, only more so. With their clashing co-stars, enormous stakes, and "must-see" status, presidential debates are nothing so much as television writ large.

Part I

PREPRODUCTION

Chapter One

THE PREDEBATE DEBATE

A few weeks after losing the 1960 election, Richard Nixon went for a sail off the coast of Florida with a group of associates that included a trusted adviser named Leonard Hall. As David Halberstam recounted in a 1976 essay on the Kennedy-Nixon debates,

> There were just a few old friends around and they all went out on a boat. Finally, Hall asked the question he had always wanted to ask— Why did you decide to debate? For a long time Nixon simply looked up at the sky, his eyes closed, his face drawn and tense. And Hall waited, but there was never an answer.[1]

In retrospect, the participation of Richard Nixon in the 1960 debates qualifies as one of the great political miscalculations in campaign history. Even at the time, the vice president seemed to be acting against his instincts. Early in the race, Nixon assured his handlers that debates with Kennedy were out of the question. "In 1946, a damn fool incumbent named Jerry Voorhis debated a young lawyer and it cost him the election," he reminded staffers, citing his own experience.[2] Nixon obviously understood what later front-runners and incumbents would come to regard as gospel: TV debates favor the underdog.

In the summer of 1960 John F. Kennedy, by far the lesser known contender, immediately accepted the invitation of the broadcast networks for a series of televised debates. A few days later, over the objections of President Eisenhower and Republican advisers, Richard Nixon followed suit. Press secretary Herbert G. Klein recalled that his "mouth dropped open" when Nixon announced at a news conference in Chicago that he would debate JFK; senior campaign aides had not been notified. "I could attribute his reversal only to the fact that he did not want his manhood sullied by appearing as if he were afraid to win such an encounter," Klein wrote.[3] According to Nixon biographer Earl Mazo, "The vice president could find no way of rejecting the television network offers."[4]

By the end of the Kennedy-Nixon series, provocative new lessons about television and politics had come into focus; but on the future of presidential debates, opinion split down the middle. The more optimistic observers saw debates as inevitable. Walter Lippmann predicted that "from now on it will be impossible for any candidate . . . to avoid this kind of confrontation with his opponent." Others, like Eisenhower press secretary James Hagerty, reached a different conclusion: "You can bet your bottom dollar that no incumbent president will ever engage in any such debate or joint appearance in the future."[5]

As it happened, the pessimists came closer to the mark than the optimists, and another sixteen years would pass before candidates for the White House again agreed to debate. It is interesting to note that before his assassination President Kennedy had verbally committed to a second round of appearances in 1964. Furthermore, according to Republican nominee Barry Goldwater, Kennedy and Goldwater had seriously discussed a plan to barnstorm the country together in a series of matches around the country. "We even talked about using the same airplane and doing it the old-fashioned way—get out on the stump and debate," Goldwater reported.[6]

But the 1964 election rolled around with an unanticipated Democratic nominee. Lyndon Johnson, nobody's idea of a glittering television personality, gave campaign debates a wide berth as the incumbent president. In 1968 and 1972 once-burned Richard Nixon likewise refused to meet his opponents for a joint appearance. "The 1960 Great Debates had taught him a bitter lesson," wrote the authors of a Twentieth Century Fund study of presidential debates. "He would take no more chances with programs that might show him in an unfavorable light, literally or figuratively."[7]

Both Nixon and Johnson hid behind a legal technicality that blocked the TV networks from airing candidate forums: Section 315 of the Communications Act, which granted all participants in a race, even those on the fringe, "equal opportunities" to television time. Since the 1950s, broadcasters had been lobbying against this restriction. Their original hope in sponsoring the Kennedy-Nixon debates was to rid themselves of Section 315, but Congress agreed only to a temporary suspension for the 1960 campaign.

In 1975, in the so-called Aspen ruling, the Federal Communications Commission finally exempted debates from the equal access requirement. Incumbent President Gerald Ford, badly trailing Jimmy Carter in the polls, departed from his acceptance speech during the 1976 Republican convention and challenged his opponent to a face-to-face TV debate. Using one live media event to advance another, Ford declared, "The American people have the right to know where both of us stand."[8] Carter quickly signaled his acceptance, and in each election since, presidential debates have occurred in one form or another.

Gerald Ford resurrected the institution of presidential debates not out of a sense of civic duty but for political advantage. "The Ford campaign needed something dramatic," said Republican adviser Michael Duval. "We needed something that would cause the country to reserve its judgment. The debates seemed to be the answer."[9] As this remark indicates, the decision to meet one's opponent comes down to self-interest. Debates hinge on the assumption that the presidential nominees will see fit to take part, but in fact only tradition and political pressure require them to do so. As veteran CBS news producer Lane Venardos says, "The candidates have all the high cards, including the ultimate high card—whether to participate."[10]

From Richard Nixon to Jimmy Carter to George Bush, the ambivalence of politicians toward engaging in live debates is not difficult to comprehend. Even for battle-scarred presidential nominees accustomed to the relentless scrutiny of the cameras, the perils can be enormous. "In no other mode of presentation," wrote communications scholar Walter Fisher, "does the candidate risk or reveal so much of his character."[11] Debaters understand that the lens will magnify their every word, gesture, and facial expression, not just for the duration of the broadcast but for the ages.

Ford and Carter managed to revive the debate tradition because, as competitors, they were fairly evenly matched. In subsequent elections a different dynamic has taken hold: The campaign in the lead, which is to say the one with the most to lose, seeks either to shirk debates or to participate only on highly favorable terms. Candidates thus adopt an attitude of petulance that creates a contentious climate in the weeks leading up to a debate series. Unfortunately for the public, as long as presidential debates are controlled by their stars, the leading players will have license to behave as prima donnas.

DEBATES IN DOUBT

In 1980 disagreement over the inclusion of independent John Anderson gave President Jimmy Carter and challenger Ronald Reagan a pretext for cutting short that year's debate series. Only two matches would take place: an inconsequential meeting in late September between Reagan and Anderson that Carter boycotted and a climactic debate with Carter and Reagan one week before the election.

Carter's refusal to join Reagan and Anderson in a three-way debate irked the sponsoring League of Women Voters, which retaliated by announcing its intention to place an empty chair onstage at the Baltimore Convention Center as a reminder of the candidate's absence. Editorial cartoonist Pat Oliphant sketched this as a baby's high chair, while Johnny Carson wondered in his *Tonight Show* monologue, "Suppose the chair wins?"[12] Under pressure from Democrats and the White House, the League eventually withdrew its threat, and no extraneous furniture materialized on the Reagan-Anderson set.

At least in the short term, Carter sustained little damage by skipping the debate. "Despite some predictions to the contrary," said the *Christian Science Monitor*, "no widespread, high-intensity wave of criticism against the president has emerged."[13] Instead, the media found a new narrative thread: the will-they-or-won't-they possibility of a two-way Carter-Reagan encounter. Publicly both candidates maintained a posture of favorability, but in private neither side could muster much enthusiasm for a debate.

Although Carter dismissed Reagan as his intellectual inferior, other Democrats were understandably apprehensive about the former California governor's performing prowess. Carter at first sought a schedule of multiple debates, hoping that "over a more extended period of time, [Reagan] and I would have to get down to specific issues, where my knowledge of foreign and domestic affairs would give me an edge."[14] Like Nixon before him, Carter mistakenly assumed that substance would prevail over image.

By the time the two campaigns agreed to debate, only a single appearance could be scheduled before Election Day. "If we're going to debate him," said Carter pollster Patrick Caddell, a staunch opponent of any face-to-face meeting with Reagan, "it's damn important that we get rules that increase the possibility that he'll say something dumb or screw up." Caddell drafted a strategy memorandum a week before the debate that warned of the dangers ahead, calling the event "fraught with great risk" and cautioning that "the risks far outweigh the possible advantages."[15]

Reagan handlers had reasons of their own to fear a debate. The Republican candidate had made a number of ill-advised statements during speeches and press conferences. According to Reagan aide Michael Deaver, a debate proponent, "It was particularly the international subjects that we felt we would have a problem with."[16] Among the strongest dissenters was pollster Richard Wirthlin, whose data indicated that Reagan could be elected without debating. "One of the keys to winning a campaign is that you deal to those things you can control," Wirthlin said, "and, quite frankly, a debate is a game of roulette. There's no telling which way that marble will bounce."[17]

What turned the tide for Reagan was the white-tie Alfred E. Smith political banquet in New York City, attended by both presidential candidates in mid-October. Concerned that Carter would use his platform to issue an impromptu debate challenge, Reagan's people armed their man with a four-hundred-word acceptance speech. When Carter failed to mention the subject, Reagan instead delivered a program of self-deprecating jokes that sharply contrasted with the humorless tone of the incumbent. In the words of columnists Rowland Evans and Robert Novak, "genial Ron" bested "uptight Jimmy" in this, their only joint appearance of the campaign other than the debate.[18] The next morning the die was cast. After listening to his aides weigh the pros and cons, Reagan said, "Well, everything considered, I feel I should debate. If I'm going to fill the shoes of Carter, I should be willing to meet him face-to-face."[19]

In the end, after one of the most successful debate performances in history, Reagan knew he had made the right call. Just as Richard Nixon got scorched by the heat of JFK's stardom, so did Carter find himself singed by the superior media presence of the former Hollywood actor. Asked afterwards if he had been nervous sharing the stage with the president of the United States, Reagan gave a response that put the matter in perspective: "Not at all. I've been on the same stage with John Wayne."[20] Beneath the humor lay a simple truth: In TV debates, star power carries the day.

If presidential debates can be said to have a savior, the honor goes to Ronald Reagan. By agreeing to appear with Walter Mondale in 1984, then-president Reagan shored up campaign debates as a permanent institution. The popular incumbent stood so far ahead in the polls that he most likely could have survived the fallout from not participating that year, a course many advisers recommended. William F. Buckley Jr. wrote,

> I am glad Reagan has scheduled a debate because I like circuses and gladiators and drums and cymbals and roller coasters. But if I were Reagan, I'd say no. I'd say, "Let's get it straight: Debates between presidential contenders should be restricted to debates between men who have not served as president. Men who have served should be judged by what they have done."[21]

Why, then, did Reagan debate? According to Deaver, "I think he believed in debates. I think he just decided, in fact I can hear him saying, you have to debate, people expect it now, it's become part of our system."[22] Furthermore Reagan had reason to be confident. As the "Great Communicator," he approached the event with five decades of experience at the microphone and an undefeated track record as a political debater.

At the first 1984 debate in Louisville, Ronald Reagan would turn in the worst performance of his long career, appearing disengaged, disjointed, and discombobulated against Walter Mondale, an opponent whom voters and the press had largely written off. Not since Richard Nixon had a presidential debater stepped off the stage so battered. That such misfortune could befall a speaker of Reagan's stature proves the riskiness of debate participation. If a star performer like Ronald Reagan can stumble, what tribulations await a candidate of lesser skills?

THE DEBATE INSTITUTION TAKES SHAPE

By 1988 debates had more than ever become a public expectation. That year negotiators for incumbent Vice President George Bush played hardball at the bargaining table, giving the Democratic campaign of Michael Dukakis a take-it-or-leave-it offer: two presidential debates and one vice presidential match in the standard press conference format. Bush, no fan of presidential debates, emerged unscathed; even a maladroit performance by running mate Dan Quayle did not adversely affect Republican prospects.

Four years later, when foot-dragging by the Bush campaign cast doubt on the 1992 debates, the price of nonparticipation had gone up. The case of George Bush offers an object lesson for any candidate seeking to shirk what the press and the public now consider a presidential aspirant's obligation to debate. In September 1992 the chief executive of the land found himself being chased around America by chickens—more accurately, humans in chicken costumes, offering themselves as metaphors for Bush's reluctance to debate Bill Clinton.

The phenomenon began with a single freelance protester in East Lansing, Michigan, a city that had been selected as the site of the season's first debate. When stalling by the Bush campaign caused the event to be canceled, Clinton showed up anyway, and so did the prototype "Chicken George." Lansing TV stations jumped on the story, airing video of the costumed demonstrator on their evening newscasts. Inspired by this example, Clinton "counterevents" forces set up an operation called "Get on TV," and soon a veritable flock of imitators around the country started turning up at Bush rallies, and on television. Craig Smith, national field director for the Clinton campaign, told the *New York Times*, "You know what they say: Let a thousand flowers bloom. This one bloomed pretty nicely."[23]

When President Bush took to addressing the chickens personally, the Clinton people knew they had scored a hit. One of the more bizarre vignettes of the 1992 presidential campaign featured George Bush squabbling with a giant fowl during a whistle-stop tour of the Midwest. The protester's sign—"Chicken George Won't Debate"—caught the president's eye and precipitated this classic example of Bush-speak: "You talking about the draft-record chicken or you talking about the chicken in the Arkansas River? Which one are you talking about? Which one? Get out of here. Maybe it's the draft? Is that what's bothering you?"[24] Inevitably the exchange made the newscasts: the leader of the most powerful country on earth having it out with an anonymous citizen in a poultry outfit.

However goofy, 1992's "Chicken George" episode shows the pressures facing presidential candidates as they ponder the pros and cons of participating in TV debates. George Bush discovered that even the appearance of hesitation was enough to give the opposition a toehold. The news media, unable to resist any story that combines conflict with visuals, eagerly played its role in the drama, promoting the perception that the president did not want to debate. Eventually Bush's high command concluded that they had no choice but to commit.

In a backhanded way, the Republican delays may have served a positive purpose. By waiting until late in the game to fix a schedule, negotiators were forced to bunch up the debates on the few available dates that remained, creating a tournament-like sequence of four telecasts within nine days. The unforeseen result was to build audience interest from one program to the next, a trend further enhanced by the introduction of experimental formats.

The 1992 series brought another important innovation, the first three-way debates. When Ross Perot reentered the presidential race in early October, representatives for Clinton and Bush were applying the finishing touches to their two-man debate agreement. With approval from the sponsoring Commission on Presidential Debates, the campaigns quickly expanded the cast of characters to include the picturesque Texan and his running mate, Admiral James B. Stockdale. Although the Reform Party candidates were given no say in the negotiations, the invitation delighted Perot. "Basically, they resurrected him by letting him in the debates," said Perot adviser Dan Routman.[25]

In 1996 the Bob Dole campaign struggled to avoid a repeat of three-way debates, touching off a brief controversy over whether Perot merited an invitation. According to criteria established by the debate commission, an independent or third-party candidate had to demonstrate "evidence of national organization, signs of national newsworthiness and competitiveness, and indicators of national public enthusiasm or concern" in order to qualify for inclusion. In the judgment of an advisory committee that surveyed opinion among academics, journalists, and political professionals, Perot did not have a "realistic chance" of being elected in 1996. On this basis he was deemed ineligible to participate.

A headline in the *New York Post* told the story: "Perot Gets Heave-Ho." In a San Francisco speech, an angry Perot compared himself to a "cur dog" among "registered puppies." "As a result of this commission's ruling on the presidential debates," Perot said, "I expect that we should bring in Bosnia and Haiti to send poll watchers to help us clean up the election process in the U.S."[26]

With Perot's exclusion resolved, the 1996 wrangling took on a perfunctory quality. Negotiators for Bill Clinton and Bob Dole quickly settled on a schedule of two debates at the presidential level and one for the running mates. In view of Clinton's formidable skills as a television performer, for the first time debates were not viewed as an inherent risk for the incumbent.

Approaching the election of 2000, as presidential debates enter their fifth decade, a case can be made that de facto institutionalization of the tradition now exists. Each successive round of debates would seem to solidify the likelihood of future joint appearances. According to this argument, avoiding debates would exact too heavy a political toll on a reluctant candidate. No amount of spin could offset what voters and journalists would interpret as an unacceptable subversion of the norm.

On the other hand, no guarantees exist. James A. Baker 3d, the former Republican adviser and a key shaper of presidential debates, believes that joint appearances can still be avoided, "but there would be a big political price to pay." In Baker's view, the stronger candidate in an extraordinarily lopsided race might be able to escape debating, though "it will be more difficult as time goes by."[27] Clinton debate negotiator Mickey Kantor likewise sees some wiggle room. "I think it depends on the candidate—what is perceived to be their strengths and weaknesses, and how their opponents are perceived," Kantor says.[28]

Naturally candidates prefer to keep debates optional. Republican adviser Charles Black believes it is "absolutely essential" that nominees call their own shots about participating. "It's simply too important a part of your campaign to let someone else decide or to make those decisions in advance," Black told a 1990 symposium,[29] echoing the general belief of political pros. Increasingly, however, this point of view may be anachronistic. An entire generation of American voters has grown accustomed to debates as a standard feature of the presidential campaign. Woe to any candidate who attempts to deprive the public of a television spectacular it now regards as an expectation.

THE DIFFICULTY OF DEBATE NEGOTIATIONS

Even in years when both sides want to debate, the ritual known as the "debate over debates" plays out as a kind of promotional trailer for the main event to come. Like the debates themselves, preproduction negotiations have winners and losers, surprise moves and tactical blunders, high stakes and colorful characters. Each round of presidential debates generates a victor not just on the battlefield of television but also at the bargaining table. It is generally believed that Kennedy's team won the 1960 negotiations; Republicans and Democrats more or less tied in 1976; Reagan's handlers triumphed in 1980 and again in 1984; Bush's took the 1988 talks; and the Clinton staff prevailed in 1992 and 1996. In every instance the successful side in predebate negotiations has gone on to carry the vote.

With so much riding on the outcome, candidates and their surrogates have from the outset been fiercely protective of preproduction decision making. Here is where the functions of campaign handler and television producer merge. Because the issues in question—structure, schedule, timing, staging, and so on—are political as well as programmatic, the campaigns take control of this agenda with a vengeance.

As early as 1960 it became apparent that the sponsoring organizations—the stagers of the event and payers of the bills—would be relegated to a secondary role in the planning. The "Great Debates" of 1960 may have been the brainchild of ABC, CBS, and NBC, but when it came to setting terms, these powerful institutions got foreclosed. Negotiating sessions for the Kennedy-Nixon debates started off with all parties at the table, but in the second meeting the politicos asked the broadcasters to leave the room. "When we came back in again," recalled CBS's Mickelson, "they laid down the pattern for the debates."[30]

To one degree or another this has been the procedure ever since: The campaigns hammer out an agreement that suits their own purposes, which then gets presented to the sponsoring institution as a done deal. "It is to the everlasting credit of the television networks that the debate programs were presented in the 1960 campaign, but the evidence is overwhelming that they relinquished essential control of the programs to do so," concluded debate scholars Seltz and Yoakam shortly after the Kennedy-Nixon events.[31] The same lament can be applied to every debate sponsor since: the League of Women Voters in 1976, 1980, and 1984, and the nonpartisan Commission on Presidential Debates in 1988, 1992, and 1996. At the campaigns' insistence, sponsors exist not to make substantive decisions but to add legitimacy, do the grunt work, and pick up the tab.

In the years since Kennedy-Nixon, debate negotiations by presidential campaign staffs have gotten only more Byzantine. The 1960 debates left political handlers with a heightened sensitivity to the volatile nature of live TV; in every debate since, the objective has been to install an invisible safety net that keeps the tightrope artists from crashing to the ground. Campaigns engage in what can best be described as a mix of talent management and preventive damage control, doing whatever it takes to stabilize an inherently combustible production situation for the leading players.

As Ford and Carter prepared to resume the debate tradition in 1976, strategists for both candidates looked to the 1960 series for inspiration. In a planning memo, a Carter adviser expressed admiration for the squabbles of his predecessors: "The constant bickering between the candidates' staffs and with the production crews about studio temperature, candidate facilities, furniture, sets, lights, etc., serves an important purpose: It tells the opposition that you do not trust them and that you are tough enough not to be walked over."[32] In this quote can be discerned the prevailing philosophy that has guided debate negotiations from 1960 on: Never give an inch.

James Karayn, who served as producer of the 1976 Ford-Carter series, saw great danger in leaving debate negotiations to the campaigns. "If the candidates' representatives do the planning," Karayn warned in an op-ed piece before the 1988 debates, "it won't be with the goal of informing the electorate uppermost in their minds. Their main concern is—has to be—to ensure that their respective candidates get the maximum exposure and the minimum risk."[33] Lee Hanna, Karayn's successor, took an even dimmer view based on his experience in the 1980 negotiations: "The candidates' representatives were pathetic in their desire to protect what they saw as their candidates' interests. The negotiations were exercises in frustration and hilarity."[34]

Jody Powell, who as press secretary to Carter participated in the 1976 and 1980 talks, calls debate negotiations a process of "bluff and counterbluff, scheming, conniving, and hard-nosed horse trading." According to Powell, the bargaining sessions offer campaign professionals "the opportunity, so rare in political contests, to sit down face-to-face with your adversaries. It is a chance to take their measure, assess their intelligence and flappability."[35] This comment suggests a reason apart from candidate protection that campaigns so reliably indulge in extensive predebate negotiations: They enjoy checking out their opponents eyeball to eyeball.

One of the opponents Powell was checking out in 1976 would emerge as a legend in presidential debate bargaining: James Baker, who, as the Republicans' lead negotiator in the 1980s, crafted highly favorable rules for Ronald Reagan and George Bush. Among other negotiating triumphs, Baker is credited with scheduling the last-minute Carter-Reagan debate in 1980 and whittling down the 1984 Reagan-Mondale series to two presidential matches. The 1988 negotiation, in which Baker teamed up with Roger Ailes against Dukakis managers Paul Brountas and Susan Estrich, is regarded as one of the most lopsided in debate history. Bush's team got essentially everything it wanted; the Democrats' consolation prize was an elevated podium for the shorter Michael Dukakis.

So persuasive was Baker's negotiating rhetoric that it boomeranged back at the Republicans in the "Baker-less" talks of 1992 and 1996. Mickey Kantor, lead debate negotiator for Bill Clinton, reiterated many of Baker's hard-line positions, even some of the same language, in ironing out agreements with his counterparts. Like Baker, Kantor got most of what he was seeking, especially in 1996, against Bob Dole's all-rookie negotiating team. Already disadvantaged by low poll standings, the Dole representatives compounded their trouble by introducing a number of irrelevant issues, at one point asking if the live audience could be made to abide by a dress code.

By 1996, as the naivete of Dole's negotiators demonstrated, these talks had become too highly specialized to be handled by neophytes. Debate negotiations are a blood sport, played under arcane rules by a cast of experienced Washington insiders. Recent predebate bargaining sessions have involved as many as five or six people per campaign, each with a particular area of expertise, drawn from the elite ranks of political strategists, media advisers, and high-dollar law firms. Directing the efforts is a lead negotiator, who doubles as press spokesman. Out of sight, but never out of mind, are the candidates, whose degree of involvement varies.

Depending on the vicissitudes of the political season, the negotiating advantage shifts from one side to the other. Back-and-forth maneuvering over the years has created an ongoing rivalry that ups the ante for each new round of debate talks. Says Janet Brown, executive director of the Commission on Presidential Debates, "It really is a machismo duel that has to do with the question of who bested the other guy . . . because each side felt that in an earlier cycle they got had."[36]

Debate negotiations typically stretch over several meetings: a preliminary session insiders describe as "mostly posturing," and perhaps two follow-up sessions at which the nuts and bolts of the agreement are finalized. These discussions can be lengthy and arduous. A 1992 negotiating meeting that began at 9:30 in the morning did not end until 3:45 the next morning.[37]

As the bargaining over debates has intensified, negotiators have increasingly resorted to the language of the courtroom to codify rules of engagement. A by-product of the past few debate negotiations has been a quasi-legal document called a memorandum of understanding, or memorandum of agreement, that governs every conceivable point of scheduling, format, and staging. This contract initially appeared in an abbreviated form in 1984, when the Reagan and Mondale campaigns drew up and signed a three-page document covering the rudiments of debate production.

The first substantial memorandum of understanding was drafted in 1988 by a Republican debate adviser named Robert Goodwin. Goodwin had cut his teeth as an aide to George Bush in the 1980 primary debates, then served as Bush's on-site negotiator in the 1984 vice presidential match with Geraldine Ferraro. Out of these experiences he devised a production agreement that has served as a template for the past three rounds of presidential debates.

What began as a sixteen-page contract in 1988 grew to thirty-seven pages in 1992, when untested formats and the presence of a third participant complicated events. Clay Mulford, counsel for the Perot campaign, remembers being astonished when he read that year's agreement. Said Mulford, "It was like the Internal Revenue code."[38] The documents anticipate every contingency, from what form of address the debaters will use with each other to where the candidates' spouses will sit in the audience.

The language of the contract betrays the mutual suspicion that exists between presidential campaigns. Among the particulars of the 1992 agreement: "It is agreed that neither film footage nor video footage from the debates may be used publicly by any candidate or candidate's campaign." "All other candidates and their representatives shall vacate the debate site while another candidate has his private production and technical briefing and walk-through." And: "No candidate shall have any staff member in the wings or backstage later than five minutes after the debate has begun nor sooner than five minutes before the debate concludes."[39] Clearly each side is on guard for the unanticipated competitive stunt.

Before hashing out such minutiae, however, negotiators tackle more fundamental issues. The first order of business is establishing a calendar: How many debates will take place? How far apart? How long will each program run? Next, formats are decided, along with such specific staging points as whether reaction shots can be taken, what type of microphones will be used, and how close the candidates will stand to each other onstage. Finally, with the rules in place, campaign negotiators select the moderators and questioners. Each of these steps in the planning process is a matter to be contested and resolved, another hand in the political poker game that shapes what the audience will see.

THE DEBATE OVER SCHEDULING

In his 1976 vice presidential match, Bob Dole claimed there were three presidential debates that year because Jimmy Carter "has three positions on everything." Though the quip was intended for laughs, it does get at a serious point of disputation in debate negotiations: scheduling. In their capacity as TV producers, campaign officials also become programmers, creating a calendar for the joint appearances that has more to do with political realities than the needs of either the public, the debate sponsors, or the networks.

Mindful of the lessons of the past, campaign strategists attach talismanic significance to the issue of timing. Conventional wisdom about the scheduling of presidential debates coalesces around several points: First, whoever is ahead wants fewer debates; whoever is behind wants more. Second, candidates in the lead will insist on as much distance as possible between the final debate and Election Day, in case time is needed to rebound from a disaster. Third, the busy autumn sports schedule must be navigated in choosing debate days, lest the public be tempted to watch something else. And finally, once announced, debates tend to freeze a campaign, as candidates go into rehearsal hibernation and voters wait to assess the performers side by side.

The "freeze" theory was first promulgated by James Baker, who, in 1980, worked the principle to his advantage by scheduling the single eleventh-hour debate between Ronald Reagan and Jimmy Carter one week before the election. "They do freeze a campaign," Baker says, "but they also have the ability to move the numbers. So the front-runner is always going to be more hesitant to extend the period of time for the debates, and the number of debates, and even the fact of debates."[40]

In 1980 this campaign paralysis hardened Reagan's lead at a critical point in the race. "After the debate was agreed to," wrote Reagan biographer Lou Cannon, "press coverage and the candidates' speeches became virtually perfunctory, with everyone waiting for the big event. The beneficiary was Reagan."[41] In postmortems of the 1980 race, Carter campaign officials admitted they had been outfoxed. "That late debate was the worst thing that happened to us in the campaign," a Carter aide told journalists Germond and Witcover. "When we wanted to debate Reagan, I think they very smartly suckered us into the late debate."[42]

The schedule might have been even worse for Carter. Baker's initial proposal called for a debate on November 3, the night before the election, "when most voters are making up their minds," as Baker told reporters. Predictably Carter's camp nixed this idea. Jody Powell said that a debate so late in the season "would leave no time for anybody to be called for misstatements, contradictions, or inaccuracies," a not-so-subtle hint that Reagan played loose with his facts.[43]

Negotiating for Reagan in 1984, Baker won the reverse concession, denying Walter Mondale's wish for a debate close to Election Day. Baker told the *Washington Post* that his side preferred an earlier encounter so as to avoid "undue impact on voters' decision."[44] At the bargaining table for George Bush in 1988, Baker got an even better deal: The last debate of the season took place more than three weeks before the election. "Though Baker did this out of concern for his own man, it's also better for the country," concluded journalist Elizabeth Drew.[45] Drew, like other observers, feared that a debate too close to the vote could have dangerous electoral implications.

In 1992, after the "Chicken George" issue forced Bush's hand, the Republicans came back at the Clinton campaign with an unprecedented counterproposal: four debates to be televised on the last four Sundays of the campaign. The final debate would air November 1, two days before the election. Paul Brountas, Dukakis's negotiator in 1988, told the *New York Times*, "The minute I heard about Baker's proposal, I recall his sitting with me and saying, 'Paul, there is no way I will let my candidate debate in the last week or ten days of the campaign, because if a statement is made that's incorrect, he won't have time to correct it.'" Four years later Brountas continued, "Something has changed—it's an interesting twist."[46]

As it turned out, the "Four Sundays" plan gave way to an even more revolutionary timetable: four debates held in rapid succession between October 11 and 19. The compressed sequence fulfilled the prophecy of Hollywood producer Harry Thomason, a debate negotiator for Bill Clinton, who predicted that the schedule would play out like a TV miniseries.[47] "Americans everywhere are wild about the drama," wrote David Von Drehle in the *Washington Post* during the 1992 debates. "All day, they speculated with the urgent palaver of a klatch of soap-opera fans. What would happen next?"[48]

In 1996 Democratic negotiators won a schedule that deliberately slotted the second and last Clinton-Dole debate against a baseball play-off game. After the election, journalist Roger Simon asked Clinton aide George Stephanopoulos why the president's team had insisted on competing with a major athletic event. Stephanopoulos's reply is a classic of convoluted election-year reasoning: "We didn't *want* people watching the debates. We wanted the debates to be a metaphor for the campaign. And we didn't want people to concentrate on the campaign."[49]

Not all debate scheduling is driven by political logic. In 1984 Nancy Reagan's personal stargazer offered her input into the timing and location of that year's matches. Astrologer Joan Quigley would claim responsibility for President Reagan's stumbling performance in Louisville on October 7, calling the selection her "one important error the entire seven years I did the Reagans' astrology."[50] White House aide Michael Deaver confirmed that he routinely ran important dates on the political calendar past Quigley, "but if she had called back and said, 'My God, all the stars in the sky are coming together at that time,' there wasn't anything I could do."[51]

How many debates is too many? The most debates in any year were the four between Kennedy and Nixon in 1960; 1980 offered the fewest, one between Reagan and Carter, another between Reagan and Anderson. Never has more than a single vice presidential debate taken place in a given year; no vice presidential matches at all were held in 1960 or 1980, though consideration was given to having the 1960 running mates, Henry Cabot Lodge and Lyndon Johnson, appear together for ten minutes at the beginning of one program before yielding to the top-of-the-ticket nominees.

Even as the 1960 series was under way, Kennedy negotiators were pressing the idea of adding a fifth debate to the schedule. Five had been JFK's ideal number all along. "Basically, Kennedy wanted as many debates as possible to gain the television exposure, and we wanted as few debates as possible, possibly only one," said Herb Klein, Nixon's press secretary.[52] Through the end of October 1960, the issue of a fifth debate remained alive, sparking a flurry of bargaining sessions and accusations in the press; when agreement could not be reached, the series ended at four.

Nixon's team had already made a costly blunder about the debate schedule, wrongly reasoning that the final match of the series would draw the largest audience. As it turned out, nothing could wipe away the impression left by the first encounter. "When the debates were held," Nixon wrote, "at least twenty million more people listened to and watched the first than any of the others, including the fourth and final appearance. I turned in my best performance before the smallest audience."[53] Even today, political strategists believe that the first debate weighs most heavily and that the first twenty to thirty minutes of any debate are the most critical.

In 1984 Mondale negotiators initially proposed a whopping six presidential and two vice presidential debates. The outrageousness of the demand, particularly from an underdog campaign, illustrates how debate negotiations resemble haggling in a Middle Eastern carpet bazaar. According to Mondale aide Richard Leone, six was never a realistic consideration; the Democratic side hoped for three and settled on two, along with one vice presidential debate.[54]

Beyond number, another reliable point of campaign disagreement is program length. In 1960 each of the four debates ran only an hour, the shortest in history. They might have been even a few minutes shorter: NBC's Robert Sarnoff argued for "appropriate" commercial sponsorship of the debates, an idea quickly scuttled by debate co-sponsor CBS.[55] Since Kennedy-Nixon, all but two of the programs have been ninety minutes long; the exceptions are the sixty-minute 1980 Reagan-Anderson debate and the 1976 vice presidential debate, which at an hour and fifteen minutes represented a compromise between Dole, who wanted an hour, and Mondale, who wanted an hour and a half.

As President Reagan learned in his first 1984 match with Walter Mondale, one and a half hours is an extraordinarily long time for any individual to perform at capacity on live television. That event, which ran beyond its scheduled time slot, clocked in at one hundred minutes, making it the longest of all presidential debates. Reagan's doddering performance—"the worst night of Ronnie's political career," in the words of Nancy Reagan[56]—brought into the open a previously unmentionable topic: the seventy-three-year-old president's ability to withstand the physical and mental rigors of the office.

According to Elizabeth Drew, "Getting the debates to last an hour and a half was one of the Mondale negotiators' major strategic achievements, even though they held few cards; they figured that Reagan would not have sufficient stamina to last that full time in good form."[57] The Republicans wanted the debates to last sixty minutes, but swapped the extra half hour for the safety of a panel of questioners. In the trade-off, Reagan's own delivery posed more of a challenge than anything his opponent said.

THE DEBATE OVER FORMAT

Since format can be thought of as a presidential debater's security blanket, it comes as no surprise that campaigns obsess over how the programs are structured. Functioning in their executive-producer role, political strategists design debates that are comfortable for the candidates first, and educational for the voters second. In practice, this meant that for three decades presidential debates remained locked in a single, candidate-friendly format: the joint news conference, with a panel of reporters posing a series of disconnected questions.

The press conference format endured because candidates took comfort in its strictures. By directing their answers to a panel, debaters could avoid confronting each other in ways that might prove unseemly in front of a viewing audience. Furthermore, with three or four reporters asking a succession of disparate questions, the discussion could not dwell on any single issue for very long, allowing candidates easy segues into their predigested campaign messages. Douglass Cater, a questioner in the second Kennedy-Nixon debate, complained that the panel's mission "was hardly more than to designate categories—animal, vegetable, or mineral—on which the two might or might not discourse."[58]

Thanks in large measure to the intercession of Bill Clinton, the 1992 debates inaugurated looser program structures: the "town meeting" or "people's debate," in which a studio audience full of uncommitted voters ask questions, and the "single moderator," used twice in 1992 and in two of the three 1996 debates. The original 1992 proposal by the debates commission called for a single-moderator format throughout the series. George Bush resisted this idea, telling CNN's Bernard Shaw, "I thought when you and others asked tough questions at the 1988 debates, it livened things up. I saw nothing wrong with the former format."[59]

Clinton himself suggested the town hall meeting that would produce the year's most talked-about debate. According to Mickey Kantor, the candidate raised the issue in a phone call during a break in one of the negotiating sessions. "He thought you'd probably get more substantive questions," Kantor said. "That had been our experience. He thought he'd do quite well in it, and that it would show the difference in his ability to relate to people and President Bush's. To my surprise, the Bush people accepted immediately." Recalled Clinton aide Paul Begala, "When the word came back that the president's folks had agreed to it, we were hooting and hollering. We couldn't believe it."[60]

Why did Bush negotiators go along with the Richmond town hall debate? According to 1992 debate producer Ed Fouhy, "They thought that Richmond, a conservative city, could be relied on to produce uncommitted voters sufficiently in awe of the president to ask softball questions." James Baker said that Bush agreed because he was "really good with small groups. When we started his presidential campaign, we had something called "Ask George Bush" forums, and they were extremely successful."[61] In the end, Bush would have reason to rue the town hall debate.

The single-moderator format made its debut with the rollicking vice presidential debate of 1992. According to Fouhy, it was Dan Quayle who persuaded the Bush campaign to accept the idea. After suffering at the hands of a press panel in his 1988 debate with Lloyd Bentsen, Quayle had cause to favor a less rigid format. As Fouhy put it, "Quayle knew that his hopes for helping the ticket and building his own candidacy for the future were riding on his debate performance."[62] Indeed, Quayle improved considerably in the give-and-take of the single-moderator structure, though many critics condemned the program as a free-for-all.

The innovations of 1992 finally dragged presidential debates into the modern era. At the end of the series, *New York Times* political reporter Richard L. Berke wrote an analysis of how the three candidates had fared in the various formats: "Before the debates, President Bush's aides wanted a panel of journalists to pose questions; now they say that approach was least helpful to their man. Governor Bill Clinton's side wanted a single moderator to ask the questions but ended up preferring another format, too." Concluded Berke, "Presidential campaigns don't know what's good for them."[63]

THE DEBATE OVER STAGING

No detail being too small to attract the notice of campaign negotiators, a number of other production points bear mention in our discussion of predebate bargaining. One of the most negotiated matters in televised presidential debates is height. Because history shows that the taller presidential candidate tends to prevail at the ballot box, campaigns strive to mitigate a debater's relative shortness.

The height issue first cropped up in the 1976 series between Gerald Ford and Jimmy Carter. Although Ford was only three and a half inches taller than Carter, negotiators for the Democratic challenger sought compensatory measures. The two sides reached what became known as the "belt buckle compromise": Ford's lectern was built to intersect his torso two and a half inches above his belt buckle, while Carter's podium intersected an inch and a half below his buckle point. In exchange for this concession, the Carter camp agreed to let Ford's people choose the color of the backdrop, something the Republicans wanted in order to mask the incumbent President's thinning hair. "We worried about the height, they worried about the hair," Carter aide Gerald Rafshoon told *Newsweek*.[64]

George Bush's six-foot stature posed a height challenge to both of his first two debate opponents, Geraldine Ferraro and Michael Dukakis. In 1984 Ferraro's people demanded and got a riser on the stage that made her five-feet-four-inch frame appear less diminutive. The piece was designed as a gently sloping ramp so that Ferraro would not have to take a noticeable step up to her podium; instead, the candidate had to concentrate on staying in place once atop the riser, lest she appear to be listing.

Michael Dukakis, at a six-inch stature disadvantage, got a similar ramp four years later, though Baker and his team did not yield this concession until the final round of the debate talks. "What are you going to do when you have to negotiate with Gorbachev?" Baker taunted his opponents. "Call for a little platform?"[65] Not inaccurately, Bush aides referred to the riser as a "pitcher's mound"; at the second debate, a Republican advance man sneaked a softball onto the set intending to leave it on Dukakis's lectern, but no opportunity arose to make the drop. In the end, stratagems to downplay the Democratic nominee's relative shortness were of mixed value. At the close of the debate, when Dukakis stepped down from his podium to shake Bush's hand, the height difference between the two men seemed all the more pronounced.

Typically presidential debaters stand for the length of the program, though negotiators regularly revisit the question of whether they might be better off sitting down. In 1960 Kennedy handlers sought to have the candidates stand in order to exploit Nixon's knee injury. Said JFK aide J. Leonard Reinsch, "If Nixon had to shift his weight every now and then, it would give the impression that he was uncomfortable and ill at ease."[66] Reinsch was surprised when the Republicans raised no objections; Nixon did visibly shift his stance on the air, adding to his impression of physical debility.

Representatives for Carter and Ford argued at length over whether the candidate who was not speaking ought to be seated, as was the policy in 1960. According to debate scholar Sidney Kraus, this discussion "probably consumed more time than any other single point in the substantive or technical negotiations and necessitated a series of telephone calls to each of the principals."[67] In 1996, after the successful introduction of sit-down formats in primary and state-level debates, the Commission on Presidential Debates again sought to seat the candidates, an effort that failed when both campaigns objected. According to co-commissioner Frank Fahrenkopf Jr., "Experts tell us that the nature and context of discussion changes when people are seated around a table. We threw it out—the candidates were not interested."[68]

Republican adviser Robert Goodwin, who has been involved in every round of presidential debates since 1984, strongly favors standing. Bush negotiators in 1988 originally planned for that year's debaters to be seated, until Goodwin intervened with an impassioned plea to keep them on their feet. Goodwin believes a candidate looks more statesmanlike at the podium. In a memo lobbying for stand-up debates, he wrote, "Having [Bush] seated at a table could invite hunched shoulders, leaning back in his chair, papers scattered on the table, and essentially the look of a city council debate rather than a presidential debate."[69]

This preference for lecterns has led debate negotiators to pay close attention to matters of podium design. The 1976 Republican team, mindful of Ford's reputation as a klutz, made sure to insist on a brace for securing the presidential water glass. Carter's people successfully demanded smaller than normal lecterns in order to display more fully their candidate's physical grace. "Jimmy uses his hands and body language beautifully," a Carter official told *Time* magazine. "The president [Ford] has zero body language."[70]

Carter negotiators also won the skirmish over whether Ford would be allowed to affix an official presidential seal to his lectern. Four years later, handlers for then-incumbent President Carter co-opted this tactic for themselves. According to a 1980 prenegotiation strategy memorandum, "The presidential seal should be on his [Carter's] podium. Obviously, we won't get this but it's something to trade away."[71]

In recent years podium design has been fixed by the predebate memorandum of understanding. According to the terms of that contract, lecterns have to be identical only from the perspective of the television audience. This allows campaigns to customize the interior of their lecterns however they see fit, while maintaining visual equality on the outside. Still to be settled with each new round of debates is the issue of which candidate stands where. George Bush's negotiators, for example, preferred the position on stage right, an angle that de-emphasized their candidate's receding hairline.

Over the years negotiators have also grappled with whether to allow debaters to bring notes or props onto the stage. John F. Kennedy used this trick in a 1960 West Virginia primary debate, producing a government-surplus food package to make a point about federal programs for the undernourished. Dan Quayle's aides sought approval to have props in the 1992 vice presidential debate; they planned for Quayle to read passages from a copy of Al Gore's controversial book on the environment. Gore negotiators agreed, on the condition that their man could bring a potato, the vegetable Quayle had misspelled in a widely publicized incident earlier in the year. The matter was quickly dropped.

THE DEBATE OVER QUESTIONERS

The television networks that sponsored the 1960 debates originally hoped to enlist a prominent jurist or university president as the program moderator. It was the campaigns' uneasiness with this idea that handed the job to journalists instead. Fearful that even a highly respected national leader could not suppress his bias, representatives for Kennedy and Nixon argued that members of the press would be less inclined to play favorites. The networks, recognizing an opportunity to promote their own personnel, gladly assented, inaugurating a longstanding tradition of journalistic participation in presidential debates.

In keeping with the general pugnacity of the 1960 deliberations, a new controversy soon erupted: the campaigns' demand that newspaper and magazine reporters be included in the debate panels along with TV people. After initial resistance from the broadcasters, an accommodation was reached that gave the networks all four panelist slots in the first and fourth debates, and two slots to print reporters in the second and third. When neither the networks nor the handlers wanted the responsibility of picking the print panelists, names were drawn at random from a list of the reporters traveling with the candidates.

Never again would campaigns take so lightly the task of selecting moderators and panelists. The resumption of presidential debates in 1976 brought a radical change in procedure: for the first time the participants had an active hand in choosing their questioners. When network news officials learned that the League of Women Voters had invited the Ford and Carter campaigns to submit suggestions for debate panelists, a brief public spat ensued. Again in 1980 media outlets objected to the League's collaboration with the campaigns to pick questioners, but, as before, the journalists soon relented.

In 1984, when Reagan debated Mondale, panelist selection blew up in the campaigns' faces, erupting in the media as an ugly sideshow. On the eve of the first debate, the League of Women Voters broke the longstanding code of silence between sponsors and negotiators and called a news conference to denounce the campaigns' high-handedness in rejecting eighty-three journalists for the first panel. Dorothy Ridings, the organization's president, publicly chastised both sides for having "totally abused" the process.[72]

The League had initially supplied the campaigns with a list of twelve possible panelists for each of the year's three debates. All but one of the thirty-six names were rejected. League officials submitted more names, only to meet with further rejections. "It was one of those things that takes on a life of its own," recalled League debate producer Victoria Harian. "They weren't really legitimate concerns—it just became a game between the two campaigns." Ridings said journalists were stricken from the list for reasons "that had nothing to do with their professional capabilities."[73]

In protest, news organizations like the *New York Times*, the *Washington Post*, and CBS announced that their employees would not serve as panelists. (CBS let correspondent Diane Sawyer appear in the first debate because she had signed on before the ban.) Press reaction to the panelist selection story was predictably harsh. A piece in the *Post* compared the exercise to both a college fraternity rush and the Nixon enemies list.[74] Network newscasts the evening of the first 1984 debate showed footage of the panelists' desk being reconfigured after one of four participants resigned in a last-minute boycott. The shrunken desk provided a visual metaphor for the predebate tussle between campaigns and reporters.

The troubles of 1984 notwithstanding, Ridings defends the right of presidential campaigns to have a hand in selecting debate panelists. "We always had the opinion that it was appropriate for the campaigns to tell us" if they objected to a particular journalist, Ridings said. "We wanted to make sure that the candidates had the most comfortable situation for themselves in terms of feeling they weren't being sandbagged. We did not want the person asking the questions to be the story." The problem in 1984, she said, was one of degree.[75]

Like others on the political side of the fence, James Baker maintains that campaigns deserve veto power over moderators and panelists. "I've never been a believer that you turn all of this over to some allegedly nonpartisan, objective group. There's too much at stake," Baker said. "The campaigns have a legitimate right in making sure they're not going into a debate with moderators or questioners who are biased. And don't tell me that these people don't have biases, because they do."[76]

Following the controversy over panelist selection in 1984, the campaigns tightened their grip, giving themselves a more active hand in the decision making. The debate agreement of 1988 devoted a full page to codifying the process for selecting questioners. The document's legalistic language illuminates the intricacy of the procedure:

> Representatives of each candidate will submit a list of at least six and not more than ten possible panelists to each other. Each side will then have the opportunity to approve or delete names from the other's proposed list. When two or more possible panelists on each side are agreed upon from each list, these final two names on each list will be submitted to the sponsor who will then select one from each list to be a panelist for the first presidential debate. If necessary, this process will be repeated until the agreed upon number of names are submitted to the sponsor.
>
> To select the third panelist, the sponsor will submit a list of ten possible panelists to representatives of each of the candidates. These representatives will then mutually agree on two or more possible panelists from the sponsor's list. The sponsor will then pick one panelist from this list and that individual added to the two selections from the process indicated in the previous paragraph will constitute the three panelists for the first presidential debate.
>
> The same process will be followed for each of the three debates.[77]

Recent changes in debate formats, particularly the phase-out of press panels, have simplified the negotiations over supporting players. In 1996 PBS's Jim Lehrer moderated all three of that year's debates, after proving his mettle as a moderator in both 1988 and 1992. Whether he will return in 2000 remains to be seen; like all debate questioners, Lehrer serves at the pleasure of the candidates.

Although predebate negotiations have become standard operating procedure in presidential campaigns, at the end of the day the nitpicking and deal making can provide only so much security. Democratic media consultant Robert Squier offered this advice to candidates headed into the debate arena:

"The first thing to remember in a debate is that once you're on stage, everything that's been negotiated is out the window. There are no rules, except the rules of fair play."[78]

In other words, presidential debates are live television. And, inevitably, live television trumps written contracts.

Chapter Two

STRATEGY AND PREPARATION

*I*n the seconds leading up to the 1980 presidential debate, President Jimmy Carter and challenger Ronald Reagan strode onto the stage from opposite sides of the Cleveland Music Hall to assume their positions at the lecterns. Instead of stopping at his podium, Reagan bounded across the set, directly to Carter, whose hand he unexpectedly shook. "Carter's look of surprise suggested that he thought he was about to be knifed," wrote communication scholar Kathleen Hall Jamieson.[1]

As with all political kabuki, such moments are part of a candidate's master strategy—in this case, to knock the president of the United States off his game just before a live debate. Again at the end of the program, in violation of the agreed-upon rules, Reagan marched over and shook hands with Carter, this time on camera, under the watchful eye of the largest television audience ever assembled for a presidential debate. The move served a dual purpose: making Reagan look amiable and flummoxing Carter.

The 1980 handshakes epitomize a fundamental quest of debaters on live

TV: seizing control of the narrative. In an unscripted setting like a presidential debate, candidates attempt to impose their own story line through the use of calculated gestures, prepackaged sound bites, and audience-tested messages. What makes debates compelling in spite of their choreography is the skill with which the leading players apply these tools. Debaters operate simultaneously as competitors and collaborators, coauthors of a work in progress that each wishes to steer in a different direction. Any small narrative edge, such as Reagan's on-camera handshake at the end of the Cleveland debate, can affect the audience's perception of which star deserves top billing in the drama.

But an obverse tendency tempers this principle: Live television creates its own momentum, apart from the strategic desires of the candidates. Presidential debates have thus spawned a litany of gaffes both serious and mild: Richard Nixon declaring that "America can't stand pat," inadvertently making a double entendre of his wife's name. Gerald Ford's erroneous claim that Eastern Europe was not under Soviet domination. Bob Dole blaming the country's war dead on the Democratic party. Jimmy Carter's discussion of nuclear weaponry with daughter Amy. Ronald Reagan, meandering down the Pacific Coast Highway in a closing statement that had to be curtailed by the moderator. Michael Dukakis reacting dispassionately to Bernard Shaw's question about the hypothetical rape and murder of Kitty Dukakis. Dan Quayle venturing unwisely into the land of Camelot for a JFK analogy. George Bush looking down at his watch during the 1992 town hall debate.

Though debaters strive to inoculate themselves against blunders of this sort, the high-combustion nature of live television renders such incidents impossible to prepare for. Candidates instead devote their predebate energy to planning *positive* tactical moments, moments that will play favorably during the live telecast as well as in postdebate media coverage. Says long-time Democratic debate coach Tom Donilon, "You hope in a debate there will be a moment . . . where your candidate can make an impact. You don't know when it's going to come."[2] The savvy debater does not wait for the high points to occur naturally; he manufactures them, polishes them, and finds a way to deploy them.

CLASSIC DEBATE MOMENTS

Like Reagan's surprise handshakes, most classic debate moments share a common heritage as the products of careful plotting. At the end of that same

1980 debate with Carter, Reagan asked the audience a question that struck its target with the accuracy of a heat-seeking missile: "Are you better off now than you were four years ago?" The line, scripted by speechwriter David Gergen, had the feel of folk wisdom, like the insightful query of a common-sense neighbor. In fact, the language stemmed directly from polling data: by a two-to-one margin, Americans considered themselves in worse shape than they had been at the beginning of Carter's presidency.

Obviously opening and closing statements lend themselves particularly well to strategic planning. But Reagan's other, seemingly more spontaneous rejoinders were also devised ahead of time, albeit by the candidate himself. In the Reagan-Carter debate, Carter tartly reminded the audience that his opponent had begun his political career campaigning around the country against Medicare. "There you go again," Reagan replied, more in sorrow than in anger. This simple line accomplished two Reagan objectives: diminishing Carter by questioning his veracity and bolstering Reagan's own standing vis-à-vis health care. According to Reagan biographer Lou Cannon, "The reply was the Great Deflector's high point of the debate and perhaps of the campaign itself. It seemed such a wonderful, natural summation of an opponent's excess that overnight it became part of the political language."

Cannon described the phrase as having "all the careful spontaneity of a minuet."[3] During debate rehearsals Reagan had resisted advice that he bone up on issues and instead concentrated on one-liners, which he believed the viewing public would be more likely to remember. According to debate coach Myles Martel, Reagan was urged to use lines that could "dramatically differentiate" himself from Carter, a tactic Carter had successfully employed against Ford in the 1976 debates. Martel noted, " 'There you go again,' crafted by Reagan himself and practiced on (mock debater David) Stockman two days earlier, successfully elevated Reagan without projecting him as unduly strident or defensive—indeed a formidable challenge when refuting an incumbent president."[4]

Of the 1980 presidential debate, Reagan wrote that the event "may have turned on only four words."

They popped out of my mouth after Carter claimed that I had once opposed Medicare benefits for Social Security recipients.
  It wasn't true and I said so:
  There you go again . . .

I think there was some pent-up anger in me over Carter's claims
that I was a racist and warmonger. Just as he'd distorted my view on
states' rights and arms control, he had distorted it regarding Medicare,
and my response just burst out of me spontaneously.[5]

Four years later Reagan would make the same dubious claim of spontaneity for his response to a panelist's question about whether he was too old
to handle the presidency. The line became another instant classic: "I want
you to know that I will not make age an issue of this campaign. I am not
going to exploit for political purposes my opponent's youth and inexperience." In his memoir Reagan wrote that the words "just popped off the top
of my head. I'd never anticipated it, nor had I thought in advance what my
answer might be to such a question."

Reagan continued,

Well, the crowd roared and the television cameras flashed a shot of
Mondale laughing. I'm sure that if I had been as stuffed with as many
facts and figures as I was before the first debate, I wouldn't have been
able to come up with that line; your mind just isn't flexible enough if
it's saturated with facts because you've been preparing for an exami-
nation.[6]

Reagan aide Richard Wirthlin recalls the story somewhat differently:
After a practice session, Wirthlin reminded the president that he would
surely be asked a question on age. "His eyes twinkled, and he said, 'Don't
worry, Dick. I've got a way to deal with that question, and I'm just waiting
for it to come up.' Now he said that it just popped off his head—and it did.
But when that thought came to him it was at least two days before the actual debate."[7] Whatever the timing, observers agreed that the riposte hit its target. Wrote David Broder, "It well may have been that the biggest barrier to
Reagan's reelection was swept away in that moment."[8]

The unforgettable line of 1988—Lloyd Bentsen telling Dan Quayle
"you're no Jack Kennedy"—also had a less than spontaneous provenance. In
an August appearance at the Missouri State Fair, Quayle boasted to his audience, "I'm very close to the same age of Kennedy when he was elected, not
vice president but president."[9] The remark, like others from Quayle's stump
speeches, was duly recorded by Bentsen's campaign staff and passed along
to headquarters. In debate rehearsals, when Quayle surrogate Dennis Eckart

drew a JFK comparison, Bentsen responded, "You're no more like Jack Kennedy than George Bush is like Ronald Reagan."[10] In the televised debate, Bentsen omitted the Bush-Reagan reference, and another catchphrase entered the political lexicon.

These and other debate triumphs stand out not just for the rewards they bestow on a particular candidate but for the damage they inflict on the opponent. As journalist Sam Donaldson points out, "It's not just the clever line, it's the reaction. Had Jimmy Carter come back with a line that topped 'There you go again,' Carter would have the headlines. Had Dan Quayle . . . been able to handle 'You're no Jack Kennedy,' that would have made it, too."[11]

In fact, Walter Mondale used just such a tactic in 1984, turning Reagan's "There you go again" around on its speaker. Attempting to invoke past glories, Reagan walked right into a Mondale trap by using the line again. "Remember the last time you said that?" Mondale asked, and Reagan nodded. The effect on camera was unsettling: Suddenly the president seemed vulnerable. "You said it when President Carter said that you were going to cut Medicare . . . And what did you do right after the election? You went out and tried to cut twenty billion dollars out of Medicare." The bit that had worked so beautifully in 1980 now came flying back in Reagan's face.

Then there are the debate moments that never were, strategic maneuvers contemplated but not executed. After Mondale's win against Reagan in the first 1984 debate, Democratic advisers briefly considered dropping a bombshell in the follow-up encounter. In the course of the debate, Mondale would produce a letter the president had written in 1960 to Richard Nixon, a letter that compared John Kennedy's ideas to those of Karl Marx and Adolf Hitler. Mondale himself dismissed the suggestion as undignified.[12]

The threat of another mystery document surfaced in 1992, when aides to Bill Clinton fretted that George Bush might flourish a letter in which the collegiate Clinton had weighed renouncing his American citizenship. "They're signaling like crazy that they have something dramatic," Democratic strategist James Carville warned his candidate before one of the 1992 debates. "But I think it's a seventy-five percent chance they're just playing mind games with us."[13] Indeed, no such letter materialized.

The Bush team did discuss a different surprise involving Bill Clinton and a letter. In this scenario Bush was to send his opponent a debate-day demand that he honor an earlier promise to release his complete draft records. During the telecast Bush would then challenge Clinton to set the matter straight. "The handlers liked the idea," wrote *Newsweek*, "but Bush, worrying about op-ed types fussing over McCarthyism, decided the ploy would only worsen his press."[14]

In 1988 Bush advisers feared that Michael Dukakis would break format at the beginning of one of the programs by challenging the vice president to dismiss the press panel and debate him one-on-one. When a Bush aide overheard a rumor to this effect from a member of the technical crew, the Republicans cobbled together a last-minute counterstrategy: if the governor abrogated the rules, Bush would step out from behind his lectern and ask Dukakis to come down from his podium. Viewers would then see that the shorter Dukakis had been perched atop a height-enhancing riser.

During the technical rehearsal preceding the second Bush-Dukakis debate, Bush aides checked their man's microphone to see if it could be disengaged and swung around in case Bush needed to move out in front of his podium. This repositioning caught the attention of Democratic handlers in the hall. Assuming that *Bush* was planning to break format, they cautioned Dukakis to expect the worst, possibly even the presence in the debate audience of the victims of Willie Horton, the Massachusetts prisoner who jumped furlough during Dukakis's tenure. The governor's aides thought Bush might ask his opponent to justify himself to the victims in front of the nation.

"This is the level of obsession, I guess, that presidential campaigns go through in these things," Dukakis coach Tom Donilon later said of the incident. Republican strategist Charles Black agreed: "Part of the problem is you get there the last afternoon and evening, and there's nothing to do, so you think up all these cute things."[15]

Before the final 1992 debate, Democratic operatives got word that the Bush campaign was planning to seat Clinton paramour Gennifer Flowers in the debate audience, next to Barbara Bush. "The notion was preposterous," wrote Jack Germond and Jules Witcover, "but the fact the rumor was circulating at all was an indicator of the high stakes in the debate."[16] In 1996 Bob Dole's campaign actually did plant an antagonistic figure in the audience: Billy Dale, who, in a minor dustup at the beginning of the Clinton presidency, had been fired from the White House travel office. Dale's presence at the Hartford debate was supposed to disconcert Clinton; in fact, the president had no idea what Billy Dale looked like.

UNDERSTANDING THE OBJECTIVE

Debate strategy is situational: A participant must deliver not just a memorable moment but the precise memorable moment that the circumstances require. Every candidate comes to a debate with a distinct objective. The 1980 Reagan-Carter match offers a textbook instance of a debater making the most of his opportunity. In that encounter Ronald Reagan dispelled voter concerns that he was a trigger-happy warmonger.

Of course no candidate steps before the camera an unfamiliar commodity. "By the time they engage in presidential debates," wrote political communication scholar Robert V. Friedenberg, "most presidential candidates are reasonably well known and already have firmly established images with the public. Consequently presidential image goals often involve modifying existing images."[17] Friedenberg dates this trend back to 1960, when Nixon sought to change his "political assassin" image while Kennedy tried to offset doubts about his lack of executive experience.

Candidates lose debates when they fail to shake off a negative perception: Bob Dole as a hatchet man in 1976, Ronald Reagan as too old for the job in 1984, Dukakis as unfeeling in 1988, Bush as disconnected from voters in 1992. Candidates win when they manage to overcome a bad rap, as Reagan did in 1980. According to Richard Wirthlin, "We knew that Ronald Reagan was a lot more powerful than he had ever been judged, which was a real advantage. It's always nice to be underestimated and exceed expectations."[18]

The Reagan-Carter match illustrates the risks incumbent presidents face in TV debates. In five election years—1976, 1980, 1984, 1992, and 1996—sitting presidents have appeared alongside challengers, in an admirable tradition of democratic sportsmanship. With the exception of Bill Clinton in 1996, the incumbent is generally thought to have faced the more difficult task. Says political scientist Austin Ranney, "Most pundits naturally believe that either the challenger or the underdog has an inherent advantage—the biggest advantage, of course, going to an underdog challenger. Challengers allegedly have that advantage because they get to stand next to a sitting president, increasing their credibility and their visibility."[19]

Carter strategist Patrick Caddell has defined debates as "the vehicle of challengers. . . . They are the best device for a challenger to reach and cross the Acceptability Threshold."[20] Until Bob Dole took on Bill Clinton, one could argue that just such a threshold was crossed by every upstart candidate. For these would-be chief executives, understanding the moment meant positioning oneself as equal in stature to the most powerful individual on the planet.

In 1976, when Jimmy Carter became the first challenger to debate a sitting president, Carter's team properly identified its mission as isolating Ford from the trappings of his office. Still they feared a backlash if the upstart candidate appeared overly antagonistic toward so revered a figure as an American president. According to journalist Jules Witcover, "Carter himself was uncertain what the chemistry would be at that moment when he finally stood on the stage with President Ford and matched wits, statistics, and barbs with him. He had no sense of awe toward Gerald Ford the man ... But separating that man from the presidency was vexing."[21]

For their part, Ford handlers took pains to frame their candidate's participation in the 1976 debates as an act of political noblesse oblige. Media consultant Doug Bailey wrote that the debates were "not between two candidates but between one candidate and the president. Everything said, done, and projected by the president should emphasize that fact. If the president is consistently, persistently presidential, Carter (no matter what he does) will not measure up."[22]

Four years later incumbent President Carter staked out this same territory for himself against Reagan. In a 1980 memorandum, Caddell wrote, "The president's role is not to debate Ronald Reagan. We are letting the American people compare responses to similar questions. Reagan is the foil for the president."[23] As it happened, executive aloofness afforded no protection against the potent Reagan charm, and Carter's attempt to marginalize his opponent backfired.

Incumbent status does offer certain advantages to a presidential debater. As Reagan adviser Richard Wirthlin suggests, "Incumbency helps in terms of the simple accrual of knowledge that a president gets." High-level briefings, meetings with foreign leaders, unfettered access to a broad range of information—all these represent valuable assets for an incumbent debater. Furthermore, sitting presidents typically hold a strong hand in the negotiation process.

But there are negatives, Wirthlin warns: "When a president sits in the Oval Office, in most cases, he lives in a White House cocoon. Everyone is deferential to him. Very seldom is he attacked one-on-one. And suddenly he is put in a position where not only his issues are being questioned, but his motives are being questioned as well." In the first debate of 1984, Wirthlin said, this sense of isolation bedeviled Ronald Reagan: "He wasn't used to someone talking to him as forcefully as Mondale did, and it took him off balance."[24]

Despite the windfall of Reagan's poor performance in the first 1984 debate, Mondale could not accomplish what every challenger must: persuading the electorate to trade in its president for a new model. The next time an incumbent participated in a TV debate this mission proved less daunting. George Bush, rarely a lucky man in debates, found himself doubly threatened in 1992, having to defend against both Bill Clinton and Ross Perot. Bush's failure to understand what was required of him until too late in the process greatly benefited the opposition.

Like other presidents before him, Bush allowed personal disdain for his competitors to blind him to the attraction Clinton and Perot held for much of the electorate. By underestimating the threat, Bush got left at the starting line, particularly in the town hall debate that so heavily abetted Clinton. Clinton, meanwhile, used the 1992 debates to "close the deal" with voters. Said Clinton campaign manager Mickey Kantor, "In a sense, we had a Ronald Reagan 1980 problem; the final sale had to made that Bill Clinton was credible."[25]

Because they usually have recent experience in primary forums, challengers tend to be better toned for debates than their out-of-practice competitors. Such was the case with Clinton, who had shown his prowess in breaking from the pack in the crowded Democratic primaries of 1992. At an Illinois appearance, Clinton took command when he rebuked former California governor Jerry Brown for questioning Hillary Clinton's professional probity. "I don't care what you say about me," Clinton snapped, "but you ought to be ashamed of yourself for jumpin' on my wife." Gwen Ifill in the *New York Times* described this as a "calculated but seemingly genuine explosion of anger"[26]—which is to say that Clinton understood the moment and availed himself of it.

As the first of her gender to participate in an executive-level debate, Geraldine Ferraro stepped up to the lectern both blessed and disadvantaged. On the plus side, as Ferraro told campaign journalists Germond and Witcover, she "could hit (George Bush) as hard as she liked, and he would not be able to return her fire in kind for fear of being cast as a bully."[27] At the same time enormous pressures fell on Ferraro, not only as a political standard-bearer but as a symbol of womanhood. According to Ferraro's debate coach, the candidate "could be ladylike, which would make her appear uninformed and too delicate to do the job; or she could be assertive, which would make her appear bitchy."[28]

Opponent Bush had his own hobgoblins to tame. As debate scholar Judith S. Trent wrote, "He needed to find the acceptable "twilight zone" between being perceived as an unacceptably aggressive attacker or an unacceptably passive lap dog." Moreover, Trent added, Bush aides worried that Ferraro's assertive style might unhinge him, "and thus reveal the kind of high-strung and nervous manner that had hurt him in other debates."[29] Bush was advised to win but not to have Ferraro lose. Observed Bush, "I don't think they would have said that if I had been debating Tony Coelho."[30]

Beyond gender, the Bush-Ferraro debate embodied a second strategic consideration, one that applies to all encounters between vice presidential candidates: "junior" debaters have substantially more room for maneuver. As political scientist Michael J. Robinson wrote of the Dole-Mondale encounter, "Small stakes make for more fun and quicker moves."[31] Indeed, this first vice presidential debate in 1976 proved far livelier than any of that year's Ford-Carter programs; the 1984, 1988, and 1992 vice presidential matches also surpassed the bigger-name broadcasts for sheer entertainment.

Part of what makes second-string debates more watchable is the latitude the running mates have to "go negative," particularly against the opposing presidential candidate. This freedom has generated sparks in vice presidential debates that could not ignite in the more rarefied air of the top-of-the-ticket appearances. In 1992, for example, Dan Quayle proved to be a formidable attack dog on the issue of Bill Clinton's character; four years later, Jack Kemp was criticized for failing to do the same. Debate researcher Diana Carlin explains that second bananas can be more aggressive "because they aren't expected to be presidential the way the presidential candidates are. And they can say things about their own candidate that the candidate cannot say about him- or herself."

As a baseline requirement, vice presidential debaters must reassure voters about their suitability for stepping into office. "This is not just another presidential debate with surrogates," says Carlin. "There should be a question in every single vice presidential debate about why you are qualified to take over—the Dan Quayle question."[32] A running mate who can demonstrate his or her presidential timber passes the test.

In the end, even successful vice presidential debaters bump up against the political equivalent of a glass ceiling. "The truth of the matter is that the vice presidential debates are really unimportant in the big picture," says James

Baker. "It's great theater, but it doesn't matter. People aren't making their voting determinations based on who's vice president."[33]

In a 1980 *Washington Post* column, television consultant Jack Hilton offered a series of suggestions to that year's presidential debaters. High on the list was the imperative "Be Liked." As Hilton saw it: "The emotional content of the debate will remain in the viewers' memories for longer than the ideas expressed. A candidate can fail in all of his objectives for the debate and still win if the viewers at home feel empathy or sympathy for him."[34]

The ethos of television demands that its star performers be "likable"; hence the cookie-cutter joviality of TV news anchors, commercial spokespersons, game show hosts, and sitcom actors. For presidential debaters, likability functions as a wild card, a commodity much prized yet impossible to generate on cue. Those lacking charisma, charisma as defined by television, face an uphill battle.

Such was the case with 1988 Democratic nominee Michael Dukakis, whose strategic objective entailed, in effect, a personality overhaul. To the candidate's credit, but also to his misfortune, Dukakis did not attempt to remake himself into Mister Congeniality in order to please the audience and the press. According to biographers Oliphant and Black, "Dukakis was more serious than Bush, more articulate, more overtly aggressive, scored many more debating points, and, ultimately, was less likable."[35]

This supposed deficiency became a discussion topic during the debates themselves. "Wouldn't it be nice to be perfect?" Bush asked viewers sarcastically. "Wouldn't it be nice to be the Ice Man so you never make a mistake?" Margaret Warner, a questioner in the second 1988 debate, put the issue directly to Dukakis: "Governor, you won the first debate on intellect and yet you lost it on heart . . . The American people admired your performance but didn't seem to like you very much." By way of reply, Dukakis declared himself a "reasonably likable guy." But when a candidate must publicly defend his appeal, the matter has already been decided.

ATTITUDE TOWARD OPPONENT

Democratic media consultant Tony Schwartz has described the presidency as "the only job in the world for which all of the applicants show up at the interview and attack each other."[36] Indeed, the nakedness of the clash is a distinguishing feature of TV debates. Presenting one's own case will not suffice; one must also bash the opposition, and do so in a way that passes the smell test of tens of millions of viewers. Each debater walks a tightrope between disparaging the competition and being properly respectful. Balancing these contradictory imperatives calls for a good deal of tactical forethought.

"At all times be courteous, respectful, friendly in manner, even when vigorously disagreeing or criticizing, even when unfairly attacked," Theodore Sorensen counseled Jimmy Carter in 1976. Sorensen had been brought into the campaign as an adviser because of his experience in the 1960 debates with John F. Kennedy. "Do not call your opponent names or slur his character or criticize his wife. But beware of appearing too agreeable to the point of passivity; be vigorously assertive and positive; take the initiative, avoid being on the defensive."[37]

Before the Cleveland debate in 1980, Reagan's campaign brain trust advised their candidate to "show righteous indignation" in responding to suggestions that he was dangerous or that questioned his California credentials. "Looking directly at Carter in such instances can be very effective," Reagan's coaches told him. "Humor or a confident smile can also disarm Carter when he thinks he's got you where he wants you."[38]

In 1984 Mondale made the decision to surprise Reagan by treating him with gracious deference. Strategists devised what they called the "gold watch" approach: The popular incumbent had done his job, but now it was time to move on—"sort of embracing a grandfather and gently pushing him aside," in the words of Democratic adviser Caddell.[39] Caddell suggested that Mondale begin the exchange with an informal greeting to Reagan, perhaps even present his opponent with a humorous gift. Mondale did not go that far, but in the opening debate he conceded that the president had "done some things to raise the sense of spirit and morale—good feeling—in this country," and added, "I like President Reagan." According to Elizabeth Drew, although Mondale had not planned the latter remark, he ad-libbed the extra compliment when he realized his affability was rattling Reagan.[40]

"The critical element to making the debate an overwhelming success is surprise," Caddell had written in advance of the first Reagan-Mondale debate. So successful was this strategy in unnerving Reagan that Caddell recommended still bolder moves for the second debate. "Mondale must not simply beat Reagan, he must take him apart. . . . The key for Mondale is to convince voters that Reagan has 'lost it' and that he ought to be retired."[41] As it happened, a perfectly delivered one-liner by the supposedly senile Reagan shattered Mondale's plan. "It was clear in the first fifteen minutes of the debate that Reagan was much more in command," said Mondale aide Richard Leone. "Nothing was going to come out of it except a reassurance people needed to vote him in for another four years."[42]

In 1988 Democratic adviser Tom Donilon articulated a definition of victory for Michael Dukakis that would seem to apply to debaters across the board: Whoever emerges the "appropriate aggressor" wins the match. Being an appropriate aggressor means going on the offense without being offensive; making moves that are bold but not reckless; appearing confident but not prosecutorial. "If he could be nice, okay," Donilon said, but the top priority for Dukakis was to answer Bush's attacks on his character. "To the degree that we had to sacrifice likability for that, we did."[43]

George Bush, by contrast, faced not a deficit but a surfeit of niceness. Fearing their candidate's good manners would be misconstrued as passivity, Republican debate coaches in 1988 worked to uncork Bush's repressed competitive juices. According to adviser Lee Atwater, Bush needed to be a "counterpuncher." Said Atwater, "The nature of the man is such that he does not go out and start a fight, he doesn't start controversy or confrontation, but if he gets hit, he hits back."[44]

In the 1992 election, incumbent President Bush continued to resist an aggressive stance. His complacent posture in the first debate allowed Bill Clinton to pull off a maneuver that dominated postevent coverage. When Bush questioned Clinton's patriotism in the first debate—a ploy Bush had also executed against Dukakis—the Arkansas governor forcefully reminded his opponent that Senator Prescott Bush, the president's father, had led the fight against Joseph McCarthy during the communist witch hunts of the 1950s. "Your father was right to stand up to Joe McCarthy," said Clinton. "You were wrong to attack my patriotism." For most of this exchange, Bush self-consciously scribbled notes, as Clinton stared him down. According to George Stephanopoulos, the confrontation played out "word for word, the way we wanted it."[45]

As though surrounded by a protective force field, Bill Clinton never got stung in any of his five presidential debates. In 1996 predebate hype called for Bob Dole to assail Clinton on the "character issue," but no such lambasting took place. "Dole could not attack his opponent's character at the eleventh hour without bringing his own character disastrously into question," concluded *U.S. News and World Report*.[46] Politically Dole's decision made sense. Studies of debate audiences conducted by Diana Carlin found that voters are put off by candidates who launch personal broadsides. "They don't mind attacking," Carlin says, "but they want people to attack ideas."[47]

Twenty years after the fact, Bob Dole still bore the scars of his abrasive, misconceived performance in the 1976 vice presidential debate. A *New York Times* headline from October 1996 indicates the pressure Dole faced vis-à-vis his own reputation: "Searing Images from Debates Past Are Continuing to Haunt Dole." The story revisited not only the infamous match with Walter Mondale but also Dole's controversial 1974 Senate debate in Kansas. In that encounter the candidate was booed by an audience at the state fair for snarling at his opponent, a Topeka obstetrician, "I want to know how many abortions you've done."[48]

Although he exceeded 1996 expectations by not devolving into "the mean Bob Dole," the senator could make little headway against the gilded television persona of President Clinton. If anything, observers were disappointed that the irascible Bob Dole of old had gone soft. Political writer Joe Klein said, "Dole seemed to be a halfhearted gladiator, too decent (and no doubt wary) to be a very effective hatchet man and too limited a political performer to provide a very compelling alternative to Bill Clinton."[49] Like every born entertainer, Clinton understood the first rule of stardom: Grab the lead role for yourself, and the other fellow gets cast as second banana.

The examples of Clinton, Reagan, and Kennedy suggest that the public responds favorably to debaters who display a high degree of self-possession. As Michael Deaver, Reagan's long-time media adviser, observed, "What is important is how comfortable the person is with himself. (David) McCullough, in his book about Truman, said there was nobody in the world he'd rather be. That's what we're looking for. If you can get that across in the debate, that's what people are hungry for."[50]

By virtue of their competitive structure, television debates provide a natural forum for the expression of leadership. This is why candidates struggle to control the narrative; when a debater takes ownership of the event, audiences are witnessing executive ability in action. "What wins a political debate," says Democratic strategist Richard Leone, "is if one candidate seems in command—of himself, of the environment, of his opponent." Republican adviser Roger Ailes expresses it another way: "People reduce it down to fairly simplistic language: I want a president who can hit a home run."[51]

RHETORICAL STRATEGIES

Like soldiers armed with hand grenades, candidates march into televised debates bearing an arsenal of rhetorical ammunition. Whatever the question being asked, debaters are instructed to answer with the desired, predetermined response. This goal of staying on message, borrowed from the world of advertising, ties debaters to a set of narrowly conceived themes, themes that have been audience-tested and painstakingly rehearsed.

In 1976 Gerald Ford's "basic message" was divided into seven points. According to press secretary Ron Nessen, "No matter what specific question was asked, the president was to answer it briefly, then slip into one of the seven points." Each of the seven points came equipped with its own one-liners: "A president cannot be all things to all people"; "There is no button in the Oval Office marked 'maybe' "; "Surely Mr. Carter understands why vetoes are necessary. As governor of Georgia, he vetoed his own legislature one hundred thirty-eight times in four years"; and so forth.[52]

Carter, meanwhile, chose a strategy of identification with "the people." Scholar Stephen R. Brydon noted that Carter used the word *people* more than seventy times over the three encounters, compared to Ford's thirty. "The challenger claimed that the people were the source of his own strength and knowledge," Brydon wrote. "Carter portrayed himself as one of the people, representing their needs, hopes, and aspirations."[53]

In 1980, running against Reagan, incumbent President Carter shifted to a top-down, leaderly approach. The Democratic candidate was coached to "leave personal and policy footprints" during the debate, using definitive language to enforce his air of authority: "I strongly believe . . ."; "I have always stood for . . ."; "I have always had a firm commitment to . . ." Carter strategists devised phrases that would paint Reagan as too much of a simpleton to serve as president: "You make it sound as easy as one, two, three"; "You make it sound as easy as apple pie"; "That sounds good but nostalgia won't solve our problems."[54]

For his part, Ronald Reagan's verbal strategy in 1980 called for the repeated use of a single reinforcing word: *peace*. In his first response of the 1980 debate, the Republican candidate got straight to the point: "I'm only here to tell you that I believe with all my heart that our first priority must be world peace," Reagan said, informing viewers that "I have seen four wars in my lifetime. I'm a father of sons. I have a grandson." Wrote Lou Cannon, "Reagan mentioned 'peace' so often it sounded like he had invented the word."[55]

Throughout his career, Reagan's rhetorical deftness vexed his competitors. Before the 1984 debates the Mondale campaign sought advice from former California governor Pat Brown, who had debated Reagan in the 1966 gubernatorial race. "Everybody who had experience with Reagan had essentially the same story, which was, there's only so much you can do," said Mondale aide Richard Leone. "You can't draw him into an intellectual tennis match at the net, and his lobs are going to drive you nuts because you can't really pound them back." According to Leone, Brown's advice to the Mondale campaign was grim: "Don't think there's anything you can do that will get him off his script."[56]

As it turned out, Reagan's rustiness gave Mondale an unexpected edge in the first debate of 1984. Mondale spooked Reagan, causing him, in essence, to forget his lines. In the wake of this disaster, media coach Roger Ailes urged the president to get back to rhetorical basics: "You didn't get elected on details," Ailes reminded Reagan. "You got elected on themes. Every time a question is asked, relate it to one of your themes."[57] This advice apparently worked, for in the second debate, Reagan discarded the flawed facts-and-figures approach for what scholars Smith and Smith described as "his familiar cinematic language."[58]

Audience researcher Diana Carlin says that voters strongly approve of debaters who, like Reagan, are able to translate abstract issues into the language of everyday lives: "They like the metaphors, they like the stories."[59] On this count, Bill Clinton fared particularly well in the audience participation debates of 1992 and 1996. Clinton psychobiographer Stanley Renshon saw evidence in these town hall performances of the candidate's gift for "strategic empathy,"[60] a skill highly prized among television audiences weaned on confessional talk shows.

At the opposite end of the strategic empathy spectrum is a debater like Michael Dukakis. Democratic adviser Frank Mankiewicz aptly defined the problem when he told *Newsweek*, "Dukakis has a tendency to say things like 'We must be concerned about health care for the elderly.' He needs to say, 'What about your ninety-year-old mother?' "[61] In practice sessions before the 1988 debates, Mario Cuomo encouraged Dukakis to tell stories, while Bill Clinton exhorted him to get angry.

Democratic coach Sam Popkin instructs debaters to bone up on the price of simple consumer goods, in case such a question comes up. "The single defining moment of Francois Mitterand's defeat of Valery Giscard D'Estaing was when Mitterand asked in a debate 'Do you even know the price of a metro ticket?' and Giscard hadn't a clue," Popkin wrote in a 1996 memo for Clinton. "Knowing the prices people pay for products and services every day is important evidence for continued connectedness."[62]

Staying connected to the audience also means not insulting them. In the 1976 vice presidential match Bob Dole's disdain for the entire debate process unwittingly extended to the body politic. Dole referred to the viewers as "those who may be still tuned in" and "those who may still be with us." As political communication scholar Kevin Sauter wrote, "The implication that those watching the debate should probably have tuned out earlier may not have been a direct affront ... but after an evening of Dole's sharp attacks on the Democrats, to make an unflattering remark about the audience was not an astute rhetorical move."[63]

Dole's intemperate 1976 performance serves as a warning to other candidates about the perils of too much spontaneity. In a television debate, contrived moments seem to play better than unplanned ones: Reagan's "There you go again" and the joke about his opponent's "youth and inexperience"; Bentsen's "You're no Jack Kennedy"; Clinton feeling the audience's pain—these are the strategies that have triumphed. A candidate of the old school, Dole held fast against the phoniness of predebate gamesmanship—the play-acting, the rehearsing, the cosmetics—and said what popped into his head. Admirable as such resistance might be, Dole paid a price for repudiating the rules of presidential debates.

Dole's 1976 debate also highlights the riskiness of wisecracks as a rhetorical device. In that program Dole let loose with a steady flow of sharp-edged remarks. He accused Mondale of enlisting union leader George Meany as his makeup man. Referring to Jimmy Carter's controversial *Playboy* magazine interview, Dole said, "We'll give him the bunny vote." And so on. The net effect of the sarcasm was to turn viewers off. According to James Hoge, who moderated the Dole-Mondale debate, "Humor is a very dangerous thing in politics, particularly if it's ironic or sarcastic. With that huge an audience, most good politicians tend to avoid it."[64]

Natural wit being a rare commodity among presidential contenders, debaters have relied heavily on scripted zingers. This practice hit rock bottom in 1988, when George Bush dropped all pretense a few minutes into the first debate and asked, "Is this the time to unleash our one-liners?" Bush then proceeded to unleash: "That answer was about as clear as Boston

Harbor." Michael Dukakis had prompted Bush's outburst with his own creaky one-liner: "If he keeps this up, he's going to be the Joe Isuzu of American politics," Dukakis said, invoking the prevaricating star of a series of popular TV commercials. In both cases one could almost hear the grinding of the gag writers' gears.

For the 1992 debates Bush was given a laundry list of suggested jokes, most of which, mercifully, he ignored: "That last answer was almost as inflated as prices would be in a Clinton presidency"; "I'd find broccoli easier to swallow than that last answer"; "Listening to Governor Clinton talk about integrity is like listening to Madonna talk about chastity."[65] Roger Ailes weighed in with his own suggestion: "You can't turn the White House into the Waffle House," which Bush did manage to work into the second debate but not quite as Ailes had planned. Before delivering the gag, Bush was supposed to set it up with three prior uses of the word *waffle*; instead, he offered the punch line minus the appropriate set-up.[66]

As it developed, the scripted bons mots of President Bush were no match for the organic, almost relentless wit of rival Ross Perot. Perot's skill with homespun one-liners reflected the candidate's true personality and not the labor of anonymous jokesmiths. Addressing his lack of government experience, Perot declared in the first debate, "I don't have any experience in running up a four trillion dollar debt," as the audience roared with laughter. A few minutes later, he shot back with what would become the signature sound bite of the night. Asked about his proposal to offset the deficit by raising gasoline taxes, Perot said, "If there's a fairer way, I'm all ears."

What was the effect of Perot's jocularity? As political communication specialist Dan F. Hahn pointed out, the zingers drew audience applause and gained extensive replay as sound bites in later media accounts. "Yet it is not clear whether these bites, successful in the short run, ultimately redounded to his benefit or came to be seen as just a little too simple for someone who would be president."[67] By the end of the series the jokes had worn thin. In a focus-group discussion after the third debate, a Boston woman remarked, "It's nice that someone has some humor and lightens things up, but now it seems like every opportunity he had to speak he had a quick one-liner."[68]

The looser formats of recent debates appear to have lessened candidates' dependence on scripted zingers; in 1996 only a handful of obvious sound bites emerged. Bill Clinton, anticipating questions about his character, got off a much-replayed line in the San Diego town hall debate: "No attack ever created a job or educated a child or helped a family make ends meet. No insult ever cleaned up a toxic waste dump or helped an elderly person." But by the usual standards of presidential debates, 1996 contained few moments of deliberately memorable rhetoric.

James J. Pinkerton, who covered the San Diego debate for *Newsday*, wrote that he "groaned out loud when Dole started to tell his little gag about the need for litigation reform." Reminding the viewers of his tumble from a stage in Chico, California, Dole said, "Before I hit the ground, my cell phone rang and this trial lawyer says 'I think we got a case here.' " As Pinkerton noted, Dole had used the line hundreds of times on the campaign trail—"and yet the bit got a healthy laugh. Real people, who pay only intermittent attention to the campaign, hadn't yet heard it. The moral of this media story: repeat, repeat and repeat—and then repeat some more."[69]

But repetition has its dangers. In the 1996 vice presidential debate Al Gore repeatedly referred to Bob Dole's tax plan as a "risky scheme"—"a zillion times," according to ABC's Sam Donaldson, who said the vice president seemed to be "reading a teleprompter in his mind." Lisa Myers on NBC described Gore as a "digitalized telephone operator,"[70] while other critics reached for unflattering metaphors of their own. Instead of reinforcing his point, Al Gore's transparently predigested rhetoric became the object of ridicule.

DEBATE BOOT CAMP

A lasting legacy of the Kennedy-Nixon "Great Debates" is the immersion of candidates in debate boot camp as a prerequisite to the actual event. Since 1960, all but a handful of presidential debaters have followed John F. Kennedy's lead in setting aside time to tone up for this most strenuous of telecasts. Although both staffs in 1960 compiled massive briefing books—JFK's people called theirs the "Nixopedia"—only Kennedy practiced for the debate with his advisers. According to Nixon campaign manager Bob Finch, "We kept pushing for (Nixon) to have some give-and-take with either somebody from the staff . . . anything. He hadn't done anything except to tell me he knew how to debate. He totally refused to prepare."[71]

Where Kennedy's predebate preps consisted of informal drills with aides reading questions off index cards, today's candidates go through detailed simulations that duplicate the format, timing, and production circumstances of the televised program. Stand-ins for the moderators, panelists, and even town hall questioners grill the debaters in sessions that are video-taped, then played back for critiquing. Each campaign amasses a team of experts to attend to its candidate's every need: political strategists and poli-cy specialists, speechwriters and voice coaches, lighting technicians and makeup artists.

From Nixon in 1960 to Bob Dole in 1996, nominees have ignored, at their peril, the preliminary conditioning presidential debates require. With so much riding on performance, only the most cavalier of candidates—or, like Perot and Stockdale, the most unorthodox—fail to subject themselves to a predebate regimen. The goal of rehearsal is simple: to ready the debater for any contingency. As Bill Carruthers, TV adviser to President Ford, put it, "When the president walks out onto that stage, nothing can be a surprise to him."[72]

The lessons of Kennedy and Nixon loomed large for the candidates and their staffs in 1976. Aides on both sides pored over the 1960 preparation materials, while the star performers, like football players studying classic game footage, watched at least part of the historic broadcasts. In Plains, Georgia, Carter held a Saturday night screening of the Kennedy-Nixon debates for a handful of relatives, aides, and friends; included in the group was actor Robert Redford, who had recently starred in *The Candidate*.[73]

It is Gerald Ford, not an individual normally associated with theatrics, who became the first presidential contender to stage full-scale practice debates, complete with lecterns, stand-in questioners, cameras, lights, and makeup. Earlier in the year, Ford had used a video setup to rehearse his acceptance speech before the Republican convention, with positive results. Advisers now scheduled a series of predebate run-throughs to be staged, recorded, and dissected in the White House family theater.

Videotape of these rehearsals shows a no-nonsense, highly professional operation at work. The Ford team took advantage of its practice sessions to deal with both content and stylistics. At the end of one gathering, Ford crumples a paper at his lectern and says, "Okay, let's see how the clothes look, and any other comments that you have." When not practicing with a live Jimmy Carter stand-in, President Ford shares the stage with a television monitor set up to play sound bites from a Carter appearance on *Meet the Press*. The mock panelists ask questions of the monitor; Carter's taped response plays back. As coached, Ford gazes forcefully at the TV version of his opponent during these replays.

The president does not always seem to be enjoying himself in the rehearsals. At one point he stops a session in progress, looks down at his watch, and announces, "I think this is enough," at which point the proceeding immediately ends. But reflecting on the experience later, Ford credited the preparation process. "Over a four-day period, I spent nine hours under the lights, and the grueling interrogation boosted my confidence," Ford wrote in his autobiography.[74]

Because rehearsals of this magnitude were unheard of in 1976, the White House sought to downplay Gerald Ford's debate preps. Carter forces, meanwhile, attempted to capitalize on what they viewed as efforts to program the Republican candidate. Of his own debate preparations, Carter pointedly assured a reporter, "I am not going to go off and practice against a dummy opponent or memorize any cute speeches or anything like that."[75]

True to his word, Carter at first would not even let his aides run questions by him, preferring instead to read his briefing books in private—the Richard Nixon approach. After the opening 1976 debate in Philadelphia, in which Carter seemed cowed by Ford and reticent to attack, he did agree to parry questions with his senior staff. But for the duration of the series, Carter steadfastly refused to participate in a mock debate.

In 1980, against show business veteran Ronald Reagan, Jimmy Carter dropped his objections. The president's team scheduled a series of mock debates, first at Camp David and then at Carter's hotel in Cleveland just before the co-appearance with Reagan. For the ninety-minute, real-time session at Camp David, lights, cameras, and lecterns were installed at Hickory Lodge, and political science professor Sam Popkin arrived from California to portray the Republican nominee.

Popkin, an expert in the rhetoric of Ronald Reagan, had come to Carter's attention with a strategy memo called "Popping Balloons," the aim of which was to help the president navigate the rocky shoals of Reagan's deceptively benign communication style. Among other suggestions, Popkin advised, "You don't beat a story with a fact—you beat a story with another story." In their first practice session, when the "stunt Reagan" trounced the president of the United States, Carter realized the challenge he would face against so folksy a rival. At the end of the practice, Popkin recalled, "I thought they were going to have the Marines break my kneecaps."

Of no small help to the Carter prep squad was the utter predictability of Reagan's language. The long-time conservative activist had spent many years on the hustings delivering essentially the same message, and for the

debates the script did not change. According to Popkin, "With one exception, every single Reagan speech I gave in every single practice was actually
used."[76]

In Carter's final run-through before the Cleveland debate, the president
told his aides about a conversation he had had with his daughter, Amy, on
the subject of nuclear war; Carter wondered if this might be something to
raise during the debate. "We had all argued against it," said chief of staff
Hamilton Jordan, "perhaps not as bluntly as we should have." According to
Sam Popkin, just as advisers were recommending against the Amy anecdote,
an inopportune phone call distracted Carter, and the message never sank in.
"That's why when you watch the tape, he clutches when he brings it up,"
Popkin said. "He knew he wasn't supposed to."[77]

To no one's surprise, Hollywood candidate Ronald Reagan perfected the
art of full-scale debate rehearsals in 1980, mounting elaborate mock debates
at the Reagans' rented home in the Virginia countryside. The Reagan campaign converted the garage into a professional quality television studio and
signed on Michigan congressman David Stockman to play John Anderson,
and later Jimmy Carter. Some twenty advisers attended these practice sessions, not counting the stand-in questioners.

Despite his years as a professional showman, Reagan was notoriously bad
in rehearsal. After the first dry run for the Anderson debate, Stockman
wrote, "You felt kind of sorry for the guy, but his lack of agility was disqui-
eting." As an outsider in Reagan's campaign circle, Stockman was astonished
to observe that none of the senior advisers wanted to take charge of the critique session. "The campaign staff treated him with kid gloves. . . . It was all
on-the-one-hand . . . on-the-other-hand."[78]

Stockman's comment underscores one of the ongoing conundrums of
debate preparations: Who will tell the emperor he has no clothes? Advisers
involved in practice sessions have found it difficult to balance candor with
deference, criticism with praise. Their diffidence is understandable. In order
to execute the stunt at hand, presidential debaters must be able to draw from
a deep well of self-confidence. Any hint of dissatisfaction during rehearsals,
anything less than a full endorsement by one's own campaign staff might
rattle the star at just the wrong moment.

In 1984 Reagan advisers so miscalculated their candidate's needs that they
prepared him in exactly the wrong way before the disastrous first debate in
Louisville. "Everybody forgot that he'd been president of the United States
for four years, so we briefed him the same way we did in 1980," said Michael

Deaver.[79] Instead of concentrating on broad themes, the debate advisers stuffed their candidate full of facts.

Reagan wrote in his memoirs that he was "hurt" by the people trying to help him in 1984:

> Everybody around me started saying, "You have to know this . . . you have to know that"; then they fill your head with all sorts of details, technicalities, and statistics as if you were getting ready to take an exam on those topics. Finally, when you're in a debate, you realize you just can't command all that information and still do a good job as a debater.[80]

After the Louisville debacle, Nancy Reagan angrily confronted Deaver back at the hotel. "What have you done to my husband?" she demanded. "Whatever it was, don't do it again."[81] As the press delved into the particulars of Reagan's preparations, Republican advisers began a round of finger-pointing. Senator Paul Laxalt, a Reagan intimate, told the media that the president had been "brutalized" and "smothered" by the briefing process.[82] Unnamed members of the debate prep team hinted that Reagan's own indolence was to blame.

To avert another disaster, campaign commanders imported a high-power guru for Reagan: Roger Ailes, a New York communication consultant who, in the 1968 election, had served as Richard Nixon's media adviser. In the words of Lou Cannon, "Ailes was to reassurance what Nixon was to foreign policy."[83] The coach began his workout by putting Reagan through a quick question-and-answer exercise called a "pepper drill." "Go back to your instincts," Ailes counseled his student. "Just say what comes to you out of your experience." For an hour, the drill continued. "Every time he'd start to stumble," Ailes recalled, "I'd ask, 'What do your instincts tell you about this?' and he'd come right back on track. He was very good. Finally I said, 'Mr. President, if you can do that Sunday night, you're home free.' "[84]

Under Ailes's tutelage, Reagan regained his confidence and showed considerable improvement. To boost the president's spirits further, the staff staged a pep rally at his hotel in Kansas City immediately before the debate. Beneath a banner marked "Hail to the Kansas City Chief," Reagan greeted supporters with an anecdote about a young American soldier who had relayed a message to him from Germany: "We're proud to be here, and we ain't scared of nothin.' " Reagan thanked the crowd, looked down at his watch, and, with a self-effacing grin, said, "I guess now I've got to go to work." Then, amid chants of "U-S-A, U-S-A!" the president departed for the auditorium.[85] According to Michael Deaver: "Reagan was always buoyed by something like that. He was, after all, an entertainer."[86]

DEBATE PREPS: BEYOND REAGAN

The 1985 autobiography of Geraldine Ferraro offers a rare firsthand account of debate preparations from the candidate's perspective. Like other debaters, Ferraro viewed her boot camp experience with mixed feelings. "It seemed like such a waste of my time, and everybody else's as well," she observed.

> I felt embarrassed sitting there, surrounded by three people the first afternoon and many more in subsequent sessions, giving thoughtful answers in such an artificial circumstance. All the candidates were doing it, of course. Mondale. Reagan. Bush. But that's what has always made these debates so phony. You get to say too little, and what you do say is so well rehearsed that I'm not sure the public has any more idea of what the candidates really stand for than it did before the debates.[87]

Mondale campaign managers assigned a cadre of advisers to Ferraro. Some, like future secretary of state Madeleine Albright, dealt with matters of substance, whereas others concentrated on style. Ferraro was urged to speak slowly and enunciate; her rapid-fire delivery may have been acceptable to New Yorkers, but for the American masses it sounded too rat-a-tat. To reinforce this notion, Ferraro's debate coach ordered the candidate to watch a videocassette of *Mr. Smith Goes to Washington*. "Jimmy Stewart was relaxed and easygoing to a fault," Ferraro said. "I fell asleep in front of the VCR and never got to see how it all came out."[88]

In spite of her misgivings, Ferraro came to appreciate the value of preparation, especially after the sessions moved into a Manhattan television studio configured to replicate the debate site in Philadelphia. "My answers got clearer and more detailed," Ferraro wrote. "People remember only those points made in the first two sentences, I had been told. By Wednesday morning everyone agreed that my replies were sharp and focused, with the key points in the first two sentences."[89]

Ferraro, like others who have run the debate prep gauntlet, saw both pluses and minuses in extensive rehearsal: "All this preparation was essential, but at the same time it magnified the significance of the debate. I'm not one for butterflies in the stomach, but I will not deny that I felt a lot of pressure."[90] As Ferraro indicates, the run-throughs designed to put a debater at ease may produce just the opposite effect.

With so many experts offering advice, debate preparations can lead a candidate to doubt his or her own instincts. "Over days of cramming and rehearsal," Dan Quayle wrote of his 1988 experience, "there was only one general idea being pounded into me: don't plow any new ground. Don't make a mistake. If you feel unsure of an answer, just fall back on old rhetoric. In other words, don't trust yourself." In his autobiography, Quayle blamed Republican handlers for not preparing him better during mock sessions before the Bentsen debate, especially on content. "The real problem with the questions they anticipated was that they were too issue-oriented," Quayle complained. "The staff didn't seem able to imagine the more general, reflective questions that have become a part of these debates."[91]

Others pointed out that Quayle himself had approached his debate preps too casually. Maureen Dowd, in the *New York Times*, reported that the candidate gave up one study session on a flight back to Washington in favor of an impromptu photo opportunity. According to Dowd, Quayle invited members of the press into his cabin "to watch and photograph him posing with sleeves rolled up and a serious expression, as if he was making notes on his briefing papers. Then he used his study time to amiably chat with the journalists about his hopes for the debate."[92]

During his rehearsal sessions, Quayle received a spectacularly bad piece of advice from Bob Packwood, the senator who served as Lloyd Bentsen's stand-in. After antagonizing Quayle in the run-through, Packwood assured him that the real debate would be less brutal. "I know Lloyd Bentsen," Packwood said. "He won't attack you the way I did today. He's a gentleman." At the same time Quayle ignored the counsel of his aides, who warned him not to make any references to John F. Kennedy. "I probably should have avoided it," the candidate said, "but I only brought it up to make a single, valid comparison about our experience in the Congress."[93]

Like Quayle, Michael Dukakis paid a toll for not heeding his coaches' advice. Strategists had worked with Dukakis to devise a response to the charge that he was soft on law and order—what the staff called "the crime question." The answer, which Dukakis had gone through at least a dozen times in the prep sessions, involved a highly personal account of his own father and brother as victims of violent crime. When moderator Bernard Shaw asked the Massachusetts governor about his stand on the death penalty vis-à-vis the hypothetical rape and murder of his wife, Dukakis was supposed to plug in the rehearsed response.

"Every step of the way he fought me on this, and fought his campaign on this, because he didn't like dealing with the crime issue this way," recalled Susan Estrich, Dukakis's campaign manager, at a 1996 debate symposium. Aggravating his problems, Dukakis had fallen ill with the flu just before the Los Angeles appearance. "And so feeling lousy that night maybe," said Estrich, "or feeling a little resentful at the last hundred times your advisers had told you to look deeply into the camera when you talk about your brother, he just didn't do it."[94]

Four years later the next Democratic presidential nominee had no such misgivings. Both in 1992, and as an incumbent in 1996, Bill Clinton set a new standard for diligence in debate rehearsal. Clinton's debate team, most of them veterans of previous Democratic campaigns, had never encountered so eager a pupil. Said Michael Sheehan, a media adviser, "For me, working with Clinton is like Kazan getting to work with Brando."[95]

According to 1992 coach Tom Donilon, Clinton spent an "enormous amount" of time preparing. "He knew how important it was, he understood that it was a special skill that had to be practiced, that it was a point in the campaign when you really did get a chance to explain yourself, and if you were going to do it within the confines of the debate structure, you really had to work at it."[96] With his elite group of debate strategists, Clinton ran drills on everything from physical posture to facial expressions.

For the first-of-its-kind town hall debate in Richmond, Hollywood producer and Clinton confidante Harry Thomason laid out the rehearsal stage in a grid so the candidate could learn to manipulate the space to maximum strategic advantage. Cameras were positioned just as they would be for the telecast, and doubles for Bush, Perot, and the audience took their places on the set. With the help of the grid, Clinton choreographed his moves so as to keep one or the other of his competitors in the camera shot at all times, a maneuver that circumvented the prohibition on cutaways of one candidate while another was speaking. According to journalist Roger Simon, the Clinton campaign hoped to catch Bush and Perot on camera with "bad facial expressions." When Bush was shown looking down at his watch, "the result exceeded their wildest expectations."[97]

President Bush had not bothered to rehearse in the town hall format, opting instead for a desultory preparation schedule that marked a retreat from the more disciplined regimen of his 1988 preps with Roger Ailes. Ross Perot did not rehearse at all for any of the 1992 debates, other than to read background papers. According to Perot aide Clay Mulford, "I was delighted if I could spend thirty or forty minutes with him the day before the debate to go over a couple of things. I thought that was an unusual concession on his part."[98]

In 1996 the Clinton debate-prep juggernaut was back in business, so methodical that rehearsal sessions for the San Diego debate took place in New Mexico in order to get the presidential body clock ticking on Western time several days before the event. The well-oiled Clinton machine provided a sharp contrast to the laissez-faire approach of competitor Bob Dole, who submitted to only the most minimal predebate conditioning. As Dole told reporters, "It's like filling up your tank with gas. It can only hold so much."[99]

However dismissive the remark, Dole does raise a valid question about debate preparations: How much better can any performer get? Modern presidential campaigns grind to a halt for days on end so that candidates may devote their full attention to test runs. Any drop of naturalness is squeezed out of the performers long before they plead their cases to the public. In all the strategizing and contrivance and plotting, what human qualities get lost?

On the eve of the 1996 San Diego town hall debate between Bob Dole and Bill Clinton, Dukakis campaign manager Susan Estrich was asked what advice she would give Dole in using the debate to stage a comeback. Her answer is eminently reasonable, if just as far-fetched:

I would tell him to get rid of all his debate advisers, to burn the briefing books, to kick out all the people who are scripting him. . . . What
are the two things he cares most deeply about? Say them. And talk to
people, not with a script and not with scripted attack points. If he's
troubled by Clinton's character, say it. Say it the way you would say it
to me if you were sitting here.

But nobody will do that because he's off closeted with fifteen people who are now reviewing the tapes.[100]

Chapter Three

PREDEBATE NEWS COVERAGE

On the morning of the first Kennedy-Nixon debate in 1960, the *Washington Post* devoted not a single news story to the broadcast that would become a seminal event in American politics. The main debate article in the same day's *New York Times* ran four short paragraphs on page 22, while the predebate edition of *Time* magazine failed to note the candidates' meeting altogether. Even the host medium of television paid scant attention; with only hours to go before the opening statements, the three network newscasts mentioned the debate only briefly, and not as a lead.

By contemporary standards of coverage, the first meeting between John F. Kennedy and Richard Nixon caught the press napping. As if to compensate, journalists in subsequent years have pursued these events with messianic fervor, casting off the shackles of subtlety that restrained the reporting of 1960. This heightened interest has accompanied a seismic shift in debate journalism, as the locus of coverage has moved, with profound consequences, from print to television.

To be sure, a few journalistic outlets grasped the importance of the first 1960 debate The *Los Angeles Times* and *Boston Globe*, each with a hometown contestant in the race, ran front-page debate-day stories, as did papers in Chicago where the event took place. In general, however, little of the momentousness that routinely attends modern presidential debates preceded this landmark telecast.

Several factors explain why the press underplayed the story. First, as with all events lacking a precedent, the novelty of joint appearances by presidential candidates presented journalists with an institutional challenge: how to report an event that had not yet occurred. Reporters in 1960 took refuge in history; a favorite predebate news angle was to compare the Kennedy-Nixon broadcasts to the 1858 senatorial debates between Abraham Lincoln and Stephen Douglas. On the eve of the televised debate, the *Chicago Tribune* ran two such stories in its Sunday edition. "It is fitting that the Kennedy-Nixon duel should kick off Monday in Chicago, the heart of Lincoln-Douglas land," one article noted. "The series of clashes between the giants of a century ago started at Ottawa, Illinois, scarcely eighty miles from today's TV studio in Chicago."[1] With no other signpost to guide them, writers sought comfort in the familiarity of a 102-year-old analogy.

Other observers cast their gaze not backward at the nineteenth century but ahead toward the twenty-first. *Boston Globe* political editor John Harris accurately forecast the gravitas of the event: "Both Nixon and Kennedy, and their staffs, busy with final preparations, are keenly aware of the high stakes. . . . They well know, skilled as each is in handling impromptu questions, that they risk losing the White House prize on the drop of an ill-chosen phrase."[2]

CBS president Frank Stanton, who for years had lobbied to bring presidential debates to television, told the *New York Times* that the discussion would create "a whole new sense of values" for the American electorate. Each candidate "will be peeled right down to the man himself," Stanton predicted, adding that televised debates would forever alter the practice of presidential campaigning.[3] What must have seemed like hubris at the time turns out to have been trenchant analysis.

For each of the 1960 debates, the networks took out advertisements in major newspapers around the country. Here, as in journalistic accounts, the tone of the promotional copy is muted: "The Television and Radio Networks and their affiliated stations throughout the United States urge you to be present during the first in a series of historic face-to-face discussions between Senator John F. Kennedy and Vice President Richard M. Nixon.

Tonight from 9:30 to 10:30."[4] The word *debate* never appears. According to Don Hewitt, producer-director of the first Kennedy-Nixon program, the networks consciously avoided the term so as not to promote a win-loss expectation among viewers.[5]

The cautious mood of advance coverage in 1960 reflects a code that no longer obtains between campaigns and the media. Audiences today expect candidates and the press to act as eager partners in establishing a predebate climate; in 1960 no such arrangement existed. One of the rare instances in which a principal player even mentioned the debates came not in a news setting but during an interview on the *Tonight Show* between Jack Paar and Richard Nixon a month before the first event. Paar asked the candidate if he looked forward to the so-called Great Debates. Presciently Nixon answered that the broadcast would be a "very rugged experience—it will be for Senator Kennedy, it will be for me." But beyond this, he was unwilling to speculate.[6]

Other factors contributed to the subdued coverage of the first 1960 debate. In the hierarchy of news stories, the telecast took a backseat to another groundbreaking event concurrently under way at the United Nations: the gathering, at the height of the cold war, of fifteen communist bloc leaders, including Fidel Castro and Nikita Khrushchev. The Soviet premier arrived in the United States exactly one week before the presidential candidates met in Chicago. Castro had already reached New York, making headlines by vacating his posh midtown hotel in a dustup over the bill and conspicuously relocating to Harlem. The every move of both leaders attracted microscopic scrutiny from the press, reducing the presidential candidates to the status of second leads in the nation's newspapers.

On the afternoon of the initial debate, even as Kennedy and Nixon underwent their preshow paces in Chicago, Castro was wrapping up a four-and-a-half-hour anti-American peroration to the U.N. General Assembly that would run alongside the next morning's debate stories. Castro's speech to the international body included an unsolicited assessment of the White House candidates: both Kennedy and Nixon, he said, "lack political brains."[7]

Probably the best explanation for the sedateness of advance debate coverage in 1960 is the higher standard of objectivity to which journalists of that era held themselves. Political scientist Thomas Patterson, in a study of the front page of the *New York Times* between 1960 and 1992, found a tenfold increase in the proportion of interpretive election stories and a concomitant reduction of descriptive stories. In the race between JFK and

Nixon, only 8 percent of front-page election stories in the *Times* could be called interpretive; in 1992 the level jumped to 80 percent.[8] By definition, most predebate reporting tends to involve speculation; the main event has not yet transpired, and observers have few concrete facts with which to work. In the absence of reportable data, the press corps of 1960 largely resisted the temptation to engage in the speculative analysis that is now de rigueur.

Television news, then in its infancy, had its own problems with advance debate coverage. Network newscasts, which at the time ran only fifteen minutes, were geared less to "futures" stories than to events that had already happened, events that could therefore be illustrated. The combination of television's visual demands and the reluctance of reporters to postulate made presidential debates an unlikely subject for advance TV coverage in 1960.

The story got a somewhat higher profile on radio, where the personalized nature of the storytelling lent itself more readily to commentary. Lowell Thomas on CBS Radio noted in the hours before the first debate, "The series that begins tonight, I suppose, could also determine the next president of the United States." Fulton Lewis on MBS Radio offered a skeptical preview: "Whether or not the occasion has been so hamstrung by artificialities and rules and red tape as to take the life out of it remains to be seen."[9]

One of the most incisive pieces of predebate journalism came from a newspaper reporter who would serve as a panelist in the third Kennedy-Nixon debate, syndicated columnist Roscoe Drummond. Drummond stressed the responsibility of the *audience* in the debate-viewing transaction: "If the candidates are prepared to encounter each other face-to-face and to let the public hear both sides simultaneously at no small risk to themselves—then we ought to be prepared to weigh, examine, compare, and ponder their arguments as free from partisan prejudice and pre-judging as we possibly can."[10] Heading into the 1960 debates, it was still possible for Americans to do this, thanks to the low-key media atmosphere that prevailed. After the fact, as journalists realized the degree to which they had underreported the story, the nation's press would quickly shift course.

The *Washington Post*, whose front page had contained only a two-sentence programming advisory the day of the first debate, came back for the second Kennedy-Nixon encounter with a full-length, morning-of story on page 1. The tone of this article by Robert J. Donovan demonstrates the rapid metamorphosis in predebate reporting: "The drama of the Nixon-Kennedy debates will go into its second act tonight when the candidates square off," the story began. Donovan wrote of the "enormous tension" building up over the confrontation and noted that Vice President Nixon "is under particularly heavy pressure to make up for a shaky start in the first debate . . . due in considerable measure to ill-advised lighting or makeup or both, which distorted his image on television screens."

The article proceeds in this vein:

> Republican leaders have been working night and day with technicians to avoid a repetition of this calamity. Furthermore, many party leaders from different parts of the country are reliably reported to have urged Nixon to be much more aggressive toward [Kennedy] than the vice president was in the first debate.
>
> They have pleaded especially that he drop the tactic he used then of expressing agreement with the senator on various basic goals. Not many expect that Nixon will be telling Kennedy tonight that he agrees with him on anything.[11]

To a remarkable degree, this report in the *Post* presages the sensibility that would come to typify most predebate news coverage. Brashly predictive, the writing addresses issues of performance and strategy and cosmetics that other press accounts in 1960 either downplayed or avoided completely. Sixteen years later, when the next round of presidential debates came to pass, the emergence of television as a mature news medium transformed the rules of the game for journalists and sources alike. All predebate reporting would sound more like the story by Robert Donovan in the *Washington Post*.

FINDING THE ANGLE

Just as Kennedy and Nixon drew comparisons to Lincoln and Douglas, so did the 1976 debaters enter the arena under the shadow of their television predecessors. The news media now had a precedent to follow, a navigational chart with which to plot coverage of the first debate series in sixteen years. The iconographic images of JFK and Nixon would hover over Gerald Ford and Jimmy Carter like gods gazing down from the video pantheon.

A month before the first 1976 debate, Joseph Lelyveld of the *New York Times* screened the first two Kennedy-Nixon broadcasts in search of clues to the upcoming Ford-Carter debates. "In one way," Lelyveld wrote, "the experience was similar to that of sitting through an old movie that was considered bold and exciting in its day but now seems mannered and coy." Lelyveld, like others before him, concluded that "the interplay of personalities, not ideas" was what had figured most strongly in the 1960 debates.[12]

Conventional wisdom from the Kennedy-Nixon series informed much of the predebate coverage in 1976. Jules Witcover, in the *Washington Post*, noted that, for Ford and Carter, substance would most likely matter less than "how each candidate looks, sounds, and handles himself vis-à-vis his opponent. That is the one clear lesson that came through in the only previous televised presidential campaign debates."[13] On NBC Douglas Kiker revisited the Kennedy-Nixon matches with a series of clips that contrasted the Democrat's grace under pressure against the Republican's unfortunate brush with reaction shots. Interestingly, among the excerpts was a 1960 debate sound bite in which JFK offered a rhetorical litany of typical American voters, a list that included "a peanut farmer in Georgia."[14]

In *The New Yorker* Elizabeth Drew sought to deflate the buildup of the 1976 debates, attributing the anticipation to a "retrospectively distorted view" of the 1960 series. "A number of people now see those debates as events in which a good guy in a white hat met and bested a bad guy in a black hat," Drew wrote. "I wonder how much enthusiasm there would be for debates this year if Kennedy were deemed to have "lost" in 1960?"[15]

All these stories use 1960 as a touchstone, just as future reports would feed off the 1976 series and its successors. With each new round of candidates, the body of debate lore expands, making presidential debates an ever more self-referential genre. Television, always keen to relive its classic moments, has been an especially effective medium for sustaining the highlights of debates past, a collection that functions as a sort of "greatest hits" reel to be trotted out with each new run for the White House.

In 1976, when the predebate story uprooted itself from newspapers to television, a reliable pattern of coverage took hold: The narrative line would begin at the negotiations; move to an intense period of expectations-setting, both by campaigns and journalists; touch briefly on candidate preparations; and conclude with debate-day photo opportunities amid a flurry of last-minute handicapping. Every four years, from the Ford-Carter debates to the present, this process has repeated itself like clockwork. The occasional wrinkle may vary the plot from race to race but essentially the press strays little from its familiar script.

To each series reporters assign a story line that sets the agenda for that year's predebate coverage; thus the emphasis in 1976 on the restoration of the debate tradition after a sixteen-year hiatus. Once a series is in motion, events in one program dictate the narrative through the remaining installments. The first Ford-Carter debate set the tone for its successor when, just as the candidates were wrapping up their final answers of the night, the sound got knocked off the air for an excruciating twenty-seven minutes.

Going into the follow-up match two weeks later, the press exhibited a sudden interest in the previously eye-glazing particulars of TV audio production. Jack Kelly, CBS's pool producer for debate number 2, recalls being "driven crazy" by media inquiries about audio arrangements. "That's the only thing people cared about," Kelly said. "I'd get calls in the middle of the night from radio stations. And it was always the same question."[16] All three networks aired footage of Jimmy Carter personally inspecting the sound board in San Francisco's Palace of Fine Arts during his tech check the afternoon of the debate, with NBC reporting that "Carter gave close attention to the maze of audio equipment and its backup system."[17]

That same day Carter furnished ABC's Sam Donaldson a sound bite that would prove prophetic in defining the next chapter of the debate saga. "If one of us makes a mistake," the Democratic challenger said, "that will be damaging."[18] Hours later Ford committed his verbal blunder about Soviet influence in Eastern Europe, giving the press an angle not just for the final Ford-Carter encounter but for the ages: the imperative not to err. Into the stone tablets of debate knowledge, journalists would carve this new message, just below the lesson about Richard Nixon's makeup.

On the morning of the last 1976 debate David Broder, in the *Washington Post*, wrote, "Both Gerald Ford and Jimmy Carter have been told by their top advisers that they can win the presidential election if they avoid a serious misstep in tonight's final television debate." ABC's Barbara Walters said, "Both sides agree that the most important element in winning is to make sure that a major mistake is not made either in fact or style." Bob Jamieson on NBC reported that another error "could be fatal" to Ford's campaign.[19]

This journalistic obsession with mistakes has colored all predebate coverage since Ford-Carter. The issue returned with a special vengeance in 1984, when Ronald Reagan's disjointed performance in the first encounter handed the press one of the most dramatic plot twists in debate history. Advance coverage of the second and final Reagan-Mondale debate two weeks later converged on a single point: Would the seventy-three-year-old Republican nominee survive the evening with his dignity intact?

Reagan's preparations for the debate in Kansas City sparked fervent media interest, as did the altered stakes for both candidates. On ABC's Sunday morning talk show *This Week*, White House correspondent Sam Donaldson raised what he called "the senility factor." Said Donaldson, "People will be watching tonight because of Louisville, to see whether the president stands up, makes sentences that make sense from the standpoint of not stammering and stuttering, and doesn't drool." (Before the first debate, in a *Los Angeles Times* interview, Donaldson had erroneously predicted a Reagan victory. "He'll get his facts wrong and his figures wrong. But so what?")[20]

Perversely the poor showing by Reagan in Louisville hurt Walter Mondale in advance coverage of the subsequent debate. As *Newsweek* put it, "Once more Mondale will look the camera in the eye, trying to project forceful leadership. His problem is that in Louisville his success was surprising; in Kansas City it will be expected. In Louisville, his style of respectful dissent seemed to take Reagan aback; in Kansas City, Reagan will be ready."[21] Clearly the debate with the strongest fascination for the press was not the president against Mondale but the president against himself.

EXPECTATIONS-SETTING BY THE CAMPAIGNS

In 1976 Carter pollster Patrick Caddell boasted to the *New York Times* of his candidate's television prowess. Carter "is very good with the camera," Caddell said. "He treats it like a person—one person. It's his strength."[22] This quote is remarkable in its braggadocio. Today we have come to expect campaigns to shade their predebate comments, deliberately lowering the standing of one's own candidate while raising the bar for the adversary.

In 1976 Jimmy Carter himself pooh-poohed his skills in a lunch interview with a trio of prominent political writers several weeks before the first debate. Over milk and a bologna sandwich at his home in Plains, Georgia, Carter offered this partisan preview: "I think President Ford is expected to know a great deal more about domestic programs and foreign programs than I do. He's been in Washington twenty-seven years. And to the extent that I come out equal to him in my apparent knowledge of issues, I think that would be equivalent to a victory for me."[23]

By the second debate Ford aide Michael Duval was arguing the opposite case, telling an ABC reporter that it was the *president* who would be operating at a disadvantage, because "when he speaks, it's the policy of the United States of America, and that is a major constraint."[24] With a single sound bite Duval sent a double-edged message: lowering the standards for Ford while reasserting his status as chief executive.

In the Duval and Carter quotes we discern competing press strategies at work, as each side jockeys for position in the media. Beginning in 1976 and continuing through the present, journalists have been coconspirators in this game of brinksmanship, serving as a kind of political message board that keeps the story alive and kicking up until airtime. This practice marks a radical shift from the cautiousness of Kennedy-Nixon coverage, when neither the campaigns nor reporters had much to say in advance of the first presidential matchups.

Today, in the weeks before a debate, politicos and the media link hands in a feverish dance of expectations-setting. Each side has something the other wants: Campaigns have information; the press has an audience. Individually these commodities are of limited value; together they form a symbiotic juggernaut with the power to predispose public perceptions. For both parties, the trick is finding an acceptable level of reciprocity in the merger.

In 1980 the campaigns' desire to position themselves favorably against the opposition assumed particular urgency, thanks to the presence of Hollywood veteran Ronald Reagan. For Reagan's two opponents, the strategic objective could not have been clearer: In the face of the Republican nominee's overwhelmingly superior media skills, the only logical choice was to prepare the audience for the worst.

"I, of course, was not the emcee for the twenty-mule team Borax," John Anderson reminded a reporter, "and I was not the host on the *General Electric Theater*."[25] President Carter told the *Washington Post*, "I'm a careful enough observer to know that Governor Reagan is a professional in dealing with the media. He's articulate and I don't underestimate him."[26] In a television story on ABC Carter ventured hopefully that the audience would not be deciding "who is the most professional debater or the best orator or the most professional television performer. The reason for the debate is to draw a sharp distinction on the issues and let the American people decide who will be the best president for the country during the next four years."[27]

In recent debate cycles the ritual of expectations-setting by the campaigns has grown ever more entrenched. In 1988 George Bush's handlers took greater than usual pains to portray their candidate as an ineffectual debater, especially in contrast to Michael Dukakis, who had moderated a public affairs series called *The Advocates* on Boston's prestigious WGBH-TV. "We capitalized on that, frankly," Bush campaign manager James Baker later admitted, "and the vice president was perfectly willing for us to do that. It wasn't an insult to his manhood for us to go out and say, 'Hey, wait a minute. Our guy's not that good a debater.' He basically let us go out and trash his debating ability, but it paid off."[28]

So contrived had the machinations become that Bush himself found it impossible to sustain the charade. At a predebate news conference, Bush went through the motions of playing up Dukakis's debating prowess, then proceeded to point out that he was "lowering expectations. My wife, Barbara, when I practice debating, she falls asleep and I have to do something about that."[29] As Dukakis press secretary Dayton Duncan commented, "When your candidate comes out and says it, there's not even any pretense to it."[30]

By contrast, members of Dan Quayle's team sought to goose their man's notoriously low standing in the 1988 predebate analysis. Perhaps the most impassioned spinner was the candidate's wife, Marilyn. Appearing on ABC's *Good Morning America* the day of the vice presidential debate, Mrs. Quayle predicted that viewers would be "incredibly surprised" by the Republican nominee. "Quite frankly," she said, "the pressure is on Lloyd Bentsen. He's been the one going around the country actually trashing Dan Quayle."[31] But however gamely Marilyn Quayle defended her husband's reputation, the worst was yet to come.

Four years later Democrat Al Gore pounced on the issue of predebate handicapping, complaining to a rally of supporters that he was at a "terrible disadvantage" in the upcoming 1992 vice presidential debate. "Dan Quayle's expectations have been pushed down to such an unreasonably low level that the news media has declared him the winner in advance," Gore grumbled.[32] Quayle attempted to protect his underdog status by drawing a tongue-in-cheek class contrast with Gore. "He has a big advantage over me," Quayle told reporters. "He grew up in Washington, D.C., and I'm a product of the public schools." As the *New York Times* pointed out, "Mr. Quayle himself had a privileged upbringing as the scion of a wealthy newspaper family."[33]

In 1996 expectations-setting reached new levels of inanity, with first-class debater Bill Clinton portrayed by the opposition as superhuman and by his own side as woefully out of practice. Bob Dole's people had the easier mission, and in raising the stakes for Clinton, they spared no rhetorical excess. Former Reagan press secretary Marlin Fitzwater, on the *Today* show, called Clinton "the greatest television performer in American presidential history." Dole spokesman Scott Reed said, on CNN, "We all know Bill Clinton is a great debater. He's capable of charming the birds out of the trees every day." Dole himself said, "He is so good, if I show up, I think I will win."[34]

During breaks in his debate rehearsals, Clinton tried valiantly to lower his standing. "I'm badly out of shape on this," the president lamented to reporters in Chautauqua, New York. Hillary Clinton did her part in an appearance on the syndicated TV talk show *Live with Regis and Kathie Lee*, claiming, "For more than thirty-five or so years [Dole] was in the Congress and was a very good debater, so I expect it will be a very tough debate for my husband." Press secretary Mike McCurry reported that Clinton "feels like he has not had the time he had allotted" for debate preparation.[35] All these lines were delivered—and reported in the press—with a straight face.

A telling photo op in 1996 showed Bob Dole blithely tossing his debate briefing papers off the balcony of his Florida condominium. Long-time Dole observers saw in this playful gesture a striking departure from the "mean Bob Dole" of yore, who twenty years earlier had approached his 1976 debate against Walter Mondale with outright hostility. Dole's preproduction press strategy for that debate is one that no candidate has dared repeat: bad-mouthing the event. "I assume the audience will be smaller," Dole quipped to one TV reporter in 1976, "but I think we can put them to sleep quicker than the presidential candidates did." In another broadcast interview Dole could scarcely contain his peevishness: "It really bugs me to have to interrupt our campaign here for a week to prepare for this. I don't think it means all that much." And: "I think we both have a mission in this debate. I haven't quite figured out what it is."[36]

More typically candidates use predebate media coverage to taunt their opponents, not the audience. Democrats in 1984 portrayed Geraldine Ferraro as itching for a debate with George Bush, a theme the press seized on. In campaign appearances around the country Ferraro repeatedly brought up the impending match. Before an Italian-American audience she needled Bush in Italian, asking, "George, are you ready to start the debate?" At another event, claiming to have gotten hold of Bush's briefing book, the congresswoman previewed what she said were her opponent's preppy-flavored attack lines: "Gosh," "Gee whiz," "Zippity-doodah," and "Let's win, win, win!"[37]

Ferraro's antics apparently succeeded in unsettling the Bush campaign, as demonstrated by a pair of incidents that occurred shortly before the 1984 vice presidential debate. In a conversation with two news agency reporters aboard Air Force Two, Barbara Bush referred to her husband's opponent as "that four-million-dollar—I can't say it, but it rhymes with rich." Mrs. Bush later said that she believed the comment had been off the record and that the word she had been thinking of was *witch*.[38] The future First Lady telephoned Ferraro to apologize, interrupting a debate rehearsal. "I was dumbfounded," Ferraro would write in her memoirs. "The issue of rudeness aside, it was an astonishing thing to say to the press. And, of course, they jumped on it."[39]

Just as the controversy began to subside, Bush press secretary Peter Teeley took aim at Ferraro in a *Wall Street Journal* story that ran the morning of the Bush-Ferraro debate. Said Teeley, "She's too bitchy. She's very arrogant. Humility isn't one of her strong points, and I think that comes through." Compounding the insult, Teeley offered a "clarification" in the next day's *Washington Post*: "What I meant by that is that . . . essentially she has to come across as not being screechy or scratchy. If you have to use the word 'bitchy,' that's adequate."[40] The press, always a sucker for conflict, had found an irresistible predebate sidebar.

COVERING NEGOTIATIONS AND REHEARSALS

The metronomic predictability of electoral reporting has made it easy for campaigns to anticipate, and thus cater to, the preproduction needs of the press. Still, two key chapters of the predebate story—negotiations and candidate preparations—take place behind tightly closed doors. To cover them, journalists must depend on morsels of information from inside sources. Television, with its addiction to pictures, has particular difficulty addressing these nonvisual portions of the tale. Cameras do not record the deal making for later excerpting; no newscast has ever aired video of a debate practice. Still photos of rehearsals are almost as rare, and those that do run exude all the spontaneity of a military parade.

It is interesting to note that in the 1976 campaign journalists criticized

Gerald Ford for staging mock debates before his televised meeting with Carter. Tom Jarriel on ABC disparaged the "top-secret coaching" the incumbent president had received: "They've told him what to wear, where to look, and have carefully edited his answers to fit into the three-minute debate format."[41] Ford press secretary Ron Nessen would write in his memoirs, "I could never figure out why reporters made such a fuss about the president rehearsing. TV correspondents and anchormen rehearsed to polish their performance for a big program. Why shouldn't the president rehearse before the debates? The stakes on a good showing were enormous."[42] After 1976 the press no longer bothered to register its astonishment at the preparation process. Today candidate warm-ups are another routine stop on the predebate trail, accepted unquestioningly by a campaign press corps excluded from covering them.

More attention is accorded the negotiation process, particularly by print journalists, who are better suited than their TV compatriots to disseminate the mostly tedious details that emerge from the talks. Although reporters lack direct access to the bargaining table, highly placed members of the press can depend on leaks from the principal players to round out the picture. "Every side wants to get out that they were less worried than the other side, so they'll leak out details," says Richard Berke, a political writer for the *New York Times* who has broken a number of negotiation stories. "And you just sort of work them against each other."[43]

In certain years—1980, most notably—negotiations constitute a driving force of the predebate narrative. In that race campaign officials argued for weeks about the conditions under which debates would take place or if they would take place at all. Carter's refusal to participate in any forum that included independent candidate John Anderson generated extensive media coverage, but after a short-term burst of negative publicity for the president, the fallout dissipated. In the *Washington Post*, Robert G. Kaiser described press reaction to Carter's decision as "the furor that wasn't." For three days, Kaiser wrote, debate developments dominated the evening news programs and the papers. "Once the news was conveyed and initially analyzed, it seemed there was nothing more to say. In the days since, the debate story has been mentioned in passing or not at all."[44]

When Carter and Reagan opened negotiations for a two-way match, media interest reignited. Reporters camped outside the closed doors of the meeting room, hungry for a breakthrough. No scrap of information was too inconsequential to be passed along. "Roast beef and turkey sandwiches were brought in as the talks dragged on through the afternoon," wrote *New York Times* reporter Terence Smith of one session. Smith and other journalists at one point overheard—and reported—Democratic negotiator Robert Strauss through the conference-room door exasperatedly telling his opponents, "I don't think you've heard anything I've said since we came in here."[45]

The press did gain access to the sanctum sanctorum for a brief photo opportunity. According to an ABC account by Susan King: "Verbal gamesmanship dominated the picture-taking ceremony, and it was clear not just the date but the debate idea itself was up for grabs. Both sides agreed on one thing: to answer no questions."[46] Negotiators in later years stopped providing even this much of a stage-managed photo op.

By tradition, campaigns zealously guard the barrier between what actually goes on in the bargaining sessions and what gets shared with the news media. One of the rare violations of this longstanding policy occurred in 1996 on CNN's *Inside Politics*, a television program tailor-made for the daily arcana of the debate over debates. Side by side on the studio set, Clinton representative Mickey Kantor and Dole representative Donald Rumsfeld conducted what amounted to a live negotiating session in front of anchorwoman Judy Woodruff and millions of viewers.

What stood out from this exchange was the sheer pettiness of the bargaining. Taking place one day after Ross Perot's official exclusion by the debate commission, the session began with a dispute over whether Perot might still be allowed to participate. Kantor did not rule out this possibility, while Rumsfeld did. The negotiators argued over the length and number of debates: Dole wanted four presidential and two vice presidential debates; Clinton wanted longer debates compressed into a shorter timetable. Woodruff asked when the next negotiating meeting would happen. Kantor said it would have to be earlier than Saturday because he had already "canceled a lot of meetings" to accommodate the Dole team. Rumsfeld responded that it was Kantor who had inconvenienced the other negotiators. "This is just plain politics," Rumsfeld said. "I think the American people are tired of that."[47]

From a public relations standpoint it is difficult to surmise why these two sophisticated campaign players agreed to go on live television to discuss arrangements, though sources on the Clinton side say they were hoping to put pressure on Dole's camp to "do the debates the way we wanted to do them."[48] Both campaigns came off as niggling and self-motivated, more concerned with winning their own narrow game than serving the broader public interest. Still, for voters, the appearance on *Inside Politics* provided unusual insight into the debate negotiating process. As Judy Woodruff later put it, "Even though you're not getting the whole thing, you're getting a little peek through the window."[49]

Several days after Kantor and Rumsfeld appeared on *Inside Politics*, Kantor and a different Dole representative, Carroll Campbell, answered journalists' questions outside the Washington office building where the bargaining sessions took place. The specifics of the negotiators' remarks are less significant than the scene as portrayed by C-Span cameras: a sidewalk stakeout by about a dozen reporters and photographers, with microphones set up for impromptu news conferences as the aides came and went. By 1996 every development in the debate over debates merited a news conference, as the media beast demanded a stepped-up schedule of feedings.

EXPECTATIONS-SETTING BY THE PRESS

We have seen how campaigns assume the role of debate producers; in the period before a presidential debate, journalists turn the tables and play political strategists. Since 1976, debate analysis has developed into a cottage industry in the press, accounting for an ever increasing share of pre-event coverage. With assistance from their campaign sources, reporters fix a conventional wisdom that departs from the standard journalistic mission of factual storytelling; in turn, this predebate "morning line" becomes the yardstick by which postdebate judgments are rendered.

Handicapping the horse race has long been a fixture of campaign journalism, but where live debates are concerned, the impulse to speculate is particularly tantalizing. Political journalists approach the debate story the way sports reporters approach a major athletic event. "This reminds me a lot of the Super Bowl," said columnist George Will on ABC the morning of the first 1992 debate. "Each year the hyperbole and rubbish and pageantry and marching bands surrounding the little kernel of football in the middle gets larger and larger."[50]

The accelerated pace of predebate coverage mirrors the explosive growth of the American news media over the past quarter-century. From three networks in 1976, each with a single daily newscast, the business has expanded to multiple journalistic outlets, twenty-four-hour news cycles, and the overheated competition of a crowded marketplace. Pressure to generate stories is enormous, particularly for television, where the dependence on visuals further complicates advance coverage of an event like a presidential debate. Because most predebate events are pictorially lacking, TV instinctively fills the gap with pundits. These talking heads cram the airwaves, spouting predictions, analyzing strategy, and revisiting debates past.

In the view of Thomas Patterson, as television news extended its influence, print journalism began taking more of its cues from the tube, with substantive reporting yielding to interpretive stories. "The television model gradually affected the print media, to the point where the difference in the styles of television and newspaper reporting is now relatively small," Patterson wrote after the 1992 election.[51] In practice this has meant more predebate stories about tactics and performance, and fewer reports that link debates with candidates' stands on the issues.

As Patterson's study shows, the shift toward interpretive analysis has been an incremental one. When presidential debates resumed in 1976, coverage was considerably more speculative than it had been for Kennedy-Nixon but considerably less speculative than what it is today. With every election, the border gets spongier between fact and opinion, description and interpretation.

In 1980, when a truncated debate season heightened the stakes, journalists handicapped the candidates' odds as enthusiastically as professional bookies. Coverage of the single Carter-Reagan debate focused on the "high noon" riskiness of the event. The *Christian Science Monitor* called it a "one-to-one shootout . . . which could decide the outcome." "A single roll of the dice with the White House at stake," said the *Washington Post*. In comments just before the debate began, CBS anchorman Walter Cronkite said, "It is not inconceivable that the election could turn on what happens in the next ninety minutes."[52]

Political analyst Jeff Greenfield, in a book critical of press coverage of the 1980 campaign, lamented the extent to which strategic considerations colored that year's predebate reporting: "So heavily was the tactical element of the confrontation played up by newspapers and television that the average voter might have been forgiven for believing he needed a scorecard or a tout sheet, rather than an informed mind, to judge the debate."[53] Also unhappy with the media's fixation on predebate maneuvers was President Carter. "Less than a month before the election," he wrote, "the press continued to ignore the substantive issues in the campaign and to concentrate almost exclusively on who might debate whom, Reagan's "blunders," and my "meanness" to my opponent."[54]

A 1980 memorandum written by Carter strategist Patrick Caddell shows the importance that was being attached to press coverage not just in the follow-up analysis after the debate but also in the days preceding the event. The goal: to tie pre-debate expectations-setting to postdebate verdicts. Caddell wrote,

> [Journalists] have an inordinate role in convincing the public not only who won on "points" but more critically, on the nature of the debate itself. Thus we cannot let the press go into the debate with the single notion of looking just for a winner and loser. Not only must we "win" on points, more importantly we must win substantively and have the press judge the debate on that criterion.[55]

Implicit in Caddell's memo is an acknowledgment of the incestuous nature of campaign-press relations. At its worst, the alliance functions as a closed conversation between insiders that only secondarily benefits the electorate. Handlers dispense pearls of wisdom to reporters; reporters dispense pearls of wisdom to handlers. Both sides fundamentally mistrust each other, but, like mutually dependent partners in a bad, indestructible marriage, neither can go it alone.

The game-playing between campaigns and the press got meaner in 1984. In a memorandum to colleagues in the Mondale campaign, Patrick Caddell ratcheted up his adversarial tone and proposed engaging journalists in a "pantomime of deception." Caddell said, "If expectations are to be overturned, then they must be built up to a maximum degree. The strategy must be protected by a 'Bodyguard of Lies.' "[56] Caddell's antagonistic language mirrors the intrinsic testiness of the campaign-press interaction. To political handlers, the press is putty that needs molding. Meanwhile, journalists regard *themselves* as the rightful sculptors of predebate expectations; campaigns merely supply the raw materials.

If hostility toward the media increased in 1984, so did the reporters' willingness to shed their reliance on campaign sources in predebate coverage. In a piece on NBC two days before the first Reagan-Mondale match, Roger Mudd delivered a classic example of insider analysis, presenting what he described as "the book" on each of the two presidential debaters. The story abandons the traditional use of interviewees, consisting instead entirely of the journalist's opinions.

According to Mudd, Reagan was expected to be camera-savvy, cavalier with numbers, a whiz with one-liners—and "from time to time he will not make sense." Mondale would have a "sharp edge" from his appearances in the primary debates and would be combative and specific. "So the contrast will be sharp," Mudd offered in his closing comment, "Mondale trying to nail Reagan with a mistake that accentuates his age and isolation, Reagan trying to make Mondale look shrill and frantic by exuding his 'Aw, shucks' optimism."[57] That Mudd was largely correct in his assessment does not lessen the radical nature of the story: predebate reporting had leapfrogged over the longstanding journalistic insistence on external sourcing.

For better or worse, Mudd's style of interpretive journalism has become the norm in contemporary predebate reporting. The press does its own expectations-setting, separate from, yet influenced by, the spin of the campaigns. For the inside players, tactical considerations and performance measures are what count.

In 1988, an exceedingly negative campaign by any standard, the journalistic weakness for speculative analysis may have hit bottom. High on the list of that year's predebate media fixations was the weightless matter of Michael Dukakis's likability. This nonissue, which mushroomed in the press beyond all reason, represents an unfortunate episode in presidential debate reporting. The story surfaced before the first Bush-Dukakis appearance but gained strength going into the second, after news analysis and polling determined that Dukakis had won the first debate on substance but lost on heart.

The debate-day edition of the *New York Times* addressed the subject in two articles. The first cited a poll in which voters named Bush the more likable candidate by a margin of 47 to 37 percent—close enough, and irrelevant enough, that one might have expected the *Times* to ignore the finding altogether. The second story, by Bernard Weinraub, dealt exclusively with Dukakis's public image as a cold fish. "There is no master plan to warm up the Massachusetts governor, whose performance in the first debate was considered skilled but rather chilly by many reviewers," Weinraub wrote.[58] Television journalists made similar points, sounding more like meteorologists than reporters with their descriptions of Dukakis's "icy" personality and need to project "warmth."

In the end, when the candidate fulfilled expectations by giving a technocratic response to the question about his wife's hypothetical rape and murder, journalists may have felt vindicated. But the test the press had applied to Michael Dukakis was a false one. How could a fifty-four-year-old man—how could anyone—suddenly make himself more likable on national television? And what did such a transformation have to do with one's fitness for the job in the first place?

DEBATERS AS CHARACTERS

The Michael Dukakis likability issue betrays a problem inherent to campaign coverage in general and debate coverage in particular: the journalistic penchant for glorifying colorful characters and punishing dullards. Sober-minded debaters like Dukakis, Carter, and Gore operate at an automatic disadvantage in such a universe, where winning smiles and clever ripostes are the coin of the realm. Reporters prefer their candidates to fall into brasher, more stereotypical categories: stars (Reagan), buffoons (Quayle), or star-buffoons (Perot).

The press also puts a premium on novelty, as evidenced by the intense attention to 1984's precedent-setting vice presidential debate between Geraldine Ferraro and George Bush. Journalists relished the prospect of this first male-female debate, eagerly laying out each performer's objectives along gender lines. In a debriefing on ABC's *World News Tonight* hours before the telecast, reporter Carole Simpson summed up the conventional wisdom for Bush: "He's really got to be careful not to attack her too much for fear of being accused of beating up on her, and yet he can't be too polite to her for fear of being called patronizing." Lynn Sherr identified Ferraro's hurdle as "proving she is qualified to be president."[59]

Beginning with Bob Dole in 1976, vice presidential debaters have almost always made better copy than candidates at the top of the ticket. In 1988 journalistic speculation about Dan Quayle built to a crescendo as his joint appearance with Bentsen approached. "For all practical purposes, the debate now features Dan Quayle versus Dan Quayle. Will he be as "bad" as expected?" asked *Newsweek* magazine, the quotation marks around "bad" supposedly softening the question.[60] A *New York Times* story by Gerald Boyd reprised Quayle's remark that he "did not live in this century" and quoted an unnamed "top official" in the Bush campaign as saying that the Indiana senator was no "rocket scientist." Boyd wrote, "The assessment explains why

Senator Quayle goes into the debate . . . as one of the most thoroughly managed running mates in history and why the contest is regarded as perhaps pivotal for the forty-one-year-old senator."[61] And these stories ran *before* Quayle had been eviscerated by Lloyd Bentsen.

The vice presidential debate of 1992 whisked Dan Quayle back to the epicenter of media attention. "Expectations for his performance tonight are so low that the vice president is almost bound to do better than expected," said Mary Tillotson on CNN. Kevin Sack in the *New York Times* wrote, "Mr. Quayle and his staff believe that the vice president is beautifully positioned because low expectations could transform a mere draw into a victory. But they recognize that Mr. Quayle will have little margin for error because of the public's perception of him as a bumbler." An op-ed piece in the *Washington Post* by Lloyd Bentsen's 1988 campaign manager argued that "Dan Quayle is in the driver's seat." "He is the only candidate who can't lose," wrote Tad Devine, "and thus will most likely emerge as a real winner when all the spin has been spun."[62]

Beyond the return of Dan Quayle, the groundbreaking debate series of 1992 offered a rich selection of story lines: three candidates for each event; the debut of the town hall and single-moderator formats; the schedule of four debates compressed into nine days. From the standpoint of news coverage, this last circumstance loomed particularly large. In previous years debates had existed as isolated events, demarcated by distinct periods of being built up and winding down. The abbreviated run of the 1992 programs threw this familiar rhythm out of whack, obliging reporters to rethink their approaches both before and after the individual broadcasts.

A *Washington Post* story headlined "Punditocracy Faces Dizzying Spin Cycle" captured the journalistic mood heading into the series. "For the men and women who fill America's airwaves with spin and opinion, this could be Gallipoli," wrote reporter David Von Drehle. Jeff Greenfield was quoted in the article as saying, "I picture guys opening booths: an epiphany, two historical analogies, and a movie reference—package deal, one hundred bucks."[63]

In deference to the timetable, advance coverage of the first 1992 match dealt not just with that encounter but with the collective effect of all of them. "The stakes are very, very high because we have this truncated debates period," said Ken Bode on CNN immediately before the first meeting of Bush, Clinton, and Perot. "This is the beginning of a dialogue that will dominate the news cycles over that period of time."[64] And indeed it did.

Journalists being suckers for larger-than-life personalities, the immediate beneficiary of 1992's predebate coverage was Ross Perot. Through his previous TV appearances, most notably on CNN's *Larry King Live*, Perot had become a familiar presence—if not exactly endearing, then compulsively watchable. How his participation would affect the debates caused much rumination in the press. Bush spinners stressed the potential negative fallout for their man. "It becomes Clinton and Perot versus Bush," Republican Lynn Martin said on the David Brinkley program, promulgating the incumbent president's party line.[65]

Journalistic observers tended to view Ross Perot as a *wild card*—a term that was picked up by the press like a mantra. "With Perot the wild card in the deck," said Brit Hume on ABC, "some kind of peculiar new chemistry could emerge here."[66] Although Perot was judged the winner of the first debate, his whimsicality lost luster over the course of the nine days. "While he scored well with viewers during the first outing," said CNN's Tony Clark, "by the second, his stories and one-liners seemed to wear thin."[67] Perot had committed a mortal sin of journalism: He allowed his act to get stale.

In the 1992 vice presidential debate, Admiral James Stockdale briefly inherited the "wild card" label from running mate Perot. CNN referred to Stockdale as "the stealth candidate." On ABC, reporter Mike Von Fremd, noting the admiral's credentials as a scholar of Greek philosophy, mused that Stockdale "could make it more of a highbrow affair."[68] The paucity of footage of this little-known candidate left TV producers scrambling, especially when Stockdale himself went into what was described as "virtual seclusion" in the days before the debate. No candidate had ever stepped onto the debate stage with so cryptic a media image, or left so pummeled.

Over the years the press's interest in predefining the story has led journalists down the occasional blind alley. CBS had egg on its face after a story that aired the day of the first Ford-Carter match in 1976. During an interview with Ed Bradley, Carter press secretary Jody Powell slyly alluded to a potential twist in the evening's plot. "In order to go beyond what's assumed and make this a dramatic point in the campaign," Powell said, "something has to happen—and perhaps some sort of an off-the-wall announcement or whatever would be a way to do it."[69] No such "off-the-wall announcement" took place, but a precedent had been established. This would not be the last time campaign staffers sought to unsettle the opposition by planting red herrings with journalists eager for a scoop.

In 1992 a predebate buzz began building over Bill Clinton's alleged inability to keep cool under fire. "There had been this idea developing in the press, about ten days before the debate, that Clinton couldn't control his temper," Clinton aide George Stephanopoulos recounted at a campaign postmortem at Harvard University.[70] In part the charge stemmed from an appearance Clinton made on the Phil Donahue television show a few days before the first debate, described by both the *Washington Post* and the *Los Angeles Times* as a "testy exchange."[71]

As the "temper" story picked up momentum, Clinton's handlers prepared for the possibility that President Bush would deliberately try to rattle the Arkansas governor, perhaps even provoke a fight on camera. In the newspapers and on television, media analysts recounted past instances in which Clinton had publicly vented his spleen. But in the actual debate, such journalistic speculation proved to be wholly unfounded, a triumph of wishful thinking over reality.

Again in 1996 reporter-strategists were deafened by the pounding of their own drums. Attempting to cook up an interesting angle in a spectacularly lackluster race, reporters touted the Gore-Kemp vice presidential debate as a preview of the presidential election of 2000. Repeatedly the pundits stressed this point, virtually anointing each candidate as his party's nominee four years before the fact. "Gore-Kemp Debate Could Preview Race for White House in 2000," read a typical *Washington Post* headline. "As of today," said Peter Jennings on *World News Tonight*, "these are the leading candidates for their party nominations in the year 2000." William Schneider on CNN said, "The next presidential race could start with tonight's debate—and it looks like it's going to be a corker."[72] On both counts, Schneider missed the mark.

Similarly coverage of that year's Clinton-Dole appearances hinged on the possibility that Dole would launch a character attack on his opponent. When such a stratagem did not materialize in the first debate, reporters reassigned the prediction to running mate Kemp, who was supposed to pursue the matter in the vice presidential match. But Kemp did not attack either, shifting the onus back to Dole in the third and final debate of the series—which once again failed to include the long-promised character attack.

In large measure this story-that-never-was reflected the journalistic fascination with Dole's "prince of darkness" reputation, incubated, among other places, in the 1976 vice presidential debate. "The press is just waiting for him to say something nasty," said Dole biographer Richard Ben Cramer on *Meet the Press* a week before the first 1996 debate.[73] Heading into the second match, media analysis centered on the riskiness of a Dole attack in the town hall format. Said Phil Jones on CBS, "Mister Dole has never been able to shed that image of a hatchet man that he got back in his 1976 vice presidential debate, and the last thing he needs tonight is a boo, a hiss, a gasp from one of the questioners who thinks he's being too mean."[74] With the press on guard for any hint of audience disapproval, Dole found himself tethered to a short leash.

Lest there be any doubt about the journalistic proclivity for dabbling in predebate strategy, consider the editions of *Newsweek* and *Time* that hit the stands just before the first Dole-Clinton appearance. "Dole has no choice but to make it Bloody Sunday," wrote Howard Fineman in *Newsweek*, fairly panting for carnage.[75] *Time*'s Michael Kramer, in the guise of an open letter to Dole, further eroded the distance between journalists and candidates:

> This is is it, Bob Dole, your final chance to move from loser to contender. The stakes couldn't be higher. Nothing else has ignited your campaign. Follow your script this week: Get tanned, get rested, get ready. And take heart. Large swings are possible. Exceed the low expectations for you this Sunday in Hartford, Connecticut, and you just might begin to roll. For the country, a lofty, substantive discussion would be great. But we're dealing with reality here. To win, you'll have to use every tactic available, even the blunt ones.[76]

Predebate coverage had come a long way from the reticence of 1960.

DEBATE DAY: THE STORY CULMINATES

Weeks of predebate coverage culminate in a home-stretch sprint that has generated its own customs and folkways: the obligatory candidate photo opportunities, often in an athletic context; afternoon technical checks in the debate hall; down-to-the-wire saber-rattling by the campaigns; and a final frenzy of handicapping in the press. Debate-day news coverage, so circumspect in the era of Kennedy and Nixon, is now a thriving subspecies of political journalism, propelled by media expansion, the rise of interpretive reporting, and TV's dominance in election storytelling.

With the predebate countdown under way, the story lines the press has worked so assiduously to develop are whipped to a climax: Will Ford make another mistake? Will Reagan make sense? Will Dukakis become likable? Will Quayle humiliate himself? Will Dole revert to form? Or will some unforeseen happening spin the tale in a different direction?

The tradition of debate-day photo ops dates back to Kennedy and Nixon, who shook hands for photographers in the WBBM studio shortly before the first broadcast. In their enthusiasm to document this historic occasion, the cameramen knocked over a number of studio lights. The raucous spontaneity of that unplanned media moment contrasts sharply with today's controlled exercises, in which candidates carefully position themselves in packaged tableaux designed to maximize strengths and minimize deficiencies. For debaters, the pre-event photo op is a chance to claim one last vestige of audience sympathy.

Gerald Ford and Jimmy Carter in 1976 appeared in the usual predebate contexts: poring over briefing books, arriving at the auditorium for tech checks, greeting crowds on the way back to the hotel. It was vice presidential candidate Walter Mondale who introduced the tradition of the athletic debate-day photo op. Newscasts the day of the 1976 Dole-Mondale match in Houston showed the Democratic nominee playing a round of tennis, pointedly unconcerned about the event at hand.

Dole's 1976 predebate coverage took a different tack, prominently featuring the senator's bride of less than a year, Elizabeth Hanford Dole. Mrs. Dole accompanied her husband to his technical check, posing next to him at the lectern for photographers. When Dole's handlers recommended a change of necktie for the television appearance, video crews followed the newlyweds to a Houston department store, where they went shopping for a substitute.

From wives to parents to children, candidates' family members have regularly turned up as characters in predebate coverage. In 1976 First Lady Betty Ford made her only debate appearance of the year at the third and final event in Williamsburg, Virginia. Mrs. Ford, described in a debate-day ABC story as "the campaign's secret weapon," joined her husband at his afternoon tech check in Phi Beta Kappa Hall on the campus of the College of William and Mary. There, as the president posed at his lectern, she stepped over to Carter's podium and scrawled a note. "Dear Mr. Carter," the note read, "May I wish you the best tonight. I am sure the best man will win. I happen to have a favorite candidate, my husband. Best of luck, Betty Ford." President Ford's press secretary displayed the note to reporters and promised to deliver it to

Carter later. On ABC, Tom Jarriel observed, somewhat cynically, "The pre-debate psychological warfare is under way."[77]

Former Hollywood actress Nancy Reagan served as a reliable co-star in her husband's predebate photo ops. For the 1980 Reagan-Anderson debate, the couple made a dramatic arrival at the Baltimore airport in a helicopter, deemed by the campaign to be a "more presidential" mode of transporta-tion.[78] On the day of the 1980 Reagan-Carter debate in Cleveland, the Reagans maintained a low profile, deliberately staying out of the media glare.

Meanwhile President Carter turned up on the evening newscasts in an especially unflattering predebate photo op. Cameras captured Carter out for a waterlogged run in the cold rain; the pictures called into question the pres-ident's common sense. Sam Donaldson made the point on ABC that "some people may not think it's very smart to go jogging in the driving rain on the morning of a day when your presidency could be at stake." NBC's Judy Woodruff linked the soggy run to a recent Carter bout with laryngitis.[79] The footage diminished the candidate, making him look silly just hours before tens of millions of voters would evaluate his suitability for reelection.

A story that aired on CBS the evening of the Carter-Reagan debate sheds light on the ambivalence journalists feel toward covering this most con-trived of political events. Dan Rather's no-nonsense report on the *CBS Evening News* began on a barely concealed note of hostility: "There are the makings of high drama here. There also are aspects of what some see as a parody of true debate." The piece then moved to the rules, overtly scolding the campaigns:

> The candidates did, in fact, heavily influence, if not outright control, negotiations on format and arrangements. The candidates wanted an audience of only nine hundred-fifty, so there will be an audience of only nine hundred-fifty. The candidates wanted few if any reaction shots from the audience, so there will be only limited reaction shots of the audience. And the candidates were even instrumental in choosing the panel of reporters who are here tonight supposedly to ask them tough questions.[80]

However contemptuous the tone, Rather deserves credit for pointing out more frankly than most the truth behind campaign string-pulling.

Rather's track record as a debate cynic extends into later years as well. Anchoring CBS's coverage of the first 1984 debate, Rather offered viewers this tart advisory just before the program began: "Inside the hall everything from the stage setting to the rules under which the candidates are appearing makes it clear that this will not be an actual debate." Before the second debate, Rather reiterated his hard-line stance: "It will not be an actual debate, not with the rules set by the candidates themselves and with the candidates having a hand in selecting their own questioners. What it will be is a candidates' forum—a kind of expanded joint news conference."[81]

Rather's comments betray an antagonism toward presidential debates that other journalists suppress. Reporters assigned to cover these events find themselves trapped in a paradox: scoffing at the manipulations of the campaigns on the one hand, while promoting their agenda on the other. As much as journalists resent being treated as puppets, they see little choice but to embrace candidate-devised rules of engagement. Occasionally, perhaps inevitably, the coverage turns nasty.

For a performer about to embark on a live TV debate, the least welcome media send-off is a last-minute round of negative press. Such was the fate of the hapless Dan Quayle heading into his appearance with Lloyd Bentsen. Two stories that aired on the evening of the 1988 vice presidential match thrust a harsh spotlight onto Quayle's image problems, just as the public was preparing to tune in for the event.

The first, on ABC's *World News Tonight*, featured uncharacteristically candid footage of the candidate inside Omaha's Civic Auditorium during his predebate technical check. As Quayle was shown at the podium practicing his lines in a low voice, his obviously memorized words appeared in the form of subtitles on the screen. Reporter Jackie Judd narrated the scene: "On the most important day of his political career, Quayle turned often to his media handler, Roger Ailes." "Hey Roger," Quayle said to his adviser. "On this, if I decide I want to gesture over there—that's all right? You don't mind that?"[82] Quayle came off in this video clip as a human marionette, nervous and profoundly insecure, in need of guidance for even the simplest thought or physical movement.

The second, more devastating television story ran on PBS's *McNeil-Lehrer News Hour*. In a report billed as a "Peer Review" of the two vice presidential candidates, correspondent Roger Mudd interviewed half a dozen senators from both sides of the aisle. The bulk of the thirteen-minute report was devoted to Quayle, who drew sharply incriminating comments from Democrat Alan Cranston. "I don't think he has been taken seriously by his colleagues," Cranston said. "Most senators have been laughing about the nomination, Republicans with tears in their eyes, and they tell a lot of jokes about him. Their private remarks are quite different than their public remarks." Without prompting, Cranston offered an example: "What were the three toughest years in Dan Quayle's life? The second grade."

Cranston continued, recalling a Republican senator's description of Quayle as "two pounds lighter than a straw hat." When Mudd asked why Cranston had chosen to break the rules of senatorial courtesy by publicly excoriating a fellow member, the California senator cited the significance of the vice presidency. Anyone with knowledge of "the capacities or incapacities" of a vice presidential nominee "has some responsibility to level with the American people," he said. Mudd, in his closing comment, sustained the negative tone: "Privately the senior senators from both parties would not be too upset if young Dan Quayle falters tonight. It is, they say, dignity and maturity and seniority and reliability and comity which are to be admired."[83] Implicit in this statement is Quayle's perceived lack of all these attributes.

Lloyd Bentsen, by contrast, attracted considerably friendlier press from Mudd and other network reporters. Where the dominant visual of Quayle's prebroadcast tech check showed the candidate consulting his TV coach, Bentsen was photographed on the debate stage playfully picking up his wife, demonstrating, in the words of an ABC story, "that at age sixty-seven he has the stamina of a man Quayle's age, forty-one."[84] With messages like these filling the air waves in the hours before broadcast, one could argue that Quayle had already lost the debate on the basis of unfavorable pretrial publicity.

Bentsen's "he-man" photo op underscores the importance campaigns attach to pre-event visuals. For the second Bush-Dukakis debate several days later, Democratic handlers concocted a less successful picture. Hoping to melt Dukakis's frosty image, the campaign arranged for photographers to take pictures of the governor tossing around a ball by the pool of his Los Angeles hotel, wearing a UCLA sweatshirt and striving mightily to look like a regular guy. But as Lesley Stahl pointed out on CBS, the visual setup left it unclear whom Dukakis was playing catch with, reinforcing a sense of isolation and loneliness.[85] Vice President Bush also selected a baseball backdrop for his preproduction photo session, attending game seven of the Dodgers-Mets playoffs on debate eve. In this venue, however, the candidate was surrounded by crowds, an undisputed man of the people.

The athletic settings in turn provided a handy theme for predebate commentary, inspiring journalists to conjure up playing-field analogies of their own. On CBS, Bob Schieffer compared the Los Angeles debate to a "ball game where [Bush] is ahead. These are the late innings, he's got to hold his lead." ABC's Sam Donaldson began his report on Dukakis's technical rehearsal with a different comparison: "Day of game. And the Democratic quarterback is on his way to check out the field." And, from Dan Rather on the *CBS Evening News*, still another sport: "Jump ball tonight here at Pauley Pavilion," Rather began, referring to the UCLA basketball Bruins who normally inhabited the debate site.[86] If athletic metaphors were good enough for the candidates, they were good enough for the press.

Candidate photo ops in 1992 presented a three-way contrast in image management. On opening day of the series Ross Perot got a haircut, George Bush made a campaign stop, and Bill Clinton went to church. In each instance the candidate was using the press to send a not-so-subtle message: Perot is unflappable, Bush is a man of the people, Clinton is a God-fearing Christian.

Four years later Clinton was photographed arriving in San Diego for the final debate of his career. As ABC's Brit Hume reported, Hillary Clinton was "conspicuously at his side, as she has been in the past when anyone attacked her husband's character. They were very much the devoted couple at the airport here."[87] The video showed the Clintons standing hand-in-hand on the tarmac, talking intimately and stealing a kiss, obviously aware of the camera's gaze. In presidential campaigns, even romantic moments can be read as predebate spin.

Part II

PRODUCTION

Chapter Four

THE DEBATERS

Walter Mondale called it "the longest walk I've ever taken": the approach to the podium in the fateful moments before a presidential debate.[1] For the layperson, it is difficult to imagine the stress that accompanies candidates as they venture onto this battlefield. A host of factors converge to intimidate: enormous stakes, vast audiences, historical implications—all under the magnifying glass of live television. For debaters, the risks could scarcely be higher.

As unscripted performances, presidential debates transcend the months of negotiation, preparation, and speculation leading up to the featured event. Once a debate begins, all previous maneuvering yields to a superior force: the on-camera prowess of the candidates. As shown by the diverse experiences of the seventeen men and one woman who have competed at this level, no strategy memo, no negotiated agreement, no amount of rehearsal can thoroughly condition a debater for the exigencies of a live television performance.

"It's like a championship fight," notes presidential historian Doris Kearns Goodwin. "You feel a sense that you're watching these candidates under pressure. And what matters even more than what they say is how they respond to that pressure."[2] Each debater appears before the nation as a solo act, succeeding or failing in an utterly personal way. For an hour and a half the support systems and defensive armor of a presidential campaign are stripped away, leaving only the mystical bond between audience and star.

The rules of debate performance defy easy explanation, and, in the last analysis, it may be impossible to articulate why viewers respond favorably to some on-screen personalities and unfavorably to others. At bottom, debates are exercises in alchemy, subject only to the hazy laws of television. With this limitation in mind, let us evaluate the individuals who have taken the "longest walk" in a presidential or vice presidential debate. What advantages and disadvantages did they bring to their matches? What sort of reviews did they draw? And what is the legacy each of the members of this elite club has left to the institution of TV debates?

JOHN F. KENNEDY (1960)

A single hour of live television was all it took to canonize John F. Kennedy as the patron saint of presidential debates. Though Kennedy would appear three more times with Richard Nixon before the 1960 election, it was that first meeting in Chicago that conferred on JFK the iconic status he maintains even today among political debaters. Subsequent candidates might outshine him in technique, but none has better understood debates as the ultimate star turn.

Like Nixon, Kennedy had proven himself in the broadcast arena well before the "Great Debates." In 1952 the young JFK successfully grappled with senatorial opponent Henry Cabot Lodge in a joint appearance that aired live in Massachusetts. Eight years later, in the West Virginia presidential primary, Kennedy met Hubert Humphrey for a televised matchup that served as a dress rehearsal for the general election debates against Nixon. Media historian Erik Barnouw wrote that Kennedy "impressed viewers with the brevity and conciseness of his replies, an engaging wit, and apparent grasp of local issues."[3] Kennedy also briefly debated his rival for the 1960 Democratic nomination, Lyndon B. Johnson, in an informal exchange that was broadcast during the party convention in Los Angeles.

In view of his less than dazzling delivery before live audiences, the senator's skill as a television communicator might not have been expected. Political scientist Harvey Wheeler wrote that the same characteristics that worked against Kennedy on the stump benefited him in the TV debates:

His unadorned style of delivery fitted well into the viewer's livingroom. And although his rapid rate of speech prevented much of his content from being assimilated, what did come through was the picture of a bright, knowledgeable young man of great earnestness, energy, and integrity.[4]

As the famous White House press conferences would later attest, Kennedy's verbal dexterity and natural wit played particularly well on live television. In an effort to seem more mature, JFK deliberately restrained his sense of humor in the 1960 debates, though occasional flashes of cleverness nonetheless peeked through. In the third debate a panelist asked Kennedy if he owed Nixon an apology for a remark Harry Truman made suggesting where the vice president could go. Answered Kennedy, "I really don't think there's anything that I could say to President Truman that's going to cause him, at the age of seventy-six, to change his particular speaking manner. Perhaps Mrs. Truman can, but I don't think I can."

The most valid criticism of Kennedy's debate performances is that they lack the common touch. Not surprisingly, some viewers interpreted Kennedy's air of detached confidence as patrician arrogance. Adviser Clark Clifford, in a memo after the first debate, suggested that "attention must be given to adding greater warmth to your image. If you can retain the technical brilliance and obvious ability, but also project the element of warm, human understanding, you will possess an unbeatable combination."[5]

Offsetting JFK's deficiency in chumminess was an abundance of attitude. "From the start," wrote Seymour Hersh, "the campaign was orchestrated by Joe Kennedy, who as a one-time Hollywood mogul understood that his son should run for president as a star and not as just another politician."[6] In every important way, the younger Kennedy approached the presidential debates from this leading-man perspective. The emphasis paid off, in the debates as in the overall campaign: presumed stardom led to genuine stardom.

Compounding his other advantages, Kennedy was blessed with fortuitous timing. The Kennedy-Nixon debates took place against a backdrop of media calm, in an era when audiences had not grown cynical about the merger between television and politics. Like no subsequent debater, JFK was given an unfiltered opportunity to connect with voters on his own terms, and he was smart enough to seize it. Reviewing a tape of his broadcast appearances after the election, Kennedy said, "We wouldn't have had a prayer without that gadget."[7]

RICHARD M. NIXON (1960)

Thirteen years before Richard Nixon met John F. Kennedy in Chicago for the first televised presidential debate, the two then-freshman congressmen held their first in-person debate in a hotel ballroom in McKeesport, Pennsylvania. Before a boisterous crowd, Nixon and Kennedy, both members of a subcommittee that had drafted the Taft-Hartley employment bill, argued the fine points of labor-management relations. That night, on the train ride home to Washington, the lawmakers shared a sleeper compartment, drawing straws to see who got the bottom berth. Nixon won.

By the 1960 campaign the career of Richard Nixon had eclipsed that of his rival, owing at least in part to Nixon's relationship with television. A riveting nationwide broadcast—the 1952 "Checkers" speech—had helped the candidate retain his slot as Dwight Eisenhower's running mate. In 1959 Nixon strengthened his anticommunist credentials in the equally famous "kitchen debate" with Nikita Khrushchev in Moscow, shown to approving audiences in the United States. As vice president, Nixon commanded the media spotlight for eight years, his tenure in office neatly coinciding with the exponential growth of American television.

Given this head start, how did Nixon go astray in the 1960 debates? As we have seen, the Republican nominee arrived in Chicago physically ill, overfatigued, and otherwise unprepared to meet his rival. But beyond poor health, Nixon had fundamentally misconceived the event, viewing it as a rhetorical exercise, whereas Kennedy approached it as a TV show. "His varsity instincts at the ready," wrote political communication expert Kathleen Hall Jamieson, "the vice president marshalled his facts against Kennedy's, contested points, and defended his ground. He instead should have showcased himself against the backdrop Kennedy provided."[8]

Harvey Wheeler speculated that the "Checkers" experience had deceived Nixon into adopting a similar style for the debates. "But the 'Checkers' speech was over a moral issue, not policy questions," Wheeler wrote. "And in that speech he was by himself on television—unchallenged by opponent or reporters."[9] Indeed, a major explanation for Nixon's failure in the 1960 debates is the relative lack of charisma he exudes alongside his co-star. Eugene Patterson, in an *Atlanta Constitution* column after the second debate, stated the matter bluntly: "The medium is good to Kennedy and most unkind to Nixon. It makes Kennedy look forceful. It makes Nixon look guilty." In Patterson's opinion, Nixon's demeanor on the small screen was that of a "salesman of cemetery lots."[10]

Visual factors conspired against Nixon in another way. Six years after the Kennedy-Nixon debates, network news producer Wallace Westfeldt had occasion to observe the former vice president as he was being interviewed on a Miami talk show. From the vantage point of a TV control room, Westfeldt watched Nixon on a pair of side-by-side monitors, one color, the other black and white. The difference was "stunning," Westfeldt recalled. "Nixon looked good in color. He looked like hell in black and white."[11] In 1960, of course, black-and-white television was the only option.

In both appearance and performance, Richard Nixon got considerably better over the remaining three debates of 1960. To combat his skeletal visage in the first encounter, he embarked on a "milkshake diet" and recovered his normal weight and collar size. He agreed to wear makeup, and a certified Republican cosmetic artist was added to the campaign entourage. Still, improvement in the later debates could not counteract the profoundly negative impression left in the first.

Although Nixon's refusal to debate in 1968 and 1972 may be understandable, the lack of these events is history's loss. Imagine Nixon in a three-way match against Hubert Humphrey and George Wallace, or one-on-one with George McGovern. As it happened, 1960 represented both the beginning and the end of Richard Nixon as presidential debater. Eventually Nixon would find bitter humor in the experience, describing himself as "a dropout from the Electoral College—because I flunked debating."[12]

GERALD FORD (1976)

As the first incumbent to meet his challenger on the playing fields of television, Gerald Ford made a significant contribution to the institutionalization of presidential debates. But even if Ford had not shot himself in the foot with his claim that Eastern Europe was not under Soviet domination, the

1976 matches would have offered this accidental president little gain against Jimmy Carter. Ford did not exactly hurt himself by debating, but neither did his lackluster performance rouse much support.

Two factors operated against Gerald Ford the debater: a loud, monotonous voice and a narrow range of facial expressions. Together, this combination rendered Ford spectacularly unscintillating on TV; by comparison, the low-key Carter leaped off the screen. Ford's relentless delivery had a narcotic effect, like the drone of a didactic speaker at a chamber of commerce luncheon. "He is forceful in his way of speaking, but he doesn't say very much," observed Elizabeth Drew, one of the panelists in the first 1976 debate. The president's debate coach warned Ford that "many viewers perceive you to be shouting." Communication scholars clocked Ford's speech rate as so slow that he needed almost thirty extra minutes to match the total number of words spoken by Jimmy Carter.[13]

President Ford's three debates with Carter cast him in the role of solid, upstanding burgher. Every inch the Midwestern Republican, Ford even wore a vest beneath his suit jacket in the first debate, as though to underscore his conservatism. In a more animated individual, Ford's lack of theatrical pretense might have seemed disarming; instead, he came off more as a local businessman than the leader of the free world. Compared to later such performer-presidents as Ronald Reagan and Bill Clinton, Gerald Ford looks and sounds like a relic from some preelectronic age.

Ford did bring one visual asset to the debate: like Reagan, he had a commanding physique that contrasted favorably with the slighter build of Jimmy Carter. James Gannon of the *Wall Street Journal*, a panelist in the first 1976 debate, described Ford as "an imposing presence" who looked as though "he could lift [the podium] over his head and throw it at me." Jules Witcover wrote that Ford gripped his lectern "like some big, menacing bear straining to leap at his adversary."[14]

Ford's track record as a klutz, reinforced in the public consciousness by Chevy Chase on *Saturday Night Live*, may have handed the incumbent president an inadvertent advantage. According to press secretary Ron Nessen, Ford "had the image of being a plodding speaker, slow-witted and clumsy. Thus, when he did not trip or bump his head, when he spoke with style and clarity, he appeared to be doing even better than he really was."[15] All the same, aides took no chances. A strategy memo drafted before the first debate addressed the specifics of Ford's stage exit at the end of the event. The memo stressed that the president would be attached to a microphone cable connected to the base of his podium, information the memo's recipient has hand-bracketed for emphasis.[16]

Videotape of one of Ford's practice sessions shows the debater in a rare candid moment, finishing up his pipe just before a run-through begins. In this footage he appears to be the very picture of relaxation and fatherly wisdom. Unfortunately for Ford, once he looked into the lens and began to speak, this easy grace devolved into dullness—and dullness is the enemy of television.

JIMMY CARTER (1976, 1980)

After the media-wise presidencies of Ronald Reagan and Bill Clinton, it is easy to forget that in 1976 Jimmy Carter was regarded as an accomplished television communicator. But strategists for Republican nominee Gerald Ford found cause for concern in their opponent's track record in three primary debates. A predebate memorandum described Carter as "controlled," "confident," and "resolute." A Ford TV adviser warned, "He does not offend anyone, either through his answers or visually. He is an appealing figure who comes across as smooth and calm."[17]

Like John F. Kennedy before him, Carter entered the 1976 debates the lesser-known commodity. Unlike Kennedy, Carter seemed subdued, even intimidated during his first encounter with Ford. "I didn't know exactly how to deal with the fact that Mr. Ford was president," Carter confessed afterward.[18] For the second debate, Carter adopted a more confrontational stance, intensified his preparations and, with unexpected assistance from Ford's Eastern Europe gaffe, emerged the clear victor. "Self-confident and acerbic, he fired aggressive and sometimes pointed charges at Gerald Ford," wrote Richard Steele in *Newsweek*.[19] Carter drew even better reviews in the third and final debate of the series. "If you were scoring by rounds," said William Greider of the *Washington Post*, "Carter seemed to be the clear winner. His presence, which was steady and confident, was less abrasive than at the second debate, more self-assured than in the first."[20]

Against the lackluster Ford, Carter had little trouble prevailing as 1976's star debater. Four years later, with Ronald Reagan as his opponent, the tables were turned. The Reagan-Carter match provided viewers with one of the sharpest polarities in debate history. An editorial in the *New York Times* saw it as a case of Carter winning on words, Reagan winning on music—and in presidential debates, music counts more. "Carter comes across like a teacher we don't really want to listen to," wrote Elizabeth Drew in *The New Yorker*. "He's not interesting to listen to, it's not fun to listen to him, he doesn't engage us."[21] Ironically Carter's strength—his command of facts and issues—became his undoing, making him seem didactic instead of commanding, humorless instead of reassuring.

Physically, too, Carter suffered by comparison with Reagan. David Broder, in the *Washington Post*, noted that while individual close-ups showed both men looking equally composed, Reagan "was the dominant figure with his greater height and bulk in the longer-range shots." According to NBC's Tom Brokaw, "When Carter bumped up against Reagan, he seemed small, and kind of wonkish."[22]

In the evening's most ridiculed moment, Carter made an ill-advised reference to his thirteen-year-old daughter. "I had a discussion with Amy the other day before I came here," Carter told the audience, "to ask her what the most important issue was. She said she thought nuclear weaponry and the control of nuclear arms." In the crowd at Cleveland's Music Hall, scattered snickers could be heard. Far more damning was the postdebate commentary, not just by journalists but by comedians and even Reagan himself, who told a rally in Milwaukee, "I remember when Patty and Ron were little tiny kids, we used to talk about nuclear power."[23]

In the end, the so-called Amy gaffe was merely a symptom of Carter's larger problem in debating Reagan. "The optimism in Carter's camp was always misplaced," said Broder. "People were ready to elect a new president, and all they needed was some assurance that Reagan was not going be some sort of crazy person."[24]

Like other debate victims before him, Jimmy Carter believed that he lost the 1980 match not on content but on theatrics. The night after the event, he dictated some thoughts about the Cleveland debate for his diary. Said Carter of Reagan, "He has his memorized lines, and he pushes a button and they come out." Carter then added what might be read as an epitaph for the 1980 debate: "Apparently made a better impression on the TV audience than I did."[25]

WALTER MONDALE (1976, 1984)

Walter Mondale's career as a debater brought him up against both ends of the personality spectrum: Bob Dole's prince of darkness in 1976 and Ronald

Reagan's sunny optimist eight years later. Largely on the basis of not being Dole, Mondale won history's first vice presidential debate. Against Reagan, Mondale had a mixed record: a remarkable, well-conceived victory in the first 1984 debate and a second debate that rendered him not so much a loser as a footnote.

Compared to both his opponents, Mondale lacked a clearly defined on-camera presence. Earnest but unexciting, Mondale had a way of seeming graceful at the lectern without leaving much of a mark. In 1976, when Dole gave perhaps too colorful a performance, this worked to Mondale's advantage. The 1984 series with Reagan cast Mondale in the role of underdog, hopelessly inferior to his opponent both in popular appeal and on matters of style.

"The public would especially expect Reagan to be glib and adroit," wrote William Henry of the first debate, "while Mondale had built up a reputation for being dull; measured against those expectations, Mondale had every chance to offer a pleasant surprise to the electorate."[26] And surprise the people he did. Mondale's performance in the Louisville debate presented a political variation of the tortoise-and-hare parable. This time, strategic preparation overtook presumptive ability.

Early in the program Mondale established a tone that shrewdly combined aggression with respect. "His principal purpose was not to explain himself," said Hugh Sidey in *Time*, "but to confuse, anger, and outscore his opponent." John Corry in the *New York Times* noted that for the first time since taking office Reagan was being openly patronized: "His strength has been in the strength of his convictions, but Mr. Mondale was suggesting that the convictions didn't amount to much."[27]

The Louisville debate, which marked Reagan's worst public performance, briefly lifted Democratic spirits. "Walter Mondale flew into New York today," reported ABC's Brit Hume the next evening, "but the way he was feeling after last night's debate, he probably didn't need the plane."[28] Needless to say, such euphoria could not last. Heading into the second and final debate of 1984, Mondale found himself trapped in a no-win situation: The bar for Reagan had been set unbelievably low.

"I believe if it hadn't been for the first debate," Mondale told journalists Germond and Witcover, "the reports on my performance in the second debate would have been far better. But I think the contrast between the two—all he had to do was stay on his feet the second time around."[29] Edwin Newman, who moderated the second debate, described Mondale as so nervous that "when he came on stage, he did not even say hello to me and the questioners."[30] Postdebate commentary suggested that the two candidates had reversed roles, Mondale seeming old and tired and Reagan sparkling with vitality.

In a news conference the day after his defeat at the ballot box, Mondale lamented the inordinate power of television in presidential campaigns. "Modern politics today requires a mastery of television," the candidate told reporters. "I've never really warned up to television. And in fairness to television, it's never warmed up to me."[31]

BOB DOLE (1976, 1996)

A candidate as naturally witty as Bob Dole faces a dilemma in the risk-averse setting of a presidential debate: whether to curb his humor or direct it at the opposition like artillery. In 1976 Dole's refusal to sugar-coat his acerbic personality led him into a series of verbal miscalculations; twenty years later, against the masterful Bill Clinton, the long-time Kansas senator reined himself in to the point of blandness.

The earlier Dole, appearing with Walter Mondale in history's first vice presidential debate, approached the event with unconcealed disdain. No other performer in the annals of debating has been so openly contemptuous of the exercise or so loath to prepare for it. According to Dole biographer Richard Ben Cramer, the candidate delayed rehearsals for the Mondale debate until the day of the broadcast, "but by then he was so offhand (or trying to look offhand), he'd just toss off wisecracks."[32]

During the debate, Dole's proclivity for one-liners manifested itself in remarks that seemed ill-considered at best, and mean-spirited at worst. Announcing at the outset that "tonight may be sort of a fun evening," the Republican candidate went on to needle his opponent: "We've been friends . . . and we'll be friends when this election is over—and he'll still be in the Senate." Dole dismissed the vice presidency as a job that is "mostly indoors and there's no heavy lifting." He insulted his hosts, the scrupulously fair-minded League of Women Voters, as being "a little bit liberal."

Most damaging, however, was Dole's offensive reference to the 1.6 million Americans killed in "Democrat wars." This charge led the laid-back Mondale to rebuke his opponent in uncharacteristically sharp language: "I think Senator Dole has richly earned his reputation as a hatchet man tonight." Wrote William Greider in the *Washington Post*, "Dole was relentlessly loose, a man whose wit is irresistible in one moment and outrageous in the next."[33]

Two decades later, when Dole made an improbable comeback as his party's nominee for the White House, the nimbus of the 1976 debate hovered over him still. In a pair of joint appearances with Bill Clinton, Dole seemed to be battling his own reputation as much as his opponent. Postdebate analysis of the first 1996 match stressed Dole's personality overhaul. Tom Shales, in the *Post*, called the Dole strategy an "attempt to dispel his image as Snidely McNasty, the meanest man in American politics." Sam Donaldson, on ABC, allowed that the candidate had not come off as a "dour troglodyte."[34] Others mentioned Dole's failure to take advantage of the opportunity that moderator Jim Lehrer had provided for a critique of Clinton's character.

Ten days later, in the second and final presidential debate, predictions that Dole would hammer the "character issue" once again failed to pan out. In the setting of a town hall forum, before more than one hundred uncommitted voters in San Diego, Dole had an even narrower window of opportunity to question his opponent's moral rectitude. "There weren't the kind of fireworks that Bob Dole promised," said NBC's Jim Miklaszewski the next morning, "because every time he lit the fuse, President Clinton managed to snuff it out."[35] Although Dole did sneak in a few references to Clintonian ethics, he got no assistance from audience members, whose own questions pointedly excluded issues of personal conduct.

By all rights, a candidate with Bob Dole's verbal agility and straight-shooting appeal ought to have been a natural in the arena of a live presidential debate. Instead, the necessity for debaters to confine themselves within a tightly delineated safety zone defanged this most watchable of politicians. Regrettably for Bob Dole, caution proved to be just as misguided a strategy as insouciance.

RONALD REAGAN (1980, 1984)

Could any presidential debater have been better prepared for the task than Ronald Reagan? The cumulative experience of fifty years as a radio announcer, film actor, television host, corporate spokesman, and political celebrity gave Reagan an edge in debates other candidates could only dream of. He started his broadcasting career at a Des Moines radio station in the 1930s, vividly describing baseball games he had not actually seen. In 1955, after a long stint in movies, Reagan served as co-host of one of early TV's riskiest live telecasts, the grand opening of Disneyland; in the face of one embarrassing technical disaster after another, the future California governor maintained an admirably cool head. Reagan more than held his own in a televised debate with Robert Kennedy in 1967, defending an unpopular stance on the Vietnam War before a hostile group of international students. Leaving the set at the end of the program, RFK warned an aide, "Don't ever put me on with that sonofabitch again."[36]

By the time Reagan entered the presidential primaries of 1980 he was completely at home in the pressure-cooker of unscripted television. That year, at a forum in Nashua, New Hampshire, Reagan demonstrated how formidable a live performer he could be. The event, sponsored by the *Nashua Telegraph* but underwritten by Reagan's campaign, had originally been scheduled as a two-man confrontation with fellow front-runner George Bush. At the eleventh hour the Reagan organization saw political advantage in extending invitations to the other Republican primary contenders, four of whom appeared at the hall at the appointed hour, ready for a showdown.

The debate began with an announcement from the publisher of the *Telegraph*: The last-minute arrivals, now standing onstage, would be allowed only to give closing statements. When Reagan protested, the moderator ordered the candidate's microphone turned off. "I am *paying* for this microphone," Reagan retorted, lifting a line from Frank Capra's political comedy *State of the Union* and drawing cheers from the crowd. Although the other candidates did not ultimately join the debate, Reagan's act of bravado instantly became the stuff of campaign legend. David Broder of the *Washington Post*, who was seated in the hall, called it "one of the most electrifying moments I've ever known in covering politics."[37]

In his two general election debates in 1980, first with John Anderson, then with incumbent President Carter, Reagan deftly accomplished a critical objective: to dispel his image as a right-wing warmonger by seeming trustworthy, avuncular, and optimistic. Reagan's closing statement in the Anderson debate, in which he described America as "a nation which is for all mankind a shining city on the hill," ranks among the Great Communicator's finest rhetoric. Said F. Richard Ciccone and Jon Margolis in the *Chicago Tribune*, "Reagan delivered his answers with the entertainer's aplomb that has made him one of the best political speakers of his time."[38]

The higher-stakes debate with Carter proved even more beneficial. Reagan's naturally cheerful disposition contrasted sharply with Carter's pinched demeanor; the difference seemed most pronounced when Reagan chided his opponent with the rueful line, "There you go again." According to historian Gil Troy, Carter unwittingly found himself cast as Richard Nixon to Reagan's John F. Kennedy. "The Carter-Reagan debate marked a clash between two styles," Troy wrote, "between a linear, formalistic print culture and McLuhan's blurry visual culture, between a politics of issues and a politics of images."[39]

As in the Anderson debate, Reagan delivered a powerful closing statement, asking Americans, "Are you better off than you were four years ago?" Broder wrote in the *Post*, "Reagan used all the skills acquired in forty years before the cameras—shrugs and smiles and easily inflected small jokes—to tell the viewers that the portrait of him Carter was drawing . . . was a political caricature." Daniel Yankelovich, pollster for *Time*, saw a radical shift in public opinion after the telecast. "The dissatisfaction with Carter was there all along," he said, "but people couldn't bring themselves to vote for Reagan. The debate changed all that."[40]

Four years later, in the first of two joint appearances with Democrat Walter Mondale, Reagan would suffer his greatest humiliation as a public figure. The seventy-three-year-old president gave a performance so disconnected that it caught his competitor off guard. "This guy is gone," Mondale commented to an aide immediately afterward. "It's scary. He's not really up to it." Reagan's defeat inspired a tidal wave of negative press. "The old actor, a ghost of his 1980 self, missed cues, flubbed lines, lost his place," wrote columnist Mary McGrory in a typical account. "He seemed lonely and afraid, just another politician clinging to his job."[41]

Reagan came into the second 1984 debate keenly aware of his mission. This time his aides agreed to "let Reagan be Reagan," a decision that accrued to the president's advantage when one of the panelists brought up the inevitable age issue. With a perfectly detonated joke—"I refuse to make my opponent's youth and inexperience an issue in this campaign"—Reagan succeeded, perhaps too easily, in silencing his critics. Even a semi-coherent closing statement, halted in progress by the moderator for running too long, did not hurt Reagan. The old magic had cast its spell.

As critic William Henry observed, "In politics, there is one gift that outshines all others, and that is the gift of luck."[42] Among presidential debaters, no one exemplifies this maxim better than Ronald Reagan.

JOHN ANDERSON (1980)

The 1980 debate between John Anderson and Ronald Reagan illuminates the problem that such events pose for independent and third-party candidates. Like Ross Perot twelve years later, Anderson upset the political applecart by threatening the traditional one-on-one structure of debates; unlike Perot, Anderson failed to win a seat at the grown-ups' table. Jimmy Carter refused to share the stage with both Anderson and Reagan, creating a lopsided, lackluster exchange between a pair of unevenly matched challengers. As Hedrick Smith in the *New York Times* put it, "The Reagan-Anderson confrontation had all the trappings of a full-fledged presidential debate except for the president."[43]

Badly trailing both his opponents, Anderson entered the event under intense pressure. "For John Anderson," reported CBS's Bob Faw, "the debate is a make or break proposition. He must not only do well but well enough to show he's a genuine contender and that a vote for him is not wasted." Anderson, who had debated Reagan in the primaries, fell far short of his opponent in the charisma department. As Faw pointed out, "The trouble is that the public John Anderson tends to sound preachy and self-righteous."[44]

Anderson's performance in Baltimore did little to dispel his advance billing as a morally superior technocrat. The candidate's closing statement makes the point:

> Do you really think that our economy is healthy? Do you really think that eight million Americans being out of work and the fifty percent unemployment among the youth of our country are acceptable? Do you really think that our armed forces are acceptably strong in those areas of conventional capability where they should be? Do you think that our political institutions are working the way they should when literally only half our citizens vote? I don't think you do think that.

Compare this with Reagan's closing statement in the same debate, in which he painted a word-picture of America as a "shining city on a hill."

The appearance with Reagan represents both the zenith of the Anderson campaign and its swan song. Within days, poll numbers for the former Illinois congressman began a slide from which they would not recover. By the time the Carter-Reagan debate rolled around a month later, Anderson's candidacy had fizzled into irrelevance. CNN, then a struggling news operation seen in only a fraction of the nation's homes, electronically inserted Anderson into a three-way version of the debate, but by this point the third man in the race had become an also-ran.

In the end, Anderson could not capitalize on the sixty-minute window of opportunity his single debate afforded. "Anderson failed in part because he did not understand debates," wrote Democratic strategist Patrick Caddell. "He was more interested in promoting his own ideas in a vacuum than in challenging Reagan. In retrospect only a total destruction of Reagan offered Anderson any hope—looking all right was fatal."[45]

GEORGE BUSH (1984, 1988, 1992)

No other presidential candidate of the twentieth century debated more, or enjoyed it less, than George Bush. After an eccentric debut in the 1984 vice presidential match against Geraldine Ferraro, Bush went on to five top-of-the-ticket debates, two with Michael Dukakis in 1988 and three against Bill Clinton and Ross Perot in 1992. His erratic track record in these encounters spanned a dizzying spectrum, from flashes of brilliance to moments of near-incoherence.

Failing to comprehend that American voters *like* evaluating their potential leaders side by side, candidate Bush never learned to mask his fundamental testiness toward debates. Bush viewed debates as irritants, roadblocks to be gotten around as quickly as possible. According to Republican adviser Mary Matalin, Bush was "generally cranky about the whole process."[46] And his crankiness showed.

In the chaotic debate negotiations of 1980, Bush managed to escape a face-to-face meeting with his opponents. Four years later he became an unwitting guinea pig in a new political tableau: the first male-versus-female debate. This juxtaposition disconcerted Bush, and against Ferraro, he gave an almost comically hyperactive performance. "In a reversal of stereotypes," wrote syndicated columnist Ellen Goodman, "Ferraro was subdued, lawyerlike, and cool . . . while Bush was shrill, strident, and, gasp, hysterical."[47]

The Ferraro debate may have been the "nadir" of Bush's career, said David Hoffman in the *Washington Post*, "in part because it spawned the notion that he was a whiny and awkward communicator in comparison with [Reagan]."[48] Emerging from Reagan's shadow in the first debate of 1988, the incumbent vice president got off to a shaky start, mangling an abortion question, demonizing Dukakis, and regularly lapsing into semi-intelligible "Bush-speak." Wrote *Post* columnist George Will, "Tracing a Bush thought back from its manifestation in speech to its origin in his thinking is like seeking the source of the Blue Nile."[49]

In the second 1998 debate Bush reaped an unexpected windfall from the unfeeling response Dukakis gave to Bernard Shaw's question about the theoretical rape and murder of Kitty Dukakis. "Bush's performance was hardly hall of fame material," observed *Newsweek*, "but he was steady, commanding and, measured against the governor, an appealingly mortal man."[50]

This "mortal man" may have been mortally wounded in his final round of debates, the 1992 series with Clinton and Perot. Just as Bush advisers had feared, the three-way structure set up a two-against-one dynamic. After the first encounter, Michael Kelly wrote in the *New York Times*,

> With both Mr. Carter and Mr. Perot taking shots at him, the president spent much of the debate playing variations on the theme that things were not as bad as they seemed. He drew mostly modest applause, and on several occasions actually finished speaking to a dead silence, a surprising thing given that a quarter of the people in the hall were friends, family, and selected Republican guests.[51]

The second 1992 debate, the Richmond town hall forum, was even more disastrous. Bush joked to an unappreciative audience that his wife would probably make a better president than he would. Then, in the night's signature moment, Bush got caught on live TV stealing a glance at his watch. When a young African-American woman asked how the national debt had affected Bush personally, his response was, "I'm not sure I get it." Clinton strategist James Carville, watching backstage at the debate hall, was heard to say, "Bush just lost the election."[52]

Recovering in time for the last installment of the 1992 series, Bush turned in the best debate performance of his career. Still, a late, isolated victory could not stop the momentum that had been gathering for Bill Clinton. "This won't be enough to give Bush the win," Richard Nixon told a colleague, "but at least he will have gone down fighting."[53]

Although Bush's inconsistent, inelegant delivery ranks him in the lower tier of presidential debaters, an endearing genuineness redeems all his performances. "Bush was not a good debater in the natural sense," said veteran Washington reporter Brit Hume, "but there was a slightly goofy goodwill that came through. You could tell he was a real person."[54] For George Bush, authenticity may have been an asset, but it was insufficient to win debates.

GERALDINE FERRARO (1984)

As the first woman on a major-party presidential ticket, Geraldine Ferraro entered 1984's vice presidential debate under microscopic scrutiny. Could she hold her own against George Bush? Would she rattle him? Would she dispel doubts about her suitability for office? "I was doing two things," Ferraro said of the match. "I had to not only debate George Bush on substance, but I had to let the public know that a woman—this woman—was able to take over the job of president."[55]

The congresswoman from Queens, selected by Mondale at least in part for her TV skills, had been dubbed by the media as "scrappy" and "feisty" and "acerbic." Hoping to soften this image, Ferraro's handlers sanded away at the sharper edges of her personality. But in their attempts to craft a stateswoman, they may have imposed too many checks. "Ferraro was in a bit of a box," wrote Elizabeth Drew in *The New Yorker*, "and her discomfort there showed."[56]

In the debate's flashiest moment, Ferraro's fighting spirit surfaced when Bush offered to help her understand the subtleties of international diplomacy. Looking directly at her opponent, Ferraro let him have it: "I almost resent, Vice President Bush, your patronizing attitude that you have to teach me about foreign policy." Was the moment planned? "Absolutely not," Ferraro said in a CNN interview twelve years later. "He kept talking down to me."[57] Particularly irritating, said the candidate, was Bush's habit of calling her "Mrs. Ferraro," despite an earlier agreement that she be addressed as "Congresswoman Ferraro."

Boston Globe reporter Robert Healy, who had covered the 1960 debates, praised Ferraro, likening her to John F. Kennedy. "Ferraro has the unusual faculty of being able to talk to the television audience as if she were sitting in their living room having a cup of coffee," Healy wrote.[58] Indeed the candidate seemed remarkably at ease before the vast viewership, especially in contrast to her opponent's high-strung zippiness.

But the general response to Ferraro was less enthusiastic, most notably on matters of style. Perhaps the salient image from the Bush-Ferraro debate was of the Democratic candidate looking not at the camera but down at her lectern, either jotting or referring to notes on a legal pad. "She had fallen back on the body language appropriate to a court of law," said campaign authors Peter Goldman and Tony Fuller. According to William R. Doerner in *Time*, "The down-and-low delivery was such a departure from her brassy style on the stump . . . that some observers thought she came across as cowed."[59]

As is so often the case in presidential debates, Geraldine Ferraro's performance could not live up to its advance hype. Although she acquitted herself admirably on content, in the end Ferraro was punished for not having mastered the stylistic niceties of TV debating. "But in terms of the substance and my handling of the issues," Ferraro wrote in her memoirs, "I think I did extremely well."[60]

MICHAEL DUKAKIS (1988)

If television is a cool medium, then Michael Dukakis ought to have been the most blessed of presidential debaters. Instead, in his two 1988 matches with George Bush, Dukakis's natural reserve functioned as an audience turnoff. Dukakis was widely thought to have won his first debate and lost his second, but in the end the distinction mattered little: win or lose, neither viewers nor the press could warm up to the unemotive governor of Massachusetts.

The first encounter gave Dukakis a much-needed opportunity to counter Bush's relentless campaign of ad hominem attacks, attacks that extended into the debate itself. Early in the program, within a single sixty-second rebuttal, Bush called his opponent a "liberal," a "card-carrying member of the ACLU," and "out of the mainstream," disingenuously adding in a follow-up, "I'm not questioning his patriotism." In what would become the evening's defining sound bite, Dukakis fired back: "Of course the vice president is questioning my patriotism. I don't think there's any question about that. And I resent it."

This newly aggressive tone helped propel Dukakis to a forty-five to thirty-six victory over Bush in ABC's postdebate poll. But the win was hollow, observed *Newsweek*, the triumph of the smartest kid in the class: "He had got A's for his answers . . . and D's in popularity." As Dukakis biographers Oliphant and Black saw it, "Dukakis made substantive points while Bush scored with emotional and folksy ones."[61]

By the second event any afterglow from Dukakis's opening performance had evaporated. The first question—Bernard Shaw's hypothetical
query about the rape and murder of Kitty Dukakis—harpooned the
Democratic candidate, and for the rest of the debate he suffered a slow,
agonizing, on-camera demise. In the view of *Boston Globe* columnist
David Nyhan, Dukakis "went into the hole on the very first question and
never climbed out. As the night progressed, Bush got better, and the Duke
got worse."[62] In her memoirs, Kitty Dukakis would describe Shaw's query
as "the nail in the coffin" of the campaign. She wrote, "Michael made a
mistake; he answered a question he should have hurled right back into the
face of his questioner."[63]

Dukakis observers were surprised that this veteran politician failed to
seize the opening Shaw had presented, especially since a response had been
rehearsed. "I think I went through fifty-odd debates with Michael
Dukakis," said campaign manager Susan Estrich. "And he was very good in
most of them; he wasn't good in every single one of them. Unfortunately,
this was the most important one of the season, and it was a disappointment."[64]

Ten years after the fact, Dukakis looked back on this, his best-remem-
bered and most damaging debate moment. "It was not an unfair question,"
he said, "but I answered as if I'd heard it for the thousandth time. There is
the danger that having done this over and over and over again, you forget
that for most of the audience this may be the very first time they've watched
you." Added Dukakis, "I've listened to the response since—and it doesn't
sound so bad."[65]

LLOYD BENTSEN (1988)

As David Broder of the *Washington Post* saw it, Lloyd Bentsen looked like
"the reliable, white-haired corner pharmacist, with a store of experience as
deep as his baritone voice."[66] In his 1988 vice presidential debate against Dan
Quayle, this kindly druggist administered the verbal equivalent of a lethal
injection.

Before the debate Bentsen had been thought of as mild-mannered, even
reserved. "Senator Bentsen is not a spellbinder and is unlikely to become
one," wrote Warren Weaver in the *New York Times* the morning of the event.
"He projects sincerity, experience and a command of complicated factual

material, but he rarely has emotional impact on an audience." *Newsweek* predicted "he may well prove boring and pedantic," while Texas Democrat Ann Richards said, "He's not going to be a standup comedian."[67]

Indeed, apart from the "You're no Jack Kennedy" line, little stands out from Bentsen's performance in Omaha. But that one exchange was all it took to stamp the debate with its signature moment. "Bentsen looked like the sorrowful uncle talking to the wayward nephew," observed NBC's John Chancellor,[68] and many viewers agreed.

Polls taken immediately after the program named Bentsen the overwhelming victor, and the candidate wasted no time savoring his moment of glory. Bentsen told postdebate audiences that Quayle "left Omaha with no forwarding address" and promised to "open the Quayle season a little early this year."[69] Dukakis campaign advertisements, which had barely acknowledged Bentsen before the debate, now prominently featured the senator's name. Political pundits wondered aloud if the Dukakis-Bentsen ticket might be more electable with the order reversed.

Though Bentsen's performance in Omaha would give Democrats a badly needed shot of adrenalin, the effect was short-lived. The principal beneficiary turned out not to be Michael Dukakis but Lloyd Bentsen. According to Elizabeth Drew,

> The emergence of this improbable star said some telling things about this election, and about how we choose candidates. Bentsen's new glory came not because he had got off his now-famous line about Kennedy; it came about because he was the most—in fact, the only— authentic figure in the race. What people were responding to was that for the first time this fall they had seen a genuine, whole person, someone at ease with himself and his knowledge.[70]

In the strange and bitter presidential race of 1988, these qualities placed Lloyd Bentsen in a class by himself.

DAN QUAYLE (1988, 1992)

Fairly or not, Dan Quayle will be forever remembered as the butt of Lloyd Bentsen's putdown in the 1988 vice presidential debate: "Senator, I served with Jack Kennedy. Jack Kennedy was a friend of mine. Senator, you're no

Jack Kennedy." With these words, the young man from Indiana, who had been cautioned not to compare himself to the thirty-fifth president, went down in stunning defeat.

Descriptions of Quayle's 1988 performance fell along two metaphorical lines: animal and schoolboy. Meg Greenfield saw "a deer caught in the headlights"; Tom Shales, "Bambi on ice"; Michael Dukakis, a "cornered chipmunk."[71] David Broder compared Quayle to the "senior class president of his high school or college," and Elizabeth Drew likened him to "a young man hesitantly reciting his lessons and knowing little else."[72] Even friendly analysts like George Will could muster no enthusiasm. "Quayle was so overprogrammed it seemed someone backstage was operating a compact disc—a very small compact disc—in Quayle's skull," Will wrote.[73] So deeply did the words sting that Quayle called Will from the road to complain.

What stands out about these assessments is their uniformity. Indeed, Dan Quayle's 1988 performance is one of the few in debate history to provoke an almost totally negative reaction. Quayle would attribute his problems to a bad night's sleep and having spent the whole of debate day "just endlessly replaying those rote answers in my mind." In his autobiography, Quayle recalled a conversation with Lesley Stahl of CBS about the peculiar effect the television camera has on certain people's eyes: "In my case, she says, it captures some look of uncertainty, even though my demeanor in person reflects otherwise."[74]

Quayle's opportunity for vindication came four years later in the three-way vice presidential debate with Al Gore and James Stockdale. "I threw away that campaign book," Quayle said, "and I focused on themes. And I was more relaxed and far more in control. I learned a lot from the 1988 debate, believe me."[75] Quayle's rock-bottom expectations also handed him a considerable edge. As Tad Devine, campaign manager for Lloyd Bentsen put it, "Such low pre-debate standing is the political equivalent of an express elevator to the penthouse of debate victory."[76]

Indeed, the 1992 reviews read like citations for "most improved" debater. "Quayle may be no Jack Kennedy, but he was no stumblebum either," wrote R. W. Apple Jr., in the *New York Times*.[77] Quayle was credited with hitting hard on the question of Bill Clinton's fitness for office, a charge Gore let slide. Gore may have been expecting another deer in the headlights, observed William Safire, but what he got was a "grizzly bear climbing up over the hood. Quayle was an imperfect but effective debater in command of his basic message: Even if you're unhappy with Bush, you can't trust Clinton."[78]

The 1992 Dan Quayle was hardly an exemplary performer. He had not tamed the tendency toward excess energy, and occasionally his voice dropped into a self-consciously melodramatic stage whisper. "He did maintain good eye contact with the camera," wrote Tom Shales, "but he still seemed essentially the same as when Bush chose him for the vice presidency four long years ago: unstable as all get-out."[79] Others found Quayle's 1992 debate turn admirable, among them a fellow victim of the debate gods' disfavor, Richard Nixon. "They should bring him out more," Nixon said of the young vice president. "People will come out to see him in droves. For better or for worse, he's interesting."[80]

BILL CLINTON (1992, 1996)

Bill Clinton's lasting contribution to presidential debates may well be the citizen participation format, a structure he pioneered in 1992 and successfully repeated in 1996. What Clinton dubbed the "people's debate" offered an ideal showcase for the Arkansas governor's vaunted television skills, uniting electoral politics and show biz in a way that perfectly suited this schmoozy Southerner's empathetic style. Working the crowd like a televangelist, Clinton redefined the relationship between debaters and debate watchers, and raised the standard for future nominees.

The effectiveness of Clinton's delivery in the town hall debate stood in counterpoint to the less fluid performances of his older co-stars, George Bush and Ross Perot in 1992, and Bob Dole four years later. Clinton, a child of television, projected total ease in the audience participation setting. That Clinton had studiously rehearsed his apparently effortless on-camera maneuvers seemed not to matter. The proof was in the performance.

After the 1992 election, Clinton told journalists Germond and Witcover that he had given a great deal of thought to the town hall forum. Clinton explained,

> It's a lot easier to be a good talker than a good listener. But in that format, with all that pressure, with one hundred million people watching, it's probably even harder to be a good listener. And one thing I thought about going into that debate was that these are real people.... I saw the American people sort of screaming for me to pay attention to them and listen to them.[81]

Clinton's debut as a presidential debater had been preceded by a rigorous roster of primary debates—three within a single thirty-hour period—and these encounters taught the candidate the value of a well-executed moment. But Clinton entered 1992's compressed round of general election debates with mixed expectations. An early October appearance on the Phil Donahue talk show provoked Clinton's short temper, making him look peevish. His voice had grown raspy and hoarse, and aides publicly fretted about the governor's well-known prolixity. "His defect is that he falls in love with his own rhetoric," political adviser Dick Morris told the *New York Times*.[82]

Clinton soon put these concerns to rest. Strong performances in all three of the 1992 programs showed this candidate to be fully at home in the debate milieu. By 1996 Clinton's reputation as a television prodigy had assumed heroic proportions. The morning after the first Clinton-Dole debate, Lisa Myers on the *Today* show allowed that "the president could talk a dog off a meat wagon."[83]

Fittingly the last debate of his career was another town hall forum, the 1996 San Diego debate with Dole; again, Clinton triumphed. As the *Boston Globe*'s Thomas Oliphant said, "Clinton never strayed from his task during this game of twenty questions—a little of his record, a little diagnosis of remaining problems, and a script for the future."[84] Though Bob Dole valiantly tried to keep pace, the night belonged to the president.

An impromptu scene immediately after this debate went off the air may have better summarized Bill Clinton than any of his studied words and gestures. Viewers watching on C-Span saw Clinton talking with individual members of the studio audience who had remained in the hall. Jeffrey Rosen described the scene in *The New Republic*: "His eyes fixed single-mindedly on his target, he continued to argue animatedly for four minutes. All told, Clinton lingered for forty minutes, debating undecided citizens, one by one. If there's a better way for the president of the United States to conduct his final campaign, I can't imagine it."[85]

AL GORE (1992, 1996)

"Debate is the perfect Gore forum," says political writer Joe Klein, "a structured setting that gives the appearance of spontaneity. It rewards creativity, but only within a context of discipline and preparation."[86] While Al Gore's debating career shows ample evidence of discipline and preparation, creativity has been in shorter supply. Offsetting this deficit is an unusually wide range of experience: over four national campaigns, in both primary and general elections, Gore has toughened into a seasoned and savvy political debater.

After earning his stripes in 1988's crowded primary debates, Gore graduated to the freewheeling, three-way vice presidential match with Dan Quayle and Admiral James Stockdale in 1992. In his opening statement Gore came out swinging, promising Quayle, "If you don't try to compare George Bush to Harry Truman, I won't compare you to Jack Kennedy." Gore then turned to Stockdale and said, "Those of us who served in Vietnam look at you as a national hero," not so subtly reminding viewers that Quayle was the only one on stage lacking Vietnam credentials. Wrote Elizabeth Kolbert in the *New York Times*, "For the innocent tone and brutal implications of his opening statement, Mr. Gore probably deserves the evening's Eve Harrington Award for adroitly undermining a rival."[87]

Other 1992 debate watchers found Gore less effective. Tom Shales in the *Washington Post* likened him to an "audio-animatronic figure at Disneyland, only less life-like," and said, "Even the TV lens glazes over whenever this guy starts to speak." Jeff Greenfield on ABC called Gore "programmed." William Safire of the *Times* preferred "android."[88]

Four years later, against Jack Kemp, Gore drew still worse reviews. In postdebate analysis on ABC, George Will described the Democratic candidate as "relentlessly, robotically, Muzak-ly on message." In the *Boston Globe*, novelist George V. Higgins compared Gore to Fred Rogers, the soporific children's host of PBS's *Mr. Rogers' Neighborhood*. David Broder of the *Post* watched the 1996 debate with a group of undecided voters in Ankeny, Iowa. "Many of them didn't like Gore at all," Broder said, "because they thought he was talking down to them. One woman said, 'He speaks to us like he thinks English is our second language.'" An observer inside the debate hall in St. Petersburg reported that even Tipper Gore, the candidate's wife, could be seen nodding off.[89]

Gore's debate performances in the 2000 primary season, though inconsistent, suggest that the candidate has profited from past mistakes. In a series of two-man meetings with Bill Bradley, Gore assumed a more energetic and aggressive posture, deploying an arsenal of props, gestures, and facial expressions to put across his points. Among the liveliest of the Democratic co-appearances was a December 1999 broadcast of *Meet the Press* in which Gore took his opponent by surprise with a challenge for twice-weekly debates.

If Al Gore has mastered the art of executing tactical moments on TV, questions remain about his ability to connect more viscerally with the viewing audience. Just as George Bush suffered by comparison with Ronald Reagan, debater Gore has had to operate in the shadow of the televisually superior Bill Clinton. According to Brit Hume of Fox News, "Clinton can bring that private magic public—and it's not easy to do for very many people. Gore, who is delightful privately, has a hard time doing it in public."[90]

Can Al Gore learn to channel his private charm into a presidential debate watched by one hundred million people? In 1993 Gore garnered widespread praise for his performance in a live debate with Ross Perot over the North American Free Trade Agreement. The program, which ran on CNN's *Larry King Live*, represents Gore's finest moment on television. In the intimate setting of a broadcast studio, absent a live audience and minus a rigid structure, Gore thrived. Should Al Gore become a presidential debater in 2000, his negotiators would be well advised to press for an informal setup in which their candidate can converse with his opponent, not speechify.

ROSS PEROT (1992)

After the first 1992 debate, Richard Nixon offered a particularly astute assessment of Ross Perot. "The guy is just interesting," Nixon told an aide. "And I've always said that the only thing worse than being wrong in politics is being dull. If Perot weren't there, it would have been dullsville." Nixon then added the inevitable postscript: "It won't affect a damn thing, though."[91]

Ross Perot's eminently watchable trio of performances in 1992 points up a curious dynamic in presidential debates: Unpredictability will almost always outmatch choreography, but unpredictability has its limits, too. Perot's irrepressible sense of humor, along with his laudable refusal to be professionally packaged, breathed new life into the ritualistic debate genre. Before the novelty paled, Perot had shown the political pros that there is value in breaking the mold.

Reentering the race less than two weeks before the first debate in St. Louis, Perot gained instant credibility from his appearance with rivals George Bush and Bill Clinton. "Let's call a spade a spade here—Ross Perot won this debate," pronounced Cokie Roberts during ABC's post-event analysis. "He made the other two sound alike." Wrote Michael Kelly in the *New York Times*, "Mr. Perot, with his hands clasped behind his back and his chest puffed out like a pouter pigeon's, played a role that was a sort of Will Rogers–Mr. Deeds hybrid. At his best lines, and there were many, the audience laughed out loud, and even cheered a bit."[92]

But in the next debate, when Perot repeated the "I'm all ears" wisecrack that had been such a crowd-pleaser in round one, the joke fell flat—an indication of the larger problem that plagued this unorthodox candidate. In the view of NBC's Tom Brokaw, "Perot didn't have a second act." Tom Shales of the *Washington Post*, describing the Texan as a "crabby Munchkin," similarly held that "his act seemed to be growing increasingly stale."[93]

If Perot could never quite replicate his initial success, he did leave an intriguing legacy for other presidential debaters to ponder. Journalist John Mashek, a questioner in the first Clinton-Bush-Perot match and a panelist in 1984 and 1988, called Perot "the most relaxed of all the people I've watched debate." According to Perot campaign adviser Clay Mulford, "He wasn't unnerved by the debates or felt that he was doing anything different than whatever else he'd do on a given day."[94] Perot's straightforward self-possession should serve as a model for other candidates, who too often approach debates like actors at a casting call, willing to twist themselves into pretzels in order to land the part.

Ross Perot proved that in a star-driven vehicle like a presidential debate, an engaging personality goes a long way. Many observers directly attributed the high viewership for the 1992 debates to Perot's presence as an offbeat character in the political drama. "He made everybody watch the debates," said Tom Brokaw, "because they didn't know when he was going to blow a gasket or say something really funny. He was great for the process because it really did bring people to the debates."[95]

JAMES STOCKDALE (1992)

"Who am I? Why am I here?" With these all too prophetic questions, Admiral James Bond Stockdale set sail on the oddest, most improbable odyssey ever undertaken in a presidential debate. *Newsweek* compared Stockdale to "a kindly old owl that had somehow blundered into a video arcade." "Flustered and unprepared," said Tom Shales. "The clear loser of the evening," in the view of Germond and Witcover.[96]

Stockdale's excruciating performance offered viewers a fascinating bounty of the unexpected. The candidate cut short an answer to a health care question by saying, "I'm out of ammunition." Stockdale missed another question because he had turned off his hearing aid. Moderator Hal Bruno had to encourage him to join the discussion. Standing mute as Al Gore and Dan Quayle jousted, Stockdale commented, "I feel like I'm a spectator at a ping-pong game."

With his shock of white hair and black, professorial glasses, this unlikely debater looked nothing like his telegenic competitors. At sixty-eight, Stockdale was a generation older and an atomic lifetime away from their experience in the national spotlight. On one level, Stockdale's babe-in-the-woods status enhanced his standing. As Gore and Quayle attacked each other's economic philosophies, Stockdale said, "I think America is seeing right now the reason this nation is in gridlock." According to Elizabeth Kolbert in the *New York Times*, Stockdale "seemed to be speaking for the frustrated viewer sitting powerlessly in front of the set, unable to intervene in an escalating squabble."[97]

Amazingly Stockdale's debate appearance marked his debut on national television. The candidate had not even known he would be debating until running mate Ross Perot announced the surprise in an interview on the ABC News program *20/20*. Stockdale practiced for the debate not in a TV studio but on a home video camera set up by his son.

Stockdale's son, an elementary school principal in Pennsylvania, wrote an op-ed piece for the *Times* a few days after the ordeal that attempted to salvage the family honor. The younger Stockdale chided Gore and Quayle— and, by extension, the system that produced them:

Two children of privilege have been handed title and authority because they play by rules of insensitivity and blind ambition. Snarling like savage poodles on choke chains one minute, and smiling with smarmy rehearsed sincerity the next, they remind us always to doubt the motives of the man who is too well-groomed. Mr. Quayle and Mr. Gore epitomized modern anger, with its hair combed.

And then there is my father. A man of compassion, truthfulness, and sincerity. He is not interested in power. He is interested in goodness, honesty, and responsibility. His experience in a Vietnam prison brought out his wisdom, a quality our modern world spurns.[98]

After the debate, Admiral Stockdale attributed his poor showing to being less packaged than the other candidates. "What I saw last night was an art form," the admiral told supporters at a rally, "an art form I've never been near before."[99] Hoping to contain the damage, Perot's campaign sent Stockdale around the country to meet with newspaper editorial boards, a setting in which this thoughtful man felt more at home. The debate, however, left an indelible mark; never had the audience seen anything like it.

The great lesson of James Stockdale for future debaters is clear: Experience has no substitute. As *Washington Post* columnist Mary McGrory put it, "Politics may seem incoherent, but it has its rules, too."[100]

JACK KEMP (1996)

Like a new cast member added to a long-running series, Jack Kemp debuted in the 1996 vice presidential debate as the year's only nonveteran. The media widely touted Kemp's appearance with Al Gore as a dress rehearsal for the 2000 presidential race, a sneak preview of coming attractions for political connoisseurs to sit back and savor. As it happened, the Gore-Kemp meeting in St. Petersburg, Florida, received some of the lowest ratings and least enthusiastic reviews of any general election debate.

As an unsuccessful presidential candidate in 1988, Kemp had taken part in his share of primary debates. But in the 1996 telecast, this former football star left an overriding impression of nervousness, hardly a reassuring trait for a would-be national leader. "Kemp was winging it," said David Broder of the *Washington Post*. "I think he had not really sat down and said, okay, what are my strategic goals, what are the three points I want to make no matter what they ask me."[101]

Moderator Jim Lehrer's opening question to Kemp provided an easy opportunity for the Republican to score points on the Clinton character issue: "Some supporters of Senator Dole have expressed disappointment over his unwillingness (in the first debate) to draw personal and ethical differences between him and President Clinton. How do you feel about it?" Kemp responded that attacks on the president were beneath Bob Dole, effectively prohibiting Dole from pursuing a character strategy in the days to come.

Conservatives disdained Kemp's kid-glove handling of Clinton and conciliatory attitude toward Gore. Bill Kristol, editor of the *Weekly Standard*, complained that "if you came down from Mars and saw this debate, you might think that Al Gore was the moderate Republican and Jack Kemp was the Democrat." Even Bob Dole, cracking wise on *Nightline*, said, "It looked like a fraternity picnic there for a while."[102]

Several days after the debate, Sam Donaldson put the charge directly to Kemp on the Sunday morning program *This Week*: "A lot of Republicans are saying they wanted a lean, mean fighting machine to show up, and they're saying that what showed up was a garrulous, unprepared wimp—you." After a few minutes of obligatory face-saving, Kemp gave in, confessing, "I'm just not an attack dog."[103]

Not all observers disapproved of Kemp's restraint. To Martin F. Nolan of the *Boston Globe*, this was "the best vice presidential debate ever, ninety minutes of serious issues rarely discussed." But those expecting sparks to fly reacted with disappointment. "The debate left little material for video editors to regale us with in 2000, should these two men meet again as presidential candidates," wrote Christopher Buckley in the *New York Times*. George Will made the point more bluntly in his postdebate analysis on ABC: "It seems to me that what happened tonight was the campaign 1996 came yet closer to being closed, and the campaign for the Republican nomination in the year 2000 opened wider."[104]

Chapter Five

THE QUESTIONERS

*T*o complement the stars, presidential debates feature cast members who function in key supporting roles: the moderators, panelists, and citizen-questioners who have been an on-camera presence in every general election debate since 1960. In some cases, these scene stealers may have affected outcomes. We can only wonder how 1988's debate series would have differed without anchorman Bernard Shaw's hypothetical question about the rape and murder of Kitty Dukakis. Or how Dan Quayle might have fared absent the sharp questioning of journalist-panelists who pressed him on his credentials. Or how George Bush would have come across had he better connected with the woman in the town hall audience who asked about his personal experience with the national debt.

In the tightly controlled world of presidential debates, the questioners and their questions function as rare, much-needed wild cards. Although the selection of moderators and panelists has always been subject to candidate approval, the interrogators have had free rein to pose whatever questions they choose. This freedom generates much of the tension that attends live debates, interjecting the element of surprise into a heavily stage-managed milieu. Campaign staffs labor mightily to anticipate questions, but in the end, the power of the query rests less with the debaters' preparedness than the interlocutors' spontaneity.

New formats used in the series of 1992 and 1996 have revolutionized the nature of debate questioning. Two basic program structures have come into favor in presidential debates: the solo moderator and the town hall forum. Press panels, which dominated debates for thirty-two years, have at least temporarily been shelved, replaced by individual interviewers and audiences made up of uncommitted voters. To many journalists, this change constitutes a long overdue liberation.

PRESS PANELS AND THE QUESTIONS THEY ASK

"Reporters should ask questions at news conferences and interviews—but not in debates," asserts political columnist David Broder. Like others in the news media, Broder believes that journalists who appear on debate panels violate the separation of church and state by involving themselves as players: "Whether the question impales a candidate or offers him escape from the tight corner of the previous change, we are affecting history, not just writing its first draft."[1] Broder's *Washington Post* was one of the earliest news organizations to ban its employees from serving as presidential debate panelists. Others, like the *Wall Street Journal*, CBS, and NBC, are more recent converts to the cause. "We don't think the campaigns ought to have veto power over our people," explained Tom Brokaw. "Simple as that."[2]

Expressions of ambivalence are not uncommon among reporters selected for the panels. Jon Margolis of the *Chicago Tribune*, a questioner in the Bentsen-Quayle debate, said he had "mixed feelings" about being picked: "I knew you had to be approved by both campaigns, and that meant either they thought I was a harmless wimp or they thought I was fair and objective. I hope it was the latter."[3] Peter Jennings recalled feeling "very honored" to be chosen for the first Bush-Dukakis debate. "It's a dubious compliment," he said, "but it meant we were acceptable to both the Republicans and Democrats, reaffirming our own belief that we were fair people."[4]

Others view the matter in a more positive light. Jim Lehrer makes the point that just as lawyers and doctors are called on to contribute to the public good, so do qualified journalists have a civic duty to serve in debates. "If we see ourselves as professionals," Lehrer says, "then we can't say no to this kind of invitation unless there's something that's improper about it."[5]

Some panelists have jumped at the chance to participate. Norma Quarles, a questioner in the 1984 vice presidential debate, received her summons shortly after being admitted to the hospital for surgery. Instead of proceeding with the operation, Quarles left her hospital bed in New Jersey to make the trip to Philadelphia. "I thought about saying no," she recalled, "but I considered this an opportunity of a lifetime."[6]

Jack White, a *Time* correspondent also selected for the 1984 Bush-Ferraro panel, felt pressure to accept on two fronts: as a magazine reporter and as an African-American. White saw himself representing *Time* but also standing in for black journalists, who had rarely been chosen for debate panels. "There were many things going on beyond 'let me get up here and ask a dynamite question,'" he recalled. "There was also 'how are you coming across representing these other groups that don't get much chance to appear in these contexts?'"[7]

With the panel format out of fashion, the issue of journalistic participation has subsided, at least for the time being. But in the shift toward other structures, has the press ceded too much ground? In 1988, the last year in which media panels appeared in all three debates, political analyst Jeff Greenfield wrote a *New York Times* op-ed column defending journalists as questioners. "The much-maligned format," Greenfield said, "produced the most significant glimpses we have had into the thinking and character of the candidates since the general election campaign began on Labor Day."[8]

As one example, Greenfield cited a question from Annie Groer in the first Bush-Dukakis debate that forced Bush to address his murky stance on a woman's right to an abortion. Groer pointed out that Bush had taken several positions on the issue over the years, including support for a constitutional amendment that would outlaw most abortions. "But if abortions were to become illegal again," Groer asked, "do you think that the women who defy the law and have them anyway, as they did before it was okayed by the Supreme Court, and the doctors who perform them, should go to jail?"

Bush's muddled response suggested that criminal sanctions indeed might be appropriate, sparking a quick postdebate clarification to the contrary by campaign manager James Baker. As Greenfield commented, "The exchange told us that in fact Mr. Bush hadn't pursued the subtleties of the abortion issue. It was exactly the kind of tough but fair prodding that debates are supposed to produce."[9]

Complaints against debate panelists' questions fall along several lines: the reporters are trying to play "gotcha"; the questions are convoluted and tendentious; the topics focus too narrowly on the day's headlines. The loudest objections have come from fellow members of the press, as in a scathing 1992 column by veteran *Washington Post* columnist Mary McGrory:

> The professional training that encourages reporters to sharpen their questions and tighten their prose deserts them on the set. Somehow the encounter is not so much to elicit information from the questioned but to display the erudition of the questioner. It is to reveal one's sophistication, one's truly impressive range of knowledge, one's exquisitely calibrated appreciation of the nuances of a question that clods might ask in two seconds.[10]

Over the years, panel members have exposed themselves to carping on several fronts. Charles Warren, panelist in the 1960 debate, received telephone calls from irate viewers after asking JFK why farms could not be operated like other businesses. One caller said, "I'm a farmer and you're a sonofabitch for asking Senator Kennedy a loaded question like that," and another warned, "You'd better watch out."[11]

Panelists draw even more notice *before* the debates, when they are inundated with suggestions for questions. A telegram delivered to the theater just before the first 1976 debate urged a questioner to ask, "How soon do you think it will take for a complete Soviet takeover of the United States?" Annie Groer was offered a hundred dollars to pose a "nasty question about the personal life of one of the candidates." Andrea Mitchell's stint as a debate panelist in 1988 coincided with the dawn of fax machines, making for a sleepless predebate night at her hotel in Los Angeles. "Special interest groups were faxing suggested questions and ideas and background papers all night," Mitchell recalled, "and the hotel kept stuffing this rolled-up fax paper under the door and waking me up. It was like having hamsters in your room."[12]

Moderators and panelists routinely discard most over-the-transom suggestions. Occasionally, however, one finds its way into the broadcast. John Mashek, a panelist in the first 1992 debate in St. Louis, used a question he had read in a *St. Louis Post-Dispatch* article in which citizens revealed what they would ask if they were on the panel.[13]

In deference to the gravity of the occasion, most journalistic participants have worked hard to polish their debate questions. Elizabeth Drew of *The New Yorker*, the first woman to serve on a debate panel, prepared for the first 1976 Ford-Carter appearance much as the candidates themselves did. With the help of a research assistant, Drew put together a notebook of information about various subjects that might come up. "And then I worked on and refined and refined the questions," she said.[14] Many other panelists report a similar process: organizing background materials by topic area, then honing specific questions.

"We all overprepared," recalled Peter Jennings. "We prepared to death. I remember an inordinate amount of constructing and deconstructing sentences, which I knew before and know subsequently is never the way to interview anybody." According to Andrea Mitchell: "The preparations are tough because what you're trying to do is come up with something that will elicit a revealing answer that hasn't been asked before and that they're not prepared for. And there's so much at stake."[15]

Sometimes a question is asked simply because it cannot be avoided. In the second debate of 1984, after Ronald Reagan had come under intense scrutiny in the wake of his faltering debate performance in Louisville, it fell to Henry Trewhitt of the *Baltimore Sun* to raise the issue of presidential competence. Because the stated theme of the debate was foreign policy, Trewhitt deliberately couched his query within that framework:

> You are already the oldest president in history, and some of your staff say you were tired after your most recent encounter with Mr. Mondale. I recall, yet, that President Kennedy . . . had to go for days on end with very little sleep during the Cuban missile crisis. Is there any doubt in your mind that you would be able to function in such circumstances?

Reagan, as we have seen, rejoined with what is regarded as a classic debate sound bite, leaving Trewhitt to deliver a less celebrated but no less amusing riposte: "Mr. President, I'd like to head for the fence and try to catch that one, but I'll go on to another question." In retrospect, Trewhitt wondered if he ought not to have pursued his original line of inquiry. "I did not respond as I should have," Trewhitt later noted. "I just let him go when I really should have said, 'Okay, fine, that's a wonderful line, Mr. President, but I really think you should try to address the question.' I didn't do that because I thought it was such a good line."[16]

Beginning with the first question ever posed in a presidential debate, the tone of journalists' queries has often been aggressive. Bob Fleming of ABC News opened the 1960 Chicago debate by asking JFK for a response to Nixon's characterization of him as "naive and at times immature." Minutes later, Sander Vanocur questioned Nixon about a remark President Eisenhower had made at a news conference a month earlier; when pressed to name an idea Nixon had contributed to his administration, Eisenhower told reporters, "If you give me a week I might think of one."

In *Six Crises*, Nixon was still smarting from the Vanocur question, which he dismissed as being "of no substantive importance" and something that would "plague me the rest of the campaign." Nixon wrote that Eisenhower had phoned him to apologize the day the remark was made.

He pointed out that he was simply being facetious and yet they played it straight and wrote it seriously. I could only reply to Vanocur's question in the same vein, but I am sure that to millions of unsophisticated televiewers, this question had been most effective in raising a doubt in their minds with regard to one of my strongest campaign themes and assets—my experience as vice president.[17]

Questions relating to a candidate's personal qualities have propelled some of the sharpest exchanges in presidential debates. In 1984 Fred Barnes asked President Reagan (and Walter Mondale as well) for a description of his religious beliefs. After Reagan delivered a homily that invoked Mother, God, and Abraham Lincoln, Barnes moved in for the kill: "Given those beliefs, Mr. President, why don't you attend services regularly, either by going to church or by inviting a minister to the White House, as President Nixon used to do, or someone to Camp David, as President Carter used to do?" Reagan never did answer the question.

The 1988 vice presidential debate, in addition to its exploration of Dan Quayle's fitness for office, offered other examples of pointed, personal interrogatories. Brit Hume asked the candidates to identify a work of literature, art, or film that had had a strong effect on them. Both debaters gave what seemed like well-coached responses that quickly segued into attacks on the opposition. But as CNN media analyst Frederic Allen pointed out: "When a debate panelist says to a candidate, 'Read any good books lately?' it's not a friendly question. It's asked with a certain degree of malice. It's asked in the secret hope that the answer will be 'I can't remember ever opening a book.'"

Hume defends the query as one he had hoped would be "revealing of character." "I spent a lot of time trying to think of questions that might take them off the script, to illuminate something beyond the rap they have predigested and prememorized," he said.[18]

Tom Brokaw's first question to Quayle dealt with the plight of American families living in poverty: "I'd like for you to describe to the audience the last time that you may have visited with one of those families personally and how you explain to that family your votes against the school breakfast program, the school lunch program, and the expansion of the child immunization program." Unconvincingly, Quayle cited a stop at a food bank in Fort Wayne, Indiana, during which no one had asked him about those votes. Brokaw later explained, "I came to that question because one of the things I'm struck by is that so many politicians are isolated from real-life experience. I thought, looking at Quayle's experience and how he lived his life, it's worth finding out. I did think it was a legitimate question."[19]

In the first 1988 Bush-Dukakis debate, Peter Jennings took a similarly prosecutorial approach to Bush, reminding the vice president that he had said he was "haunted" by the lives of inner-city children. "If it haunts you so," Jennings asked, "why over the eight years of the Reagan-Bush administration have so many programs designed to help the inner cities been eliminated or cut?" Bush's fuzzy reply fell far short of the question. Soon after the debate, Jennings said, "George Bush took a disliking to me."[20]

Not all panelists have defined their role adversarially. Max Frankel, the *New York Times* reporter whose question to Gerald Ford led to the Eastern Europe gaffe, saw his task in a different light. "I wasn't so much trained to fish for news on television, or to play any kind of game of 'gotcha,'" he said. "My thought always was that the purpose of these things is to elucidate views."[21] In the San Francisco debate, after Ford prematurely liberated Eastern Europe, Frankel gave the president an opportunity to dig himself out, an opportunity Ford did not take.

Another reporter from the old school was Harris Ellis of the *Christian Science Monitor*, a panelist in the lone Carter-Reagan debate of 1980. Ellis said he purposely shaped his debate questions to emphasize his own neutrality. "In those days, when TV on that scale was still relatively new, that is the way more journalists would have acted," he said. "Today I have the real feeling that many journalists distort their role before the television camera in challenging a president or candidate."[22]

PANELIST STRATEGIES

In their predebate meetings, panelists have tended to preview one another's questions in order to avoid duplication. But not always. Sander Vanocur, a questioner in the initial Kennedy-Nixon debate, recalls fearing someone else would preempt his question about President Eisenhower's putdown of Vice President Nixon.[23] The four newsmen in that debate had no idea what topics the others would raise, which has also been true in several subsequent programs. Essentially the matter of sharing questions is something each panel decides on its own.

Panelists in the 1976 vice presidential debate not only read their questions to one another ahead of time, they helped edit one another's copy. "We are to my knowledge the only panel that conspired to write the questions and to establish an order we wanted to ask them in," said Hal Bruno, a participant in that debate.[24] Bruno and his colleagues agreed to limit their questions to thirty seconds and pledged to avoid unnecessary follow-ups that might bog down the discussion.

Just before the telecast, the panel's prearranged sequence of questions bumped up against a last-minute obstacle. According to panelist Walter Mears of the Associated Press, two of the questioners decided to trade seats in order to maintain the order of topics they had agreed on beforehand. "But when Dole's people heard about the switch, they objected, saying they had been preparing on the basis of the original order of questioning. I never did figure out how Dole could prepare for questions I might put as opposed to those Marilyn [Berger, another panelist] might ask."[25]

The three panelists in 1976's final debate carried the concept of collaboration one step further. In a meeting before the debate, they agreed that when the broadcast reached the sixty-minute mark, whoever had the floor would yield and ask the candidates to break format and directly question each other. Five minutes before air time, Jack Nelson of the *Los Angeles Times* informed moderator Barbara Walters of the plan. "We had not told her in advance because we didn't want her to maybe scotch the idea or tell any of the producers of the program," Nelson said. "Of course, she didn't try to scotch it, but what happened was we didn't get the time cue." Thus was avoided what might have been one of the most spontaneous episodes in presidential debates. According to Nelson, "We intended to do that because we thought it would be better to have an actual exchange between the two candidates rather than what amounted to three separate press conferences."[26]

Perhaps the most unified group of questioners in debate history were the panelists in the 1988 Bentsen-Quayle match. The journalistic quartet of Judy Woodruff (PBS), Tom Brokaw (NBC), Brit Hume (ABC) and Jon Margolis (*Chicago Tribune*) functioned in a way debate panels almost never do, as a synchronized interrogation machine that hammered away at Dan Quayle's qualifications for the vice presidency. In their predebate gathering, the panelists discussed the value of follow-up questions and decided to join forces to hold the candidates' feet to the fire. According to Brokaw, at one point in the planning sessions, Woodruff proposed a question about Quayle's collegiate academic record. "Margolis and Brit and I all said, 'No way, somebody's liable to look into ours,'" Brokaw recollected. "We discovered that we had as checkered a past as undergraduates as he did."[27]

Hume said that by following up one another's questions, the panel hoped to circumvent the deliberately restrictive structure the campaigns had imposed. "I was last in the rotation, and it was agreed that I would keep my eye on questions that had been asked by my colleagues that might have gone unanswered," he explained.[28] In this capacity, Hume returned to Woodruff's opening question to Quayle about his qualifications for the job. Later Hume followed up his own follow-up; each time, Quayle offered a response that did not satisfy the panel.

Finally the rotation came back to Brokaw. "I had real mental anguish," Brokaw recalled. "I don't think Quayle's people will ever appreciate that, but I remember as it came around to me, I thought, 'Oh, God, do I want to ask this again?' But he was so inadequate in the first two answers, I thought in a way he deserved the third crack at it. Also I thought the country deserved to hear one more time what he would do as president. That's why we were there."[29] Brokaw's rephrasing led Quayle to liken himself to John F. Kennedy, which led to Bentsen's "You're no JFK" line.

At the end of the day, how much difference have panelists' questions made in presidential debates? As Walter Mears points out, "For all the self-importance a lot of us like to put in our questions, debates have been more driven by things that were beside the point."[30] Mears cites Ford's Eastern Europe gaffe and Dole's "Democrat wars" statement as examples of debate moments that sprang only indirectly from a panelist's question.

Furthermore, no matter what the question, clever candidates will always shape answers that match their political objectives. Robert Boyd of Knight-

Ridder Newspapers, a questioner in the Bush-Ferraro vice presidential debate, called the candidates' responses in that event a "classic dodge and feint." "They're pros at this," Boyd said. "There was no question they hadn't answered probably scores of times already before and there was no real way, and no desire, to trip them up."[31]

In a *Newsweek* column about her experience, Jane Bryant Quinn, a panelist in the Reagan-Anderson debate of 1980, lamented the candidates' lack of responsiveness. "When reporters put a question to a politician they don't really expect a full and frank reply," Quinn wrote. "There are, however, some general rules of the game—one of them being that even an irrelevant response should contain, somewhere, some faint indication that the original question has at least been heard."[32]

MODERATORS OF PRESS PANEL DEBATES

Under the old press panel format, some of television journalism's most venerated names stepped up to the microphone to moderate presidential and vice presidential debates. Barbara Walters, Bill Moyers, Judy Woodruff, Bernard Shaw, Howard K. Smith, Sander Vanocur, and Pauline Frederick are a few of the individuals who presided over press conference–style debates. Given the strictures of the format, their talents went largely underutilized.

With a few notable exceptions, moderators of press panel debates have made only a limited contribution to the content of the discussion, serving less as interrogators than traffic cops and timekeepers.

In 1988, for the first time, debate moderators were given the opportunity to begin the telecast with a question to each candidate. This change in rules made possible what is undoubtedly the best-known exchange between a debate moderator and a presidential candidate, Bernard Shaw's opening query to Michael Dukakis in the Los Angeles debate: "Governor, if Kitty Dukakis were raped and murdered, would you favor an irrevocable death penalty for the killer?" Equally shocking to the audience as Shaw's question was Dukakis's dispassionate reply.

In the predebate meeting with fellow panelists Andrea Mitchell of NBC, Ann Compton of ABC, and Margaret Warner of *Newsweek*, Shaw had been reluctant to share his question, "petrified" that it would become known to Dukakis in advance. When the panelists pressed him, Shaw relented and read it to them precisely as he would read it on the air. Taken aback, Mitchell asked him to consider substituting the words "your wife" instead of citing Kitty Dukakis by name. The other panelists supported Mitchell—"delicately," according to one—but Shaw held fast. "We thought it was a little unseemly, a little undignified," Mitchell said. "And you have to think back to the context. This was before shock radio, tabloid television, the blurring of lines within the multiplicity of media, so we were a little uptight and stuffy."[33]

Shaw hoped that his question would be a "stethoscope" to probe Dukakis's attitude toward capital punishment. "Bush had been beating Dukakis severely about the head and shoulders, charging he was soft on crime. Many voters perceive seeing and hearing Dukakis but not feeling him. I asked that question to see if there was feeling." The idea had come to Shaw at 2:00 A.M. on the day of the debate. His initial worry was that Dukakis would "hit it out of the park," making Shaw seem too easy on the candidate. "I didn't know how he was going to answer. What surprised me was that he didn't stop to reflect at all before answering. It was as if he didn't hear the question."

At the end of the debate, Shaw recalled, "an eerie thing" happened: As he made his way from the stage to the CNN anchor booth, the audience silently parted to let him walk past. "Nobody said 'thanks' or 'good debate' or anything like that," Shaw said. "And then I realized I had walked through the Dukakis side of the hall, through his supporters. And that's when it struck me what impact my question must have had."[34]

Reaction to the question ran heavily against Shaw. Kitty Dukakis herself called it "inappropriate" and "outrageous." In *Time* magazine, Walter Shapiro wrote, "The question was in ghoulish taste, but it proved revealing." ABC's Hal Bruno, who had been at the debate, found himself seated next to Shaw the next day on the plane back to Washington. "He's a good friend, we were police reporters together in Chicago," Bruno said. "Bernie started talking about why he asked the question. And after my second scotch I said, 'Bernie—it was a shitty question.'"[35]

Though it is the Kitty Dukakis question that most viewers remember, Shaw had a similarly gruesome opener for George Bush. Quoting the Twentieth Amendment to the Constitution on the issue of presidential succession, Shaw asked Bush to comment on the possibility of Dan Quayle becoming president in the event of Bush's death. Midway through the question, after the words "if you are elected and die before inauguration day," Bush interrupted and exclaimed in mock horror, "Bernie!" The difference between this and the mechanical Dukakis response underscored Bush's relative humanity.

Less notorious than Shaw's question to Dukakis was moderator Judy Woodruff's opening volley to Dan Quayle in the 1988 vice presidential debate in Omaha. Woodruff got the program off to a memorable start:

> Senator, you have been criticized, as we all know, for your decision to stay out of the Vietnam War, for your poor academic record. But more troubling to some are some of the comments that have been made by people in your own party. Just last week former secretary of state Haig said that your pick was the dumbest call George Bush could have made. Your leader in the Senate, Bob Dole, said that a better-qualified person could have been chosen. Other Republicans have been far more critical in private. Why do you think that you have not made a more substantial impression on some of these people who have been able to observe you up close?

Quayle's programmatic, unsatisfying response started him down what would soon become a disastrous path. According to Woodruff, the decision to query Quayle about his qualifications was obvious. "I came to Omaha pretty much persuaded that I wanted to go to that first," she later recalled. "It was particularly relevant in Quayle's case because there were outstanding questions about his background and his selection."[36] Woodruff's sharply worded opener paved the way for her fellow panelists in the Omaha debate to pursue the issue.

It is interesting to note that all presidential debate moderators but one have come from the world of television. The exception is James Hoge, who, as editor of the *Chicago Sun-Times*, pulled duty at the 1976 vice presidential debate between Walter Mondale and Bob Dole. Hoge is also unique in representing a news organization based neither in Washington nor New York.

As moderator, Hoge found himself making a decision that would affect the substance of the event. According to Hoge, the debate sponsors had encouraged him to mediate if one of the candidates attempted to "demagogue" a response. "And when Dole gave his answer, the gist of which was that Democrats were responsible for all wars, his face screwed up and nasty, I was seconds away from saying, 'Excuse me, Senator Dole, but you really didn't answer the question. Would you take another stab at it?' " In his peripheral vision, Hoge could see Mondale signaling with a vigorous shake of the head that he did not want Dole interrupted. "I made a split-second decision," said Hoge. "It's their debate, they're the ones who are going to get elected, so I didn't intervene that way."[37]

Barbara Walters, moderating the first 1984 debate between Ronald Reagan and Walter Mondale, began her opening remarks with a crisp rebuke of both camps' imperious tactics in selecting press representatives for the panel. Tersely explaining to the viewing audience the difficulties encountered in the process, Walters said: "As moderator and on behalf of my fellow journalists I very much regret, as does the League of Women Voters, that this situation has occurred."

"On reflection, I might have asked her not to do that," says Dorothy Ridings, then president of the League. Herself a newspaperwoman, Ridings sympathized with Walters's desire to stand up for journalists. "But for the historical record it probably would have been better if she didn't."[38] Ridings changed her opinion after screening the debate some ten years later with people who did not understand the context, and who found Walters's reference confusing. For their part, the campaigns scorned the moderator's impromptu editorial. "That was pretty badly received," recalled James Baker. "Everybody was a little pissed off," agreed a Mondale aide.[39]

The tartness of Walters's opening statement was consistent with her overall moderating style, an attitude that brooked no nonsense. When Mondale raised the issue of Lebanon, Walters sternly reminded him, "Foreign policy will be the subject of the next debate. Stop dragging it by its ear into this one." At another point, Walters congratulated the candidates for heeding her admonitions, saying, "You're both very obedient. I have to give you credit for that." In the view of *Washington Post* TV critic Tom Shales, Walters outdistanced both Reagan and Mondale in demonstrating leadership qualities. "She's a toughie," wrote Shales. "She laid it on the line."[40]

In some instances the influence of the moderator is not evident to debate viewers because it manifests itself behind the scenes. According to panelists in the first 1988 match between Bush and Dukakis, that program might have taken a dramatically different turn without the predebate intervention of moderator Jim Lehrer. Stories had appeared in the press speculating that the panelists might violate the format as a protest against the campaigns' high-handed tactics in choosing panelists. The *Washington Post* went so far as to suggest that the journalists "stand up at the outset, take off their microphones and tell Lehrer to launch a one-on-one exchange between the candidates—the one thing both campaigns have been trying to avoid."[41]

Joining Lehrer as panelists for that debate were Peter Jennings of ABC, John Mashek of the *Atlanta Constitution*, and Annie Groer of the *Orlando Sentinel*. In the group's preproduction meeting, Jennings pushed the idea of dispensing with the rules in order to force the candidates into direct engagement. According to those present, Lehrer steered the conversation back to an acceptance of the terms agreed to in advance. In the end, Jennings resigned himself to the inevitable. "You got hired by the rules and you played by the rules," Jennings said.[42]

As in previous years, the panelists' frustration stemmed from the restrictive format conditions imposed by the two campaigns. "We had some difficult moments because of the agreement," Lehrer said. "There was some discussion there about 'to hell with the rules, we can do any damn thing we want to,' and I kept saying we had made an agreement to come and do something. I felt it just as a matter of function, a matter of giving your word."[43]

The event came off as planned, and the panel stuck to its preassigned role. The discussions that took place among the journalists behind the scenes, however, would inspire Lehrer to write a 1995 novel called *The Last Debate*, in which a quartet of reporter-questioners deliberately undertakes to sabotage a presidential candidate during a live TV debate. The idea for the book came to Lehrer as he left the hotel en route to the debate site at Wake Forest University. He was carrying a folder that contained his opening questions; as he walked past campaign officials from both sides, Lehrer commented to his wife, " 'Boy, they would give anything to know what I've got in this folder.' That's when I started thinking . . . what if you were the candidate and you knew what the questions were going to be?"[44]

DEBATE MODERATORS IN THE 1990S

"A moderator is like a body at an Irish wake," observed Bill Moyers, who performed the function in the 1980 debate between Ronald Reagan and John Anderson. "You need it to have the party, but it doesn't say much."[45]

With the demise of the panel format, Moyers's description no longer applies; the corpse has returned from the dead. Though single moderators now operate with a reasonable degree of discretion, their task remains tricky: they must run a program devised by the participants for the participants, while simultaneously, and overarchingly, addressing the needs of the public. A moderator must be acceptable to each of the candidates and the debate sponsor, but also to constituent groups who lack direct veto power, namely, the voters and the press. Moderators must be judicious and informed, telegenic and leaderly.

Since 1992, only three individuals have held the job: Jim Lehrer of PBS, the most experienced presidential debate moderator in history; Carole Simpson of ABC, moderator of the Richmond town hall debate of 1992; and Hal Bruno, retired political director of ABC, who was at the helm of the boisterous 1992 vice presidential debate.

Lehrer has moderated six presidential debates, one in 1988, two in 1992, and all three of the 1996 matches. For his deft handling of the job, the PBS newsman has drawn overwhelmingly positive reviews. After the 1996 debates, *New York Times* television critic Walter Goodman reserved special praise for the subtlety of Lehrer's approach. "This man of modest mien keeps the spotlight on the person being questioned," Goodman wrote. "His somewhat halting conversational manner invites rather than commands. And his professional principles dispel any fears that he is out to get not just his guests' point of view but also the guests themselves."[46]

Lehrer draws a distinction between moderating a debate and conducting a journalistic interview. "I am not there to do things which I normally do," he explains. "Moderating, in my opinion, is a separate skill. I learned how to do it functioning as a journalist on the *News Hour*, but as a moderator of a presidential debate I'm not sitting there as a journalist, I'm sitting there as a journalist functioning as a moderator." Lehrer's background as a Washington insider appears to work to his advantage. "I'm not dealing with a bunch of strangers," he said, "and they're not dealing with a stranger, which gives me a tremendous leg up. They've agreed to let me do this, so they have some level of trust in me that gives me a lot more latitude and a lot more confidence to do what I want to do."[47]

Lehrer's first debate as moderator, the opening 1988 encounter between Bush and Dukakis in Winston-Salem, followed the traditional press panel format; four years later, at the initial Bush-Clinton-Perot meeting in St. Louis, he would repeat this format. Lehrer's maiden voyage as a solo moderator came in the final 1992 debate in East Lansing, Michigan. A clumsy compromise between the Bush and Clinton campaigns gave Lehrer a solo shot at the candidates for the first half of the debate; halfway through the program, the format switched, and a panel of journalists joined him onstage for the remaining forty-five minutes. It was the single-moderator half of this debate that would supply a rough model for the 1996 series, in which Lehrer returned for three rounds as the lone questioner.

Lehrer found that the relaxed rules governing the first half of the 1992 East Lansing debate broke the tyranny of the clock that usually constrains presidential debates. "I was depending on my instincts and my experience to make sure it was fair, rather than time cues," Lehrer recalled. What Lehrer calls "the hardest moment I've ever had in a debate" occurred during this telecast, when Ross Perot interrupted the dialogue to complain about the distribution of time. "Is there an equal-time rule tonight?" a testy Perot asked. "Or do you just keep lunging in at will? I thought we were going to have equal time, but maybe I just have to interrupt the other two. Is that the way it works?" As Lehrer remembered the moment, "I looked at him and I said with my eyes, 'Don't you dare accuse me of being unfair,' and he backed off."

With three participants in the 1992 debates, another of Lehrer's challenges was devising questions of equal weight for each of the candidates. Lehrer explained, "I had to ask an apple, an apple, and an apple, always. If there was an edge to one, there had to be an edge to all of them. If there were lobs, they had to be lobs for all three." Lehrer was, he said, "free to choose every subject. There was no restriction on how much time was devoted to anything." This freedom both simplified and complicated his job.

Lehrer suffered a few anxious moments shortly before the East Lansing debate, when he read his opening questions over the telephone to his wife and sounding board, novelist Kate Lehrer. Because she was in the middle of a book tour, Mrs. Lehrer had remained at the couple's home in Washington. "I told her the three questions and there was silence," Lehrer recalled. "I said, 'What's the problem?' and she said, 'You've got two apples and an orange.' She was very reluctant to say anything because she knew this was the worst time in the world." Realizing she was right, but fearing he would not have time to rewrite his questions, Lehrer set forth for the debate hall. Although the Secret Service had worked out the route in advance, they did not account for Lehrer's limo being delayed at a railroad crossing, which unexpectedly gave the moderator the time he needed to fashion a last-minute substitution.

In 1996, with only two debaters per program, and the precedent of the single-moderator format under his belt, Lehrer faced new challenges at the first Clinton-Dole debate in Hartford. To begin with, the candidates had tightened the rules, giving the moderator less elbow room than he had had in 1992. Furthermore, Bob Dole's twenty-point lag in the polls had led to press speculation about a debate "surprise," a dramatic gesture Dole might make in order to turn the race around.

With this possibility in mind, Lehrer devised a contingency plan. "If either candidate violated the rules—their rules, not my rules—I was not going to step on the event," he said. "Once they broke their own rules, I was going to let it play to its natural conclusion, then say, 'Gentlemen, you have violated the rules. We can negotiate some new ones right here in front of everybody or we can continue this wide open thing—your decision.' I was all prepared to do that. And of course, nothing like that happened."

Halfway through the Hartford debate, when Dole still had not touched on the widely discussed issue of Clinton's character, Lehrer made an "editorial decision" to introduce the subject himself. "I'd throw him a lob," Lehrer said, "but he was going to have to hit it. I wasn't going to hit it for him." Lehrer's query ("every word of this question I had down cold down") was an exercise in restraint: "Senator Dole, we've talked mostly now about differences between the two of you that relate to policy, issues, and that sort of thing. Are there also significant differences in the more personal area that are relevant to this election?"

Dole refused the bait, devoting most of his response to talking about tax cuts and then citing as a personal difference the fact that Clinton was "a bit taller than I am." According to Lehrer, "If he had said, 'Yes, I think there are matters of character involving this man,' then the whole rest of the debate would have been about character."

More puzzling to Lehrer than Dole's reticence was running mate Jack Kemp's avoidance of the character issue at the vice presidential debate several days later. Although Lehrer directly solicited Kemp's view of the "personal and ethical" differences between Clinton and Dole, Kemp offered only a tangential response. "He wasn't ready for that," Lehrer said, "which I just find weird. It's the only thing that had been talked about. He gave this stock answer, which was irrelevant to my question. I was astounded that he wasn't prepared for that."

Lehrer's raising of the character issue in the 1996 debates is consistent with his belief that a moderator should limit the discussion to subjects already in play instead of introducing new topics in a debate. "I also believe that this is not an opportunity for a moderator to show how tough he is," said Lehrer. "I feel very strongly about that, because it would be so easy to change the nature of the campaign. I could have, in Hartford, changed the whole nature of the campaign by the questions I asked—for good, bad, or indifferent. I'm not sure I could have changed the outcome of the election, I don't mean that, but changed what they would have talked about."

Lehrer makes a crucial point about the solo moderator: Anyone who serves in this role holds vast power. Given the volatile combination of live television, high stakes, and enormous audiences, such power could easily be abused.

The first single moderator of a general election debate was not Jim Lehrer but Hal Bruno of ABC News, who moderated the 1992 vice presidential match between Al Gore, Dan Quayle, and Admiral James Stockdale. Though deemed a "slugfest" and a "free-for-all" in the press, this debate also broke ground as the first to dispense with a panel of questioners. Minus any journalistic sidekicks, Bruno had his hands full with this freewheeling conversation, which is best remembered for two things: the aggressive posture of Quayle and Gore toward each other, and, more famously, the excruciating disconnectedness of Stockdale.

"About three or four minutes into it, I realized, oh my God, this is trouble," Bruno recalled. Stockdale's rhetorical opening questions, "Who am I? What am I doing here?" had caught the moderator, as well as the audience, off guard. "That's when I realized how much out of his element he was," Bruno said. "Somehow I established kind of a mystic eye contact, and I could tell when he wanted in or out. About halfway through, I really did feel that this poor guy had no business being there."[48]

As for Gore and Quayle, "They really were absolutely wild with each other," Bruno said. "Gore was going after Quayle, Quayle was going after Clinton." When Stockdale announced that he had missed a question because his hearing aid was off, Bruno stopped himself from blurting out, "You may be the luckiest man in America."

Bruno's performance as moderator drew mixed reviews. Some observers thought he ought to have been more forceful; others believed he was correct to let Gore and Quayle go at it. "It's hard to judge when you're sitting there," Bruno said. "I took the attitude that as moderator I was to be like a potted palm, just simply steer the discussion, see that they got their time."

Like other moderators before him, Bruno considered himself hamstrung by the "rigid structure" drawn up in advance by campaign negotiators. Both the major party candidates, he said, "were programmed to say certain things no matter what, so you let them do that and try to snap them back to the question. But in that format there wasn't time to get them back." Bruno also felt constrained by the set, which placed the three debaters at individual podiums, physically segregated from the moderator and from one another. Bruno would have preferred gathering everyone around a table, an arrangement whose logic was too radical for the negotiators who drafted the memorandum of understanding.

These challenges notwithstanding, Bruno found the experience exciting. "I'm not blasé about it at all," he said. As a young reporter, Bruno had been present in the studio at WBBM in Chicago for the first Kennedy-Nixon debate. Thirty-two years later, he made debate history on his own.

Carole Simpson, Bruno's colleague at the ABC News Washington Bureau, also entered the history books when she moderated the first town hall debate in Richmond with George Bush, Bill Clinton, and Ross Perot. Simpson got the job, she said, because of a "flukey thing" that happened in 1992. The three broadcast networks had proposed a series of three debates that year, each to be hosted by a major network anchorman. When the Commission on Presidential Debates rejected this proposal, NBC and CBS barred its employees from participating as moderators or panelists, leaving ABC the only over-the-air network still in the mix. As a result, ABC News was represented in each of the four 1992 debates. "Things happen for a funny reason," Simpson said. "I'm sure had they come to ABC and said, 'Give us one of your anchors to moderate this debate,' I would not have been at the top of the list."[49]

Simpson's experience was in some ways more taxing than that of either Lehrer or Bruno, since she was inaugurating a riskier, untested format. Recalled Simpson, "I had been watching presidential debates all my career, and of course they had always been panels of journalists questioning the candidates, so this was totally different. There wasn't anything to go back and look at to see how to do this." Simpson said she was surprised to see how much leeway the written debate agreement gave her. "The only things it said I had to do were to make sure they each had a closing statement of two minutes, that no one would dominate, that we would cover both domestic and foreign issues, and that I could follow up and press a question," she said. "I had all kinds of latitude to do things that I thought were necessary to get the people to question the candidates."

Though praised by many, Simpson did not emerge from the experience unscathed by criticism. In the days that followed, some Republican cam-

paign officials openly charged that Simpson had skewed the debate by the
tone she set in her predebate audience warm-up and by her choice of on-air
questioners. Simpson spent about half an hour with the town hall audience
before the telecast began. "I said, 'I want an idea of the kinds of questions
you want to ask,' and they wanted to stand up and read me their questions,"
Simpson recalled. "And I'm going, 'No, no, no, I don't want to know your
questions, I just want to get a sense of the issues you're concerned about
because my job is to see that you get answers from these candidates to the
questions that concern you the most.' " The issues the audience raised,
Simpson said, were considerably more substantive than those reporters and
the campaigns had been focusing on.

Early in the debate, when President Bush attempted to bring up Bill
Clinton's draft status, Simpson invited the audience to share with the candidates what they had told her in the warm-up. "I thought, given the guidelines, that I had a perfect right to bring up my discussion with the audience
in which they indicated that they did not want to hear about things like that.
And I said, 'Would some of you like to express to the candidates what you
told me?' and that's when the man with the ponytail got up and said, 'We
want an end to the mudslinging, we're tired of the negative campaigns.' "

Simpson's critics charged that she had preselected the audience members
whose questions ultimately made it on the air. In fact, the moderator did not
choose the questioners; that task fell to producer Ed Fouhy, who communicated his instructions to Simpson through her earpiece. As Simpson
described it, "He was just trying to balance the audience, so that we got men,
we got women, we got minorities . . . We'd go from one side to another side.
I had no control over that. I was being told who to go to, and purely based
on where they were located, not because we knew what their questions were
or anything like that." Fouhy confirmed this. "I was in her ear throughout,
and I was telling her who to go to next," he said. "To suggest that somehow
those questions were screened . . . it's simply not true."[50]

Simpson said that the accusations of question-planting hounded her
after the debate. "It was widely talked about on the Rush Limbaugh show,"
she said, "and I even got death threats. The Republicans had put out this line
that I was pro-Clinton and that I had tried to make George Bush look bad."
Bush himself sent Simpson a thank-you note, commenting that she had
done a fair, professional job. "I have it framed," she said, "because people
were so accusatory that I had made George Bush blow it. I didn't make
George Bush blow it."

In a campaign postmortem at Harvard's Kennedy School of Government, Bush aide Fred Steeper criticized the "iron hand" Simpson exercised as moderator. His reasoning offers an insight into campaign thinking on whom debates should rightfully serve. "Her interest seemed to be more to get as many questions as possible out of the audience, rather than having the candidates speak," Steeper said. "Somehow the audience's interest was more important than the interests of the three campaigns. You could tell that she didn't want give and take among the candidates. She wanted to maximize questions from the audience."[51] According to this view, even the "people's debate" belonged to the candidates.

Since the format changes of the 1990s, other, flashier television personalities have either been proposed, or proposed themselves, as debate moderators. In 1992 CNN talk show host Larry King actively pursued a slot in one of that year's debates. King's unsuccessful lobbying efforts became a running theme in a video documentary called *Spin*, in which experimental filmmaker Brian Springer spliced together footage downlinked from the CNN satellite. These scenes, never intended for public consumption, were recorded as King and the various candidates relaxed during commercial breaks in King's program. "I think I'd be a fair moderator," King tells Bill Clinton. "Yeah, I do, too," replies Clinton, ever the master politician. On a different show, King asks George Bush if the first panel had been selected; Bush says not yet, then adds, cryptically, "I did what I told you I would do."[52] Eventually King did turn up on the Bush campaign's list of potential moderators.

Oprah Winfrey was among the Democrats' choices to moderate in 1996, according to *Broadcasting and Cable* magazine, though this notion apparently did not get very far. A Clinton aide told the magazine, "Oprah would clearly appeal to a broad spectrum of people who might not otherwise watch the debate."[53] Network news anchors have also been proposed as debate moderators, despite doubts that a "media bigfoot" is the proper person for the position. Said Paul Kirk Jr., cochairman of the debate commission, "Some of these anchors are so dominant that we were fearful they might upstage the merits of what was happening."[54]

Political columnist David Broder stated the problem more bluntly: "I have to say that when television does stuff in presidential campaigns, it tends to be more for the promotion of the television personalities than it does about the candidates. That's why God invented Jim Lehrer. He's superb."[55]

TOWN HALL QUESTIONERS

With the introduction of the town hall format, average citizens have become the newest breed of debate questioners. To the delight of some observers and the chagrin of others, these ordinary Americans have supplanted journalists in querying the candidates on a wide range of subject matter. The viewer appeal of this format seems to have guaranteed its future, at least for now. "The town meeting is always the most popular for one reason," says Janet Brown, executive director of the debate commission. "People identify with the participants. They look and sound like most people who are watching."[56]

The elections of 1992 and 1996 each included a town hall debate, putting the power of the microphone directly into the hands of voters. The 1996 event, which brought together Bill Clinton and Bob Dole in San Diego, produced few memorable moments or interesting characters. However, the 1992 "people's debate" in Richmond, featuring the trio of Clinton, Bush, and Perot, briefly thrust several individuals into the national spotlight:

- Marisa Hall, the twenty-five-year-old African-American woman who asked George Bush how the national debt had personally affected his life. Although Hall's question was confusingly worded, Bush's "I don't get it" response contributed to the public perception of a White House out of touch and gave Bill Clinton ammunition that would last throughout the campaign.
- Kimberly Usry, a young single mother who early in the debate wanted to know why the candidates spent such a "depressingly large" amount of time "trashing their opponents' character."
- Denton Walthall, a ponytailed father of two, who followed up Usry's question by asking the candidates to cross their hearts and pledge to "focus on the issues and not the personalities and the mud."

In postdebate analysis on ABC, Jeff Greenfield emphasized the civilizing effect of the questioners. Greenfield credited two unanticipated reactions to the town hall participants: They knocked the candidates off their sound bites and kept attacks to a minimum. NBC's John Chancellor was even more exultant, calling the debate "a shining example of how well things can work in presidential politics." An editorial in the *Christian Science Monitor* described what happened in Richmond as a "citizens' arrest": "The candidates had little choice but to be civil and engaging—not only because of the cautionary early questions, but also because they were compelled to look honest-to-goodness voting citizens in the eye and respond to their heartfelt concerns."[57]

Not everyone approved of the town hall forum. According to Monica Crowley, an aide to Richard Nixon, the former president was "horrified" by the Richmond debate. "Wasn't that format miserable?" Nixon asked Crowley. "It made them all look bad. They claimed that it was an 'audience of undecideds.' Undecideds? Selected by whom? Come on. Undecideds don't know very much because they don't care!"[58]

Nixon has a point. By choosing only uncommitted voters to pose questions, the organizers of town hall debates run the risk of dumbing down the intellectual content of the dialogue. Town hall audiences in both 1992 and 1996 were selected by the Gallup Poll organization, which started the process with a random sample survey, then winnowed the pool to registered voters who described themselves as uncommitted. The main criterion for participation was not having decided on a candidate. (In 1996 the Secret Service removed fourteen individuals from the list of possible questioners when background checks revealed they were convicted felons.)[59]

No one claims that the town hall audiences truly reflect the national populace or even the populace of the debate city. Carole Simpson recalls meeting the Richmond questioners and being surprised to spot only five African-Americans in the group; given the town's racial composition, she had expected a more diverse crowd. "How Gallup had chosen them was to go with people who were undecided. Most African-Americans had decided they were going to vote for Clinton, so that's why they weren't part of the audience," she said.[60]

As in other matters of debate production, it is the campaigns that have decided to fill the town hall audiences with uncommitteds. Uncommitteds are preferred over partisans in order to guarantee that the random selection of questioners will not inadvertently skew toward either candidate. In this, however, the candidates make a trade-off: Questions from undecided voters are less easily predicted and therefore less easy to prepare for.

In Richmond the town hall participants successfully steered the conversation toward substantive issues of general importance. Four years later the San Diego audience came closer to fulfilling the warning of government professor Michael Robinson that "there is nothing more self-centered than an audience of untrained voters who ask the same question: me, me, me."[61] A military man asked Dole about the gap between military and civilian pay scales. A landlady wanted to know about capital gains cuts. A minister spoke about returning the country to Christian values. Two of the twenty questions dealt with gay rights. Moderator Lehrer had to actively solicit foreign affairs questions; only two were posed during the ninety-minute debate.

Carole Simpson, among others, defends the questioning of the town hall participants. "I've had arguments with my colleagues who thought the public's questions were innocuous and inane, and I have just to yell back at them that this election is about the people and their questions. They're not the questions that we might ask, but this is what they want to know, and I don't think we should have any criticism of that."[62]

Lehrer, while acknowledging that the San Diego debate was "not as successful as it might have been," believes town halls serve a separate purpose from other debates: letting voters see how the candidates respond to ordinary citizens. "There are a hundred different ways to show that, and maybe this is a good way, but that's all it does," Lehrer said. "You get questions that might not be asked by professionals, sometimes they're a little off the wall, but so what—it's a different function."[63]

The volatility of town hall audiences is one of their most intriguing qualities, not to mention one of the greatest challenges for producers. Officials from the debate commission tell the story of a member of the Richmond town hall audience who never made it on TV with his question. Shortly before air, the Secret Service informed Frank Fahrenkopf Jr., cochairman of the commission, that the man had been behaving erratically. "What happened," Fahrenkopf recalled, "is he'd brought a flask in. They'd been there since three in the afternoon, so he was drunk and we had to remove him."[64] We can only wonder how the candidates might have handled an average American citizen under the influence.

Chapter Six

THE PRODUCTIONS

With less than ten minutes remaining in the nation's first presidential debate in sixteen years, Jimmy Carter was wrapping up his final answer of the evening, talking about a breakdown in the trust between government and the people. Mid-sentence, in tens of millions of homes across America, a static buzz suddenly knocked Carter's voice off the air. Unaware of the problem, the candidate continued to speak. Seconds later, anchormen on all three networks materialized on-screen to announce the unthinkable: Audio from the program had been lost. On ABC, the network charged with pool-producing the debate, Harry Reasoner reassured viewers, "It is not a conspiracy against Governor Carter or President Ford, and they will fix it as soon as possible."[1] "As soon as possible" turned out to be twenty-seven minutes, an eternity for live television.

"I don't think I've ever been in a situation more tricky than that," moderator Edwin Newman would recall. "I immediately thought to myself, what in God's name am I going to talk about? I can't talk about what they've said, or review it, or evaluate it, since I'm the moderator and I'm supposed to be impartial." Exacerbating the awkwardness of the situation was the all too apparent discomfort of the debaters themselves. Neither man wanted to make the first move, so, for the duration of the gap, both stood in place like statues. "When I suggested that they sit down because there were chairs onstage, not only did they not sit down, they did not acknowledge that I had suggested it," Newman said.[2]

Carter and Ford would reminisce about this most stilted of public moments in a joint interview with Jim Lehrer for the Commission on Presidential Debates's Oral History Project:

CARTER: I watched that tape afterwards, and it was embarrassing to me that both President Ford and I stood there almost like robots. We didn't move around. We didn't walk over and shake hands with each other. We just stood there.

FORD: I suspect both of us would have liked to sit down and relax while the technicians were fixing the system. But I also think both of us were hesitant to make any gesture that might look like we weren't physically or mentally able to handle a problem like that.

CARTER: But the fact is we didn't know at what instant all of the power was going to come back on and the transmission would be resumed. So it was a matter of nervousness. I guess President Ford felt the same way.

FORD: Because that was twenty-eight (*sic*) excruciating minutes. You're on TV nationally, and yet you're not doing anything.[3]

In the *New York Times*, Joseph Lelyveld called the sound failure a "great equalizer": "Presidents and presidential candidates normally ride with sirens and motorcycle escorts to insure that they don't have to wait for anything. But there they were, for all the nation to see, alone with their thoughts like ordinary citizens caught in a traffic jam."[4] The episode also demonstrated to a nationwide audience that neither Ford nor Carter had a knack for improvisation.

The breakdown would be traced to a tiny piece of electronic hardware valued at less than a dollar. David Brinkley began the next evening's NBC newscast by holding up an example of the errant part whose malfunctioning had been responsible for "plunging President Ford and Jimmy Carter into unaccustomed silence" and "irritating maybe ninety million people."[5]

A new chapter had entered debate lore, one that even today serves as an object lesson for the men and women who stage presidential debates.

The audio breakdown of 1976 underscores the fragile nature of live television. Although debates are pure choreography, they also operate according to the iron rule of spontaneity, meaning that even the most carefully laid plans will sometimes be subverted. Debate technicians strive for a program whose execution calls no attention to itself; when the production becomes the story, unhappy television functionaries result. Elliot Bernstein, the ABC pool producer in charge of the Ford-Carter debate, described himself as "very depressed" after the incident. "For a couple of weeks after that I felt really awful," he said. The morning after the broadcast, President Ford invited Bernstein and a production colleague for a conciliatory cup of coffee. "The meeting with the president was like taking two aspirin," Bernstein said. "I felt better for about two hours."[6]

On the heels of the audio problem in Philadelphia, technicians outfitted the subsequent debate site in San Francisco with a triply redundant sound system. "We had to add backups to backups," recalled CBS pool producer Jack Kelly,[7] and in every presidential debate since, caution has been the watchword. Debate producers make elaborate preparations for worst-case contingencies: extra cameras at the ready, candidates and questioners on multiple microphones, carpeting and drapes that are thicker than normal in order to muffle ambient sound. For 1976's final debate on the campus of the College of William and Mary, student volunteers oiled all 650 seats in Phi Beta Kappa Hall to prevent squeaking during the telecast.

Producers of presidential debates do whatever it takes to ensure a smooth-running production. In the middle of a rehearsal for the 1988 vice presidential match, Omaha's City Auditorium lost electrical power when a bird flew into an auxiliary power supply. Determined to avoid a repeat of this during the live broadcast, executive producer Ed Fouhy placed a strongly worded phone call to an official at the local power company. The official's perfunctory reassurances did not satisfy Fouhy, who countered with a threat to distribute the man's home phone number to all fifteen hundred journalists covering the event should anything go wrong. The next day crews arrived to double-wire the facility, which, according to Fouhy, "cost them so much power that people who live in that part of Omaha weren't seeing a full picture on their television sets. They were getting about a two-inch picture on their eighteen-inch monitors."[8]

Not every potential disaster is technical in nature. Annie Groer, one of the questioners in the first Bush-Dukakis debate, remembers spending the hour-and-a-half broadcast terrified that she and her fellow panelists would fall off the set. "Our chairs were all on casters which were literally about eight inches from the apron of the stage," Groer said. "So one false move and we all would have been pitching backwards."[9] Four years later producer Fouhy had similar worries during the split-format debate in East Lansing, in which the panelists were required to walk onto the set halfway through the telecast. "My greatest fear," Fouhy wrote, "was that one of the three—all debate rookies—would walk onto the stage . . . and literally fall flat on their faces, coming from the backstage darkness and having to negotiate two steps to get to their table in the blazing onstage lights."[10]

During the 1992 vice presidential debate, Admiral James Stockdale gave producers a scare when he began wandering away from his podium. Richard Berke of the *New York Times* monitored this drama-behind-the-drama from an on-site production truck, where he was able to observe the full range of cameras simultaneously. Berke described the scene:

> As the ninety-minute event wore on, Stockdale ventured farther and farther away from his spot on the podium, as if he had had enough give-and-take and was ready for his daily constitutional.
>
> "He's going for a walk!" came the voice of a nervous network producer in New York over a squawk box in the control room here. "I don't know if anyone can suggest something be done—he's got bad legs from the war, and he's going to fall down!"
>
> Nothing could be done, but luckily for the anxiety-ridden producer, as well as for Stockdale, he never fell.[11]

DEBATE VENUES

Although presidential debates were hatched in the sterile environment of a television studio, 1960 was the first and last year the programs took place in this kind of setting. (WBBM's Studio One in Chicago, the birthplace of debates, would later become home to another form of televised joust: the weekly movie review show featuring dueling critics Gene Siskel and Roger Ebert.) Since 1976, all fourteen presidential and five vice presidential debates have been produced before live audiences at auditoriums and arenas throughout the country.

Just as campaigns shape other production decisions, so do they influence the selection of debate cities. "The role of different regions is a political factor that you have to take into account," says Janet Brown, executive director of the debate commission. "I think it's reasonable to assume that you would not choose a place where the candidates are going to balk about spending any time, because these are big stops on their schedules."[12]

In laying the groundwork for debates, sponsors face the Herculean task of having to anticipate the wishes of the campaigns. Venues for presidential debates must be booked well ahead of schedule, which is to say months before candidates have committed themselves to participate. The down-to-the-wire timing of debate negotiations means that campaigns routinely thwart the sponsors' carefully laid plans. More years than not, beleaguered sponsors have been left to mop up the negotiators' mess when political wrangling forced last-minute cancellations and facilities substitutions.

On paper, the process for site selection seems fairly straightforward. The sponsoring organization invites cities to bid for a debate based on a list of logistical criteria. Obviously a suitable hall is needed, but so are the accoutrements that come with the traveling circus of a presidential debate: transportation, hotel space, a press center with room for two thousand working journalists. To offset expenses, sponsoring cities must also make a financial contribution, five hundred thousand dollars in 1996.

Debates take place in two types of on-location facilities: theaters and field houses, each with its benefits and drawbacks. "A modern and well-equipped theater means almost a turnkey operation," says Brown of the debate commission. "You can move in and a great deal of the equipment is there. By the same token, our crew brings in a great deal of the equipment from scratch. I think in many cases it surprises them that we bring in as much equipment as we do." Even state-of-the-art facilities undergo adjustments. Beyond the needs of debate producers, network news operations require major remodeling efforts to accommodate their on-site anchor booths for pre- and post-debate analysis.

In contrast to a production-ready theater, the field house setting means building a stage from the ground up; the advantage for producers is that they can create whatever space suits their needs. For the Richmond town hall debate, for instance, crews constructed a facility-within-a-facility in the middle of a fifteen thousand–seat basketball arena, exactly to the desired specifications. But field houses also present a liability: an atmosphere that encourages the live audience to approach the debate as an athletic competition. Says executive producer Fouhy, "You put people in a sports arena, and they behave like they're at a sporting event."[13]

No better illustration of this exists than the 1988 Bentsen-Quayle match, whose spirited in-house spectators constituted the rowdiest debate audience in history. Democratic campaign officials later confessed that they had imported three hundred partisan supporters to make noise and generate pro-Bentsen energy inside Omaha's City Auditorium. For each row, a designated leader cued applause and led cheers for the Texas senator.

"That was an attempt to take advantage of television," strategist Tom Donilon acknowledged at a symposium two years after the fact. "Because if you look at that tape, you can give people the sense that all of America is supporting your man's position when you have a kind of roar behind him."[14] For the next round of debates, campaign negotiators put an end to such shenanigans by stipulating that "the supporters of each candidate be interspersed among supporters of other candidates."[15]

According to Brown, a live audience of several hundred is ideal for a presidential debate; "over a thousand is where you get into a problem." UCLA's Pauley Pavilion, site of the final Bush-Dukakis debate and home court of the basketball Bruins, regularly seats fourteen thousand. Reconfigured for the debate, the space held only fifteen hundred. Still, Brown said, "people realize they're in a cavernous space and it does change the feel of the event."

As part of the audience warm-up in Los Angeles, debate cocommissioners Frank Fahrenkopf and Paul Kirk went through their regular preshow paces of exhorting those in attendance to comport themselves civilly. According to Fahrenkopf, a particularly defiant guest at Pauley Pavilion was the actress and Dukakis supporter Sally Field. "She just turned around and stared at me, giving me the finger with her look," Fahrenkopf said. "I'll never forget that as long as I live."[16]

Perhaps the best-behaved audiences have been those in the town hall debates in Richmond and San Diego, where a seat in the hall meant the possibility of active participation. For the latter event, moderator Jim Lehrer enlisted the support of audience VIP Gerald Ford in enforcing proper decorum. In his predebate warm-up, Lehrer informed the crowd he was appointing Ford "hall monitor," and told Ford, "You can discipline anybody who gets out of line."[17]

Except for the town hall forums, tickets for debates are equally split among the sponsor and the campaigns, which then parcel them out to supporters. Often the candidates invite high-profile guests from the worlds of politics and entertainment; in the final 1976 debate, for example, singer Pearl Bailey sat with First Lady Betty Ford. With tickets in high demand, average citizens have almost no opportunity to be part of a presidential debate audience. When the first Bush-Dukakis meeting in 1988 took place on the campus of Wake Forest University in Winston-Salem, North Carolina, only thirteen seats were earmarked for a student body of five thousand. (The students did receive a consolation: Because the school cafeteria was commandeered for use as a media center, dorm residents received breakfast in bed.)

However exclusive the ticket, a spot inside the auditorium does not offer the best vantage point for debate watching; after all, the production is designed as a TV show and not a theatrical event. Acoustics and sight lines can be poor, and temperatures in the brightly lit hall are often uncomfortable. Describing the second 1976 meeting between Ford and Carter, James Wooten in the *New York Times* referred to San Francisco's Palace of Fine Arts as "the largest sauna in the country." Unseasonably hot weather had turned the hall into an oven; spectators fanned themselves with their programs "like ladies at a country church in the deep of summer."[18]

The two candidates had no such worries. Production crews had gone to great lengths to keep Ford and Carter comfortable, installing an ad hoc air conditioning system in the otherwise uncooled theater. According to debate scholars Seltz and Yoakam, "Large flexible ducts, looking like elephant trunks, wound their way onto the stage and the debate set, where they were suspended from the light grid and aimed at the lecterns."[19] Taking no chances, technicians diffused the air blowing out of these hoses so as not to tousle the debaters' hair.

This image—Gerald Ford and Jimmy Carter standing onstage beneath separate but equal air ducts—offers a useful visual metaphor for presidential debates. In the never-never land of TV debates, where reality intersects with contrivance, it is fitting that each candidate existed in what amounted to his own microclimate. Temperature-controlled and wind-free, these artificial zones of perfection underline how exacting a pursuit debate production can be.

ON-SITE NEGOTIATIONS

Once at the debate site, the campaigns intensify their efforts to anticipate the unexpected. This task begins about a week before the debate and involves anywhere from a dozen to twenty people per campaign, headed by one or two lead representatives on each side. Also on hand are the nonpolitical personnel who will execute most of the production specifics: the debate sponsors and their team, plus the crew from the pool network assigned with getting the program on the air. From 1960 on, the major networks have shared responsibility for televising presidential debates, drawing lots to see who stages which event. The network in charge supplies a director, a technical crew, and, in the end, a fully produced feed of the program that is sent out for use by all members of the pool.

The relationship among the various entities at the debate site is not one of equals. As is true throughout the process, campaigns maintain the upper hand in the on-location dealings, leaving sponsors and television networks in a reactive posture. With the negotiated memorandum of agreement as their charter, the handlers set about converting the dry prose of the contract into a live television show. Until this point, the debate has been all theory and bluster; now it becomes three-dimensional.

The differing requirements of each physical setting make it impossible for the drafters of the debate agreement to foresee every contingency. For this reason, campaign representatives continue to hammer out production details even as the hall is being set up. The goal on each side is simple: to protect one's candidate. "The stakes are such that you do literally everything you can think of to maximize the advantage, even if it's point-zero-zero-one percent," says Brady Williamson, an on-site negotiator for Democratic candidates in the past four elections. "Sometimes in hindsight, the trivial turned out to be sublime, and the sublime turned out to be trivial."[20]

At the debate venue, negotiators must settle a variety of issues, both procedural and production-related. Coin tosses determine many of the procedural questions, things like which candidate speaks first; the sequence of the candidates' arrival at the hall; the order in which the spouses take their seats; and so on. More complicated staging points may call for a session at the bargaining table—or, when practical, on the set itself.

As production arrangements come into focus, the handlers on site maintain close contact with their counterparts involved in candidate preps. The objective is to communicate details about the location that can be incorporated into the mock debates. Bill Clinton's advance teams in 1992 and 1996 were particularly effective in conveying production minutiae that was then applied in the practice sessions. For the logistically complicated town hall sessions, the Clinton prep operation received precise measurements of the debate stage that were used to lay out an accurate replica for rehearsals.

Depending on the situation, and the dynamic between opposing handlers, on-site negotiations may or may not be thorny. Generally the campaign representatives on both sides are experienced hands at presidential debates, and many of the key figures have worked with one another in the past. "I think it's fair to say we've become good acquaintances, and come to respect each other along the way," Williamson says. "If we didn't have each other's mutual respect, and dare I say trust, it wouldn't work."[21]

Still, relations have not always been smooth. On rare occasions when campaigns cannot reach agreement, the disputes never do achieve reconciliation. In 1976 advisers for Ford and Carter battled for weeks over how blue the backdrop on the set ought to be, an argument that persisted even as the four-debate series was under way. According to Seltz and Yoakam, "The Carter people . . . wanted the background to be less blue—or warmer, as they put it. The Ford handlers wanted it to be more blue." Imero Fiorentino, a veteran lighting director hired by the League of Women Voters, ended up mediating the disagreement. Said Fiorentino, "The blueness of the background changed all the time. Now if there was anything that was of interest to the candidates' representatives, and befuddled me to death, it was the blue background."[22]

In 1984 the placement of the podiums generated sparks between the Reagan and Mondale campaigns. Mondale negotiators sought a particular angle in order that their candidate might take a step away from the lectern, turn to his opponent, and address him directly in a dramatic on-camera maneuver dubbed "the pivot." According to debate coach Tom Donilon, the plan was to showcase Mondale by having him make a physical move that had never been tried in a presidential debate. "When you actually turn your body, the whole picture of the thing changes into a much more confrontational event," Donilon explained. "A little movement on television goes a long way."[23]

As a key element in Mondale's strategy to unnerve Reagan, the placement of lecterns was a serious negotiating point for the Democrats, though obviously they could not reveal why. Victoria Harian, debate coordinator for the League, recalled, "There was a lot of discussion about exactly how those [podiums] were going to be canted—what angle, how many inches, from what point were they going to be measured. It ended up being a very silly thing to have taken up so much time and to have become such a big deal."[24]

For 1984's second debate the flashpoint was lighting—the "battle of the bulbs," as the hometown *Kansas City Star* dubbed it in a news story devoted to the squabble. Mondale's people favored the lighting plot used in the previous debate in Louisville, where the Democratic nominee had been victorious; Reagan's people demanded changes. Among other things, the Reagan team wanted lights on the live audience. According to a spokesman for pool network CBS, the president's aides believed that lighting the audience would be less "stressful" for Reagan than "talking to a black hole."[25]

Eventually the Republicans got many of the changes they insisted on. Most significantly Michael Deaver, Reagan's television guru, made a last-minute alteration that worked to his candidate's benefit on the air. "I always lit Reagan from the top, never underneath," Deaver explained, "because you get that full head of hair, you don't get any lines in the face, and you get a line across the broad shoulders." Just before the debate, Deaver reconfigured the lighting according to this high-angle scheme—with the consent, he said, of the League of Women Voters and the Mondale campaign.

For Mondale, the results were disastrous: bags under the eyes, and a waxy pallor that added years to his appearance. "Mondale needed heavy lighting straight on," Deaver said, "and I had changed it, but I certainly didn't do it on purpose."[26] Frank Greer, Mondale's television consultant, later complained that the high angle of the lighting had been "extreme" and that the original setup would have been more advantageous to his candidate.[27] After this episode, campaigns took greater care to protect the lighting design from tampering by the other side.

Sometimes the site itself exacerbates tensions between campaigns. The 1996 town hall debate in San Diego took place in a theater so cramped that it obviated a rule in the contract giving each candidate his own onstage "zone." Once the reality of the space became apparent, negotiators discussed a number of alternatives, including the possibility of painting a line down the middle of the set to create a border. In the end, against the wishes of the Dole camp, the concept of clearly delineated zones was abandoned.

"We spent more time on that than anything," said Clinton representative Beverly Lindsey. "We wanted our candidate to be able to approach the audience on all sides, not just the side he was on." Dole handlers, by contrast, feared that in so intimate a space the president might be tempted to instigate a confrontation. "I think they were concerned that Clinton would walk right up to Dole and put a finger in his shoulder or something," Lindsey said.[28]

In the end, the physical maneuvering in this debate proved to be one of its distinctive qualities. As Maureen Dowd wrote in the *New York Times*, "The president kept sliding out from behind his lectern, bearing down on Bob Dole and looking as if he were going to give him a good clip from the side."[29] At one point in the program Dole stepped backed, muttering, "I'm going to get out of your way here." Nothing, it appeared, could stand between Clinton and his need to bond with the studio audience.

The San Diego debate posed a second problem for on-site negotiators. Dole's representatives made an unconditional demand that Elizabeth Dole be seated in her husband's line of sight during the telecast. This same request had been easily accomplished at the previous debate in Hartford, which took place in a standard auditorium. But in San Diego, with its theater-in-the-round setup, Mrs. Dole would have had to sit among the town hall participants, a position Democrats feared might influence the tenor of the questioning.

Negotiators struck a compromise: A platform was built above the last row of the audience where Elizabeth Dole would be visible to the senator but separated from the questioners; Hillary Clinton got an identical stand on her side of the house. During the debate, Dole's reason for wanting his wife in view became evident: Her job was to smile at him, and thus remind him to relax. For the duration of the ninety-minute telecast, observers said, Mrs. Dole never stopped smiling.[30]

One of the most heavily negotiated production points from year to year is the assignment of candidate holding rooms. As Clinton aide Brady Williamson says, "Not all space is equally desirable."[31] From the outset, debate sponsors have been sensitive to this issue. Back in 1960, ABC constructed identical "dressing room cottages" for Kennedy and Nixon on the studio set of the New York City debate. Although each cottage had its own sink, the candidates were expected to share a toilet.

Today's debaters no longer share much of anything. Backstage holding areas function as a traveling campaign headquarters, complete with private areas for the candidates and full-scale communications centers for the staff. Campaigns take extreme precautions to segregate the star participants physically from each other in the period before a debate begins. "You arrange their holding rooms so that they don't intersect each other's path," says debate consultant Bob Goodwin.[32] In some cases, curtains have been installed specifically to keep the competitors from catching an accidental glimpse of each other.

Just before the first 1992 debate in St. Louis, Ross Perot violated this long-standing protocol by paying an impromptu social call at the dressing rooms of his surprised opponents. Brady Williamson remembers standing outside Clinton's holding room, when "out of the shadow comes this small figure and it's Ross Perot. He walks up to me and says, 'May I say hello to the governor?'" Overcoming his shock, Williamson went inside and got Clinton's approval, and Perot proceeded inside for a brief predebate chat. Perot, said Williamson, "didn't approach this thing quite the way the other two did."[33]

Perot's attempt to see President Bush was less successful. This time the Reform Party candidate did not get past the holding room door.

PREDEBATE TECH CHECKS

On the afternoon of a presidential debate, several hours before broadcast, the on-site process culminates with each debater's final preshow technical check. As with other production particulars, the order of the candidates' arrival for the walk-throughs, and how much time they are allotted on the set, have been decided in advance. At the appointed hour the hall is cleared of nonessential personnel, and the star and his entourage sweep in for a briefing session with producers and technicians.

In many ways this is standard show business procedure, like the sound check that takes place before a rock concert or dress rehearsal for a Broadway play. In other ways the tech check preceding a presidential debate has no parallel, thanks to the uniquely bifurcated nature of the event, the weighty stakes involved, and the intensely felt pressure of the rival camps. For each side, the on-site walk-through represents one last opportunity to counteract any perceived inequities.

Even more important, the point of the exercise is to get the candidate as relaxed as possible in the crucial hours before the debate commences. Says Brady Williamson, "It's like trying on a new suit. You just want to make sure that you're comfortable, that it fits."[34] During the tech check, debaters receive their final instructions on such key production details as camera placement, timing, and how they will enter from offstage. Cueing devices and microphones are tested. Makeup and clothing are examined under television lights so advisers can preview the candidate exactly as he or she will appear on the air. The last step, according to Democratic debate coach Tom Donilon, is to review ground rules with the producers, "to make sure they're not going to do anything that's not to your advantage. You want to be there with the stage manager, the camera people, the director."[35]

Technical checks may run smoothly, or they may fall victim to the intensity of the moment. Victoria Harian, debate producer for the League in 1984, described an unusually nerve-racking scene when Geraldine Ferraro came in for her walk-through before the vice presidential debate in Philadelphia. Campaign advisers were having "fits and tantrums" over a variety of minor matters, Harian said, "to the point you knew they weren't serving their candidate well. You could see Ferraro was getting too much exposure to all this nattering, and most of it was just absolutely a waste."[36]

Tech checks have always had the potential to harrow. Robert F. Kennedy, accompanying his brother to NBC's Studio A in Washington for the second 1960 debate, voiced objections on two counts: lighting and studio temperature. Standing at Nixon's podium, RFK demanded to know why the Republican side of the set seemed brighter than the Democratic side. The candidate himself asked if the Nixon people had arranged the lighting for both debaters. "There's only one light pointing over here (at Nixon's lectern)," JFK said. "Let's not have four lights in my eyes."[37] Technical director Leon Chromak agreed to reposition a stand light on the studio floor, in what he later called a "psychological lighting change" to appease the Kennedys.[38]

Mindful of Richard Nixon's on-camera perspiration in the first debate, Nixon handlers had requested that the air conditioning be set at a cooler level in Washington. As John Kennedy entered the studio, he commented, "I need a sweater." Bobby Kennedy asked an aide, "What are they trying to do? Freeze my brother to death?" The Democrats insisted that adjustments be made, and the temperature came up a few degrees.[39]

For the transcontinental third debate of 1960, with Nixon in California and Kennedy in New York City, each candidate got his way: the temperature of Nixon's studio remained at fifty-eight degrees, while Kennedy's registered at seventy-two. Otherwise, ABC took great pains to create identical studio arrangements. The network purchased cloth for the two backdrops from the same mill run, in enough quantity to dress both sets. The same can of paint used on the New York set was hand-carried on a plane to Los Angeles so the colors would precisely match.

Even at that, physical distance and equal facilities did not prevent a long-distance tiff. After the debate Republicans charged that JFK had violated an agreed-on rule by bringing notes into the studio in New York. A few minutes before the program began, Nixon evidently caught a glimpse of

Kennedy on a monitor shuffling papers at his lectern. Once the program went off the air, Nixon discussed the matter with journalists, as reported in the *New York Times*:

> "The vice president insisted that "I'm not angry about it," but his face was rigid, his lips taut, and his voice rose as he continued talking about the use of notes.
>
> "I'm not complaining," he told reporters in the ABC studio. "I never complain about debates after they are over.
>
> "But before the next debate we had better settle on the rules."[40]

More recently the paranoia over bringing notes onto the set has found its way into the negotiated memoranda of agreement. The 1996 contract lays out an explicit procedure for the campaigns to follow: "Each candidate must submit to the staff of the commission prior to the debate all such paper and any pens or pencils with which a candidate may wish to take notes during the debate, and the staff of the commission will place such paper, pens, and pencils on the podium of each candidate."[41] Astute debate viewers will observe that in the sixty seconds before air, when the candidates first walk to their lecterns, they use the time to scrawl final reminders to themselves with the officially sanctioned implements. The rules permit only this much pre-debate note taking.

Over the years technical walk-throughs have grown increasingly off-limits to the media. Before the final Ford-Carter debate of 1976, Jimmy Carter's closed rehearsal nearly became a news story when audio from inside the hall mistakenly found its way to the nearby press center. To make matters worse, Carter had decided to use his tech check to engage in a dry run, offering real responses to questions asked by advisers on topics like tax reform and foreign policy. NBC, the network in charge, spent the next several hours contacting people who might have heard the rehearsal, imploring them not to report it; apparently no one did.

At the 1996 San Diego site, sponsors ejected an Associated Press photographer whom they discovered hiding under a canvas in the balcony during one of the technical checks. The photographer had concealed an automatic camera inside a curtain and was snapping pictures of the rehearsal with a remote control device. The debate commission took away the man's credentials and banned him from the premises.

One reason campaigns do not allow press coverage of the tech checks is that the scenes can become volatile, in effect extending the bargaining into the hours immediately before the event. At the tech check preceding the first 1976 debate, President Ford roiled the waters by asking that the stool behind his lectern be removed. The League's production coordinator, "in the afterglow of meeting the president of the United States," honored this request, forgetting that campaign negotiators had spent hours haggling over the seating issue.

When Carter's people discovered the stool had been removed without their consent, they angrily demanded an explanation from the other side. "I got about thirteen phone calls in forty-five minutes," recalled Ford media adviser William Carruthers.[42] The stool was returned to Ford's lectern, but moments before the telecast began, the president again signaled Carruthers to strike it. Carruthers dragged the stool a few feet away from Ford, where it remained on the stage throughout the program, forlornly turning up in some of the two-shots.

Stools recurred as a bone of contention sixteen years later in the three-way town hall debate in Richmond. According to director John LiBretto, at issue were the height and positioning of the seats, and whether each debater would have side tables on which to take notes. "That seemed to take hours to figure out," LiBretto said. "I kept saying you can't have [the candidates] hindered in any way from getting up—they have to be able to get up easily from the chairs and walk around—but that just seemed to go on forever."[43]

A couple of hours after the debaters had completed their tech checks, LiBretto said, representatives from both the Bush and Clinton campaigns returned to the hall for yet another look at the floor layout. (Perot's people had pronounced themselves satisfied, even though the stools were too high for the diminutive Texan.) Deciding the stools were still too close together, the handlers requested an adjustment. LiBretto tried adding space between candidates, but the repositioning adversely affected his camera shots. After about an hour of tinkering, the director and the handlers agreed to split the difference. "I can say that when we were done I had the chairs back where they started," LiBretto said. "I don't know they were even aware that I ended up with the chairs back on their original marks."

The candidates themselves approach their tech checks with varying degrees of seriousness. Bill Clinton was renowned for being a highly engaged participant in his predebate walk-throughs. Before the 1992 town meeting Clinton peppered director LiBretto with questions about the physical configuration of the set: "What if I did this, and what if I did that?" "Does this work?" "If I stand here and turn to the president, will that show on camera?" President Bush, LiBretto said, was far less interested in such arcana. Ross Perot did not even attend his session, sending a surrogate instead.

For the 1996 town hall debate in San Diego Clinton conducted a similarly thorough survey. "He got off the stage and walked the whole circumference of the theater," recalled Bob Asman, executive producer for the debate commission.[44] Bob Dole, by contrast, never left the stage. Where Clinton used most of his one-hour allotment of time, Dole made quick work of his on-site briefings, taking less than twenty minutes.

Unlike Clinton, Dole always brought along his wife, who, according to one observer, remained "glued to his side" during the walk-throughs.[45] Twenty years earlier Mrs. Dole had been an equally visible presence at her husband's predebate tech check before the vice presidential debate with Walter Mondale. During that session, when Dole expressed concern that the live spectators might present a distraction, Elizabeth Dole went out into the house so the candidate could see how the audience would look under the actual lighting conditions of the broadcast. Wrote debate historians Seltz and Yoakam, "The senator looked at Mrs. Dole for awhile and seemed satisfied that the problem had been solved."[46]

THE VISUAL STYLE OF PRESIDENTIAL DEBATES

The controversy over reaction shots in the first Kennedy-Nixon match initiated a tradition of visual caution in presidential debates. This timidity of approach affected not only the remaining programs of 1960 but influenced debates across the decades. Now as then, campaign representatives attempt to favorably preordain the shooting and directing of debate telecasts, hoping to press the grammar of the medium into political service. These exertions ignore a fundamental reality: Live television is inherently at odds with visual proscription.

Mindful of the widespread attention Nixon's cutaways had drawn in the opening encounter, the director of the second 1960 debate pointedly timed each reaction shot with a stopwatch as campaign handlers looked on. The third meeting of Kennedy and Nixon, potentially a gold mine of contrasting images, was even more buttoned-down. This program had offered an unprecedented opportunity for experimentation: with Nixon in Los Angeles and Kennedy in New York, history's first and only split-screen presidential debate was, for its time, a technical tour de force. It took three studios to pull off the exercise, two in Los Angeles (one for Nixon, another for the panel) and a third in New York for JFK. ABC, the designated pool network, billed the production as "the most technically complicated broadcast in history."[47]

Oddly, in spite of the intricate setup, viewers saw the split-screen of both candidates only once, in the opening moments of the program before the men began speaking. Director Sonny Diskin, whose regular assignments included *The Fight of the Week*, ABC's Saturday night boxing show, explained afterward that he did not want the side-by-side shots to be "distracting."[48] Not coincidentally, the third debate is generally regarded as Nixon's best; with John F. Kennedy a safe three thousand miles away, the vice president managed to relax and deliver.

Since 1976, when debates moved out of the television studio and onto remote locations, the trepidation over cutaways has expanded to include reaction shots of the live audience. Throughout the history of TV debates, campaigns have actively prohibited shots of the onlookers, fearful that such images might unduly influence the audience at home. In at least a couple of instances entire rows of seats were removed from the debate hall in order to prevent audience reaction shots. Only during the town hall debates have in-house spectators played a visible role in the proceedings.

Carter media adviser Barry Jagoda told *Newsweek* in 1976 that "one frown could color a whole public reaction."[49] Republican debate consultant William Carruthers, in a predebate strategy memo for the Ford campaign the same year, warned that a live audience represented "one of the most sensitive and potentially dangerous aspects of the debates. If there is any way we can preclude the appearance of an audience, we should do it."[50]

At the behest of the campaigns, the sponsoring League of Women Voters agreed to forbid cutaways of spectators in the 1976 debates, a move that set off a nasty skirmish with the television networks. Likening the ban to censorship, the broadcasters contended that they should be free to cover the debate as they would any bona fide news event. "If someone falls out of the balcony, boos or cheers, falls asleep, well, that's part of the event and we have a right to cover it," said Walter Pfister of the ABC Special Events unit, the group overseeing television pool coverage for the first debate.[51] After briefly hinting that they might refuse to carry the programs altogether, the networks backed down, and the series proceeded without audience cutaways.

From a production standpoint, the effect of this prohibition was to limit artificially the way the event played out to viewers. As Seltz and Yoakam concluded about the 1976 vice presidential debate,

> There was an obvious chance for audience reaction shots when the theater audience laughed at some of Senator Dole's remarks. A director, operating freely, might have considered taking a shot of the audience if there was enough reaction to make it a significant part of the story. To do that, he would have had to have a camera aimed at the audience, and sufficient light. Because of the no-shot rule, neither was available at that moment. To have faithfully reported the whole story of that debate, the director should have had the option of shooting the audience.[52]

A similar violation of visual grammar occurred in 1988, when Bernard Shaw asked Michael Dukakis the infamous question about the hypothetical rape and murder of his wife. For the program's director, the logical move would have been a reaction shot of Kitty Dukakis herself, seated in the audience only a few feet away. One could argue that such a cutaway, by adding visual context, might even have humanized her husband's clinical response. But the terms of that year's memorandum of understanding specifically forbade the possibility: "In no case shall any television shots be taken of any member of the audience (including candidate's family members) from the time the first question is asked until the conclusion of the closing statements."[53]

Even as the directorial style of presidential debates remained frozen in 1960, viewing audiences were learning to expect cutaways as a standard ingredient of live television programming. Sporting events, awards programs, interviews, and talk shows routinely use reaction shots to add visual depth and interest, but for most of their history, presidential debates did not follow suit. Looser formats in the 1990s have finally dragged debates into the modern visual era, particularly in the town hall forums, which, by definition, call for a variety of shots of candidates and audience members alike.

John LiBretto of NBC, who directed the landmark 1992 Richmond town hall debate, considered himself free to cut the program as he saw fit. One of the most memorable and remarked upon shots in that debate showed President George Bush looking down to check his watch; to many viewers, Bush appeared disengaged. "I was cutting to him for a reaction shot," LiBretto recalled, "and as I cut to him he looked at his watch. I remember my reaction in the truck: What in the hell is he doing? That's exactly what came out of my mouth at that moment. The effect was devastating. I felt like here I just cut to a camera and cost the man the job, but I know that's not what happened."

LiBretto later wondered, would he have taken the shot had Bush looked at the watch *before* the camera change? "My instinct, especially as a sports director, is to go to that reaction shot," he said. "If it's there, if it's on camera, you go to it because you want to show everything that's going on."[54]

Until recently only one version of a presidential debate was available to the various television entities that carried it: the program as directed by the designated pool network. Dissatisfaction with this practice dates back to 1976, when the sponsoring League of Women Voters refused to allow the broadcast networks to set up their own cameras in the debate hall. The pool was adopted as a practical solution to the problem of too much equipment competing for too little space.

In the last two rounds of debates, however, the pool network has fed not only its fully mixed version of the debate, with shots selected by the director, but also uninterrupted, "unilateral" shots of the individual participants. This allows each outlet, in effect, to direct its own version of the debate, at least to the limited degree isolated cameras permit. Flaunting the campaigns' negotiated agreement, the networks have used these so-called iso-cams to create split-screen shots of both candidates at once, a visual effect the handlers vigorously oppose.

According to debate producer Bob Asman, campaign advisers came to him after the first 1996 Clinton-Dole program "very upset" over the split-screens that turned up in some of the network coverage. Asman explained that the networks now had the technical capability to circumvent the pool feed.[55] "In hindsight," said Democratic negotiator Brady Williamson, "the Clinton campaign was not displeased, because the iso-cams ended up showing pictures that we found useful."[56] Still, the provision of these unilateral shots is an issue that politicians, sponsors, and networks will certainly revisit before the next round of debates.

No doubt the strangest example of production tinkering in presidential debates occurred in 1980, when CNN electronically inserted uninvited independent candidate John Anderson into the Reagan-Carter debate. CNN, at that point an upstart operation with only three and a half million subscribers, saw the ambitious experiment as a publicity bonanza, though the exercise turned out to be less a moment of glory than a technical farce.

As Reagan and Carter debated live in Cleveland, Anderson stood before CNN cameras at Constitution Hall in Washington, D.C., where an audience of twelve hundred had gathered to watch him shadowbox the big boys. Four producers, camped in nearby production trucks, recorded the Reagan-Carter debate on as many videotape machines. These tapes were then played back in sequence, with Anderson's answers edited in at the appropriate points. A stenographer listening to the live debate transcribed the panelists' questions from Cleveland, which were hand-delivered to CNN moderator Daniel Schorr, who read them to Anderson in Constitution Hall.

Several times the audio either failed or fell out of sync with the video. Because of an editing mix-up, Reagan was shown answering a question that had not yet been asked in the CNN debate, and moderator Schorr understandably lost track of the complicated timing. In the *New York Times*, John J. O'Connor wrote, "The effort was extremely awkward . . . But it was also an intriguing glimpse of a possible future when, armed with the multichannel capacities of constantly expanding cable, all third-party candidates will have access to a national forum that has proved impossible on limited over-the-air network television."[57]

THE TV PROS TAKE OVER

Campaigns may function as executive producers of presidential debates, but once a program goes on the air, responsibility for its execution shifts from the the political establishment to the television establishment. The candidate representatives who draft the production agreements, plan the strategies, and oversee the on-site arrangements must now pass the baton to the TV professionals, if only for the duration of the event.

The battle-zone atmosphere of the Kennedy-Nixon control rooms taught the networks to be wary of campaign interference while the program is on the air, and, since 1976, political operatives have maintained a low profile during the broadcasts. The terms of the negotiated agreement allow each campaign to have one representative in the production facility during the debate and provide for phone lines between the control room and the candidates' holding areas. In practice, these privileges are seldom invoked; handlers do not stand over the director's shoulder as he carries out his job.

This has not always stopped campaigns from expressing their concerns while a debate is in progress. In 1992's first presidential encounter, Bush campaign chairman James Baker had one of his deputies telephone the control room with an urgent message for moderator Jim Lehrer. According to the language of the debate contract, the topic was supposed to shift from domestic to foreign policy halfway through the program; five minutes past this point, the switch had not occurred. Before the message could be communicated to Lehrer, the debate moved to foreign affairs anyway. Baker's phone call "didn't have any effect on what happened on the stage," Lehrer said.[58]

More typically campaigns tend to back off during the actual telecast. For one thing, they know they are overmatched, not just by the professional experience of the crews but by the medium itself. A TV production is an organic exercise with its own energy and personality. Invariably live programming overpowers the prescriptive words of a document. As debate producer Ed Fouhy put it, "Trying to micromanage a television program with a lot of lawyers is something that's not going to work."[59]

The negotiated documents that cause so much strife for the campaigns before the debate only indirectly affect the television crews who bring the program to life. John LiBretto, director of a 1992 debate, said that he did not even see the production guidelines that governed the town hall debate he directed in Richmond. "The thirty-six-page document is in the possession of the campaigns and in possession of the commission," said Janet Brown of the debate commission. "My sound guy who has done the Super Bowl and the Olympics and all this other stuff—trust me when I tell you he's not carrying a pocket copy of a thirty-six-page thing, even though microphones are usually mentioned." Brown added that this does not mean sponsors willfully ignore the wishes of the campaigns. "It just means that it's a television event, and you get on with doing the job."

The agreements deal out the specifics of camera shots in what Brown described as "excruciating detail." Instances have occurred during debates, she said, when campaign officials have complained that visual guidelines are being violated. "There are inevitably shots that end up mid-debate that some campaign guy, because he wants to sound important, is going to object to," Brown said. "Are you going to stop the debate and bring the director on stage and say, 'You abrogated the agreement'? I think not."

Brown notes that the highly skilled network directors chosen for this assignment understand and respect the seriousness of the occasion. From the beginning, presidential debates have been staffed with top-flight professionals who operate comfortably in the high-pressure setting of live, big-ticket television. They come from newscasts and magazine programs, talk shows, sports, even the comedy series *Saturday Night Live*. Their mission is complicated: working within a tightly controlled political framework to create a TV event that will enter the archives of American history.

"The quality of our production staff is without peer," says Janet Brown, citing the crews' experience in producing inaugural coverage and summit conferences, high-profile sporting events, and Academy Awards shows. "If there's something in television they haven't dealt with," she said, "I don't know what it is." According to Bob Asman, an NBC veteran who served as the debate commission's executive producer in 1996, the pool network takes pride in putting on a polished program, "so the tendency is to really use your best people."[60]

"I don't know how many times I went to meetings and demanded that the crew be absolutely the best crew NBC had," recalled Richmond director LiBretto. "I told them about the sense of history I had about this—that we would be judged accordingly, and it had better be good. I insisted on an excellent crew and I got it."

Shortly before the groundbreaking debate, LiBretto and his team sat down for a group dinner. "It was the first time I've ever seen any of these guys nervous in all the years I've worked with them," he remembered. "Super Bowls, World Series—I've done major, major events with all these people."[61] Nothing in the world of television, he said, could quite match the pressure of a presidential debate.

Part III

POSTPRODUCTION

Chapter Seven

POSTDEBATE NEWS COVERAGE

When the first Kennedy-Nixon debate signed off the air at 10:30 P.M. Eastern Daylight time on September 26, 1960, the broadcast networks did not follow the event with news analysis. Instead, they resumed their regular programming: the *Original Amateur Hour* on ABC; *Jackpot Bowling with Milton Berle* on NBC; and, on CBS, a prerecorded interview between Walter Cronkite and Lyndon Johnson that ran as part of the *Presidential Countdown* series. For the duration of the 1960 debates, television scrupulously refrained from instant commentary and postevent news specials. Remarkable as it may seem to contemporary audiences, the millions of Americans who tuned in for the 1960 debates had to wait until the next morning's newspapers to catch the reviews.

In 1976 this programming isolation ended, and today no presidential debate exists in a vacuum. Starting with the Ford-Carter matches and continuing to the present, a live debate has come to represent only the centerpiece of the larger media marathon that begins weeks before air time and ends well after the program fades to black. The power of the press reaches its apogee in the aftermath of a debate, when two things happen: First, the pundits have their say in the period immediately following the broadcast, and, second, the ninety-minute event is reduced to a collection of sound-bite highlights that will be played over and over as a kind of shorthand for the complete program. The news media thus create a parallel version of the debate that may overtake the audience's original perception of what it saw.

This was hardly the case in 1960. That year, for the first and last time, the debate story belonged not to television but to the pencil press. At the time of the Kennedy-Nixon debates, TV news scarcely registered in the national consciousness, much less as the country's primary conduit of political news. The day after the first event, none of the three network newscasts led with the debate. CBS ran only a brief mention of the joint appearance as the tenth story in its lineup, after such items as the arrival in Washington of Japanese Crown Prince Akihito and Crown Princess Michiko, Nigerian independence preparations, and a plane crash in Moscow.[1]

TV news outlets approached the 1960 debates warily, perhaps because the programs were produced and sponsored by the very networks that would then have to provide objective coverage. By today's standards, television's underplaying of the events seems almost irrationally circumspect. Not a single newscast excerpted sound bites from the Kennedy-Nixon broadcasts. Neither the candidates nor their surrogates came forth with any on-camera spin, and anchormen and reporters studiously avoided anything but the most cursory debate references.

Newspaper accounts were considerably less diffident. Richard Nixon's anemic performance handed print reporters a story line that would sustain momentum for the remainder of the series. The morning after the Chicago debate, the *Christian Science Monitor*'s Richard L. Strout was among the first to assess the effect of the reaction shots: "The cameras showed close-ups of the listening candidate's face while the other talked . . . Nixon looking to many weary from endless campaigning, with chin perspiring under the hot TV lamps." Peter Lisagor, in the *Chicago Daily News*, wrote that Nixon's face "looked drawn, and beads of perspiration on his chin were plainly visible as he spoke." The *Boston Globe*'s Percy Shain also used the word *drawn* to describe Nixon, and added, "Kennedy was almost chubby by contrast."[2]

In the days that followed, journalists had no difficulty keeping this tale alive. Nixon's people did their part by issuing hasty proclamations of their candidate's vitality. Press secretary Herbert Klein announced that "Mr.

Nixon is in excellent health and looks good in person." Patricia Nixon told a reporter that she didn't know if her husband had lost weight "because Dick and I aren't the types who weigh in every day." Nixon himself said, "I think I lost a couple of pounds, and it may show up in my face."[3]

Three days after the first debate, the *Chicago Daily News* goosed the narrative with a copyrighted front-page article that ran under the headline "Was Nixon Sabotaged by TV Makeup Artist?"[4] The story quoted an official from the Makeup Artists and Hair Stylists union in New York as saying that he believed Nixon had been worked on by a Democrat. "They loused him up so badly that a Republican couldn't have done the job," the union rep told the paper. Although no evidence was advanced to support this claim, the *Daily News* nonetheless used the quote to trump up the possibility of a conspiracy. Network officials denied the charge, and the vice president's aides stepped forward to admit that they had done their own cosmetic work.

The matter of Nixon's camera presence snowballed in the press. By the time the weekly news magazines published their accounts of the first debate, the conventional wisdom had been set in concrete. "Within minutes after the candidates went off the air," wrote *Newsweek*, "the whole country seemed to be chattering about who did what to whom. But the one question that was on almost everyone's lips was: Why did Nixon look so haggard, so worn, and so grim?"[5] Even Nixon himself got into the act. During a visit to the set of the TV series *77 Sunset Strip*, the vice president joked to actor Efrem Zimbalist Jr., "How come you look like yourself with makeup and I don't?"[6]

The tale of Richard Nixon's on-camera visage illustrates the highly self-referential nature of postdebate news coverage. Today, as in 1960, the cumulative effect of journalistic reporting is to reinforce existing perceptions and perpetuate particular story lines. In each debate reporters hope for an angle that will provide grist for the news mill; the best stories are those with a whiff of controversy and a prolonged shelf life. In Nixon's lack of preparedness, the political press corps of 1960 found a narrative thread with which to weave a veritable tapestry. Even now, forty years after the fact, the disparity in appearance between John F. Kennedy and Richard Nixon remains the legacy of history's first televised debate.

But an even bigger headline to come out of the 1960 debates is one that eluded the news media of the day, perhaps because the story was too close at hand to be properly observed. Russell Baker, who covered the Kennedy-

Nixon debates for the *New York Times*, would write nearly thirty years later of the significance of the first broadcast. "That night," Baker said, "television replaced newspapers as the most important communications medium in American politics."[7] Indeed, few such transitions in the nation's history have been so clearly demarcated. Not only newspapers were knocked off their throne; so was radio. And so, for that matter, was the accepted formula for waging a presidential campaign.

At the time only a few journalists sensed the shifting ground beneath their feet. "Both sides have found that television has added a new element to politics—one that is not yet fully appraised," wrote a contributor to *U.S. News and World Report*.[8] *Atlanta Constitution* publisher Ralph McGill confessed, "We and the candidates are up against the fact that we do not understand all we would like to know about the impact of television." McGill recounted the outcome of an informal experiment he had conducted, one that would quickly enter the received wisdom of presidential debates. He had arranged for "a number of persons" to listen to the first Kennedy-Nixon debate on radio, to see if they would react differently than television viewers. "It is interesting to report they unanimously thought Mr. Nixon had the better of it," McGill concluded. Despite later, more scientific data to the contrary, this early finding took root as a shibboleth.[9]

McGill's poll, specifying neither sample size nor methodology, reflects the casual approach the news media of 1960 took toward the audience reaction story. Instead of slavishly collecting and reporting survey data, journalists favored random "man-on-the-street" roundups of public opinion. The *Los Angeles Times* published one of the more commendable examples of this genre, devoting a full page to viewer responses the morning after the first debate. Next to each comment, the article featured a photo of the interviewee watching television. A brief introduction stressed that "in this effort to learn what people said and thought during and after the first of the Great Debates, the *Times* deliberately ignored political leaders, candidates, and active party workers."[10]

In years to come this same constituency that the newspaper so assiduously shunned would be dubbed "spinners," and their comments, along with those of the journalists themselves, would dominate the postdebate agenda. Sixteen years after the Kennedy-Nixon series, when TV news had grown up, debate coverage underwent a radical change. Presidential debaters no longer played to win just the audience at home; they played to sway the media as well.

THE BIRTH OF INSTANT ANALYSIS

In a wholly unplanned way, the twenty-seven-minute audio gap that interrupted the first 1976 presidential debate begat the era of punditry that viewers now take for granted. Network anchors and reporters, desperate to plug the hole caused when the sound failed, started their coverage with predictable filler: sketchy statements about the technical problem and cautiously worded, well-balanced summaries of the debate to that point. But as the minutes ticked on, the on-air personnel found themselves drifting further into uncharted waters in an attempt to stay afloat.

A review of NBC's coverage during the audio gap demonstrates the pitfalls of off-the-cuff reporting. A few seconds after the problem arises, David Brinkley comes on-screen to repeat the obvious: The cause of the failure is unknown. After a bit of vamping, Brinkley throws to reporter Douglas Kiker inside the debate hall, and the two of them kill time. Brinkley asks if his colleague has a screwdriver and a pair of pliers, and Kiker launches into a lengthy recap of the debate, which ends when Ford press secretary Ron Nessen steps into the lobby where Kiker is standing. Kiker collars Nessen for an impromptu interview, asking, "How is your guy doing so far?" "It's a clear-cut victory for the president," Nessen says, adding that Ford had come across as "being in command of the situation, being in control." Kiker, trying to soften Nessen's partisan tone, points out that the same could be said of Carter.

Next, Kiker insinuates himself to a nearby interview in progress between CBS's Lesley Stahl and Democratic National Chairman Robert Strauss, who calls it a "good night for the American people and a great night for Jimmy Carter." Kiker listens, then grabs Strauss for himself. A few seconds into the questioning, Kiker gets a cue to return to the candidates. Announcing that the audio is back, he throws to the debate stage, where in fact the problem has not been fixed.

David Brinkley reappears and, continuing to stretch, adds his judgment to that of the campaign managers. Brinkley calls it a "pretty lively debate, each one landing a few blows on the other, though I don't think anyone was permanently disabled, politically speaking." After yet another recap, Brinkley tosses back to Douglas Kiker, who interviews Republican adviser James Baker about Ford's debate preparations. Baker tells Kiker, "I think the president did an excellent job."

Kiker then commandeers Carter press secretary Jody Powell, again away from Lesley Stahl. Kiker follows up Powell's pro-Carter spin by asking if he knows why the microphones went dead. Powell demurs: "I assume it was a technical problem, as sometimes happens." Strangely, Kiker then proceeds to raise the possibility of "a conspiracy at work," telling Powell, "It's been my experience in a situation like this that there's always a theory held by a lot of people that, oh, there was a conspiracy to cut him off. We have no proof of that, it was just simply a technical foul-up as far as we can determine, isn't that correct?" Powell's comeback is biting: "Not only do you have no proof, but nobody's brought up the subject that I know of, have they?"[11]

The 1976 audio gap, with its twenty-seven minutes of ad hoc political spin and reporter commentary, marks a turning point in media coverage of presidential debates. Even without the technical malfunction, however, changes were poised to happen. The networks that had been so averse to postdebate programming in 1960 now inaugurated a tradition from which there would be no retreat: instant analysis.

Roger Mudd of CBS was among the first reporters to offer his opinion when the opening Ford-Carter debate came to an end. "It certainly wasn't the most scintillating television that we've ever witnessed," Mudd declared. "In fact, I think we could honestly call it dull." Though the TV pundits of 1976 were willing to pass general judgments of this sort, they steered clear of outright proclamations of winners and losers. "To some measure," said Walter Cronkite in a characteristically tactful observation, "each probably succeeded."[12]

In the years since the Ford-Carter debates journalists have overcome their shyness about calling victors. With the help of instant polls, on-camera reporters now routinely assess the performances within minutes of the closing statements, and print analysts, like theater critics, rush to write their accounts for the next day's papers. Even though presidential debates are nowhere near as conclusive as football games or beauty pageants or awards shows, the press cannot resist the impulse to attach resolution to conflict, to wrap up the yarn with a definitive ending.

The problem with declaring winners and losers, according to David Broder of the *Washington Post*, is that, more often than not, the outcome is murky. "I thought that Clinton in Richmond was an easy one to be confident about," Broder said, "although by way of self-criticism I did not notice and therefore did not remark upon what everybody remembers from that debate, which was George Bush looking at his watch. That went right by me."[13]

As this comment of Broder's points out, even seasoned journalists can miss things. In his book *Behind the Front Page*, Broder outlined the difficulties of rendering postdebate judgments:

> A reporter has to jump three hurdles to handle the debate assessment well. We are trained to make a balanced judgment, so we score the debate by rounds, as if it were a prize-fight: we say A did well on Points one, four, six and seven, but B probably came out ahead on Points two, three, five and eight. As a result our verdicts tend to be cautious and fuzzy.
>
> Second, being somewhat familiar with the issues, we are inclined to give some weight—perhaps undue weight—to the candidates' accuracy and skill in answering policy questions. Ironically our performance as instant analysts is handicapped by qualities our critics say we lack: a desire to be fair and an interest in substance.
>
> The third point—which took me a long time to understand—is that our overall assessment of the debate must be based on who seems more in command. That is the test. And if you realize that television news shows will quickly capsulize the whole debate into that moment or two when one candidate or the other takes command, your attention can focus on recognizing that moment and can put it into the context of the campaign situation.[14]

Scholars like Diana Carlin have noted that journalists evaluate debates differently from regular viewers. "Many of the people who do the critiquing of debates . . . are far more knowledgeable and involved than the average voter," Carlin said at a debate symposium in 1992. "Most voters are not that intimately involved in the process until the last few weeks. So for most . . . this is the first time they really know what someone's position might be."[15]

The audience's perception of debates as informational would appear to conflict with the criteria by which reporters pass postdebate judgments. As Bob Schieffer, a CBS analyst in every debate series since 1976, explained, "The first thing I always try to do is see if there's any news there. Did one of these candidates say something he hadn't said before? Next you ask, did one guy get the better of the other one, and how's this going to play on the eleven o'clock news, and what impact is it going to have on the campaign?"[16] The general public may watch for information, but journalists watch for different things: departures from the norm and strategic maneuvers.

Critics have long charged reporters with prizing performance over substance. Scholar James B. Lemert found that, in 1976, 38 percent of postdebate journalistic statements about the first two Ford-Carter debates pertained to issues. Four years later that amount dropped by more than half. By 1988 the percentage of content coverage had dipped to less than 10 percent of all the postdebate reporting on television news. Over the same period the number of references to performance and tactics rose dramatically.

Lemert made another interesting observation: In 1976 and 1980 the networks followed the debates with only brief remarks from the anchors, waiting until after the local newscasts had aired to return with full programs of postdebate commentary.[17] More recently an increasing share of follow-up analysis has taken place immediately after the event, giving reporters little or no time to collect thoughts and contemplate judgments before communicating them live on the air. The stepped-up rhythm of modern television demands glib, on-the-spot analysis.

Perhaps the least savory example of postdebate punditry occurred in 1980, when George Will of ABC went on camera after the Reagan-Carter debate and praised Reagan's "thoroughbred performance," neglecting to disclose that he had helped prep the Republican candidate. "Far from resulting in Will's losing his job, the controversy only added to the Willian lore, further blurring the lines between the watchdogs and the watched," wrote media critic Eric Alterman. "By the end of the controversy, Will's political status was so great he was also beyond virtually all accepted journalistic rules and practices."[18] Nearly two decades later George Will remains a high-profile debate commentator.

THE EARLY YEARS OF POSTDEBATE SPIN

In the hours after the first 1960 debate Nixon press secretary Herbert Klein gathered up a handful of aides and made the rounds of Chicago's hotel bars to talk with some of the reporters who had covered the event for the morning papers. "I thought it was highly important to put on a confident front and to find out what they really thought," Klein wrote. "Most of them had concentrated so much on the content of the debate that they offered few opinions on the outcome, and the initial stories generally treated the "joint appearance" with balance."[19] Interestingly Klein and his team made no attempt to directly influence journalistic opinion; by the time the conversations took place, the reporters had already filed their stories.

Compared to today's tarantella of spinning, the political establishment of 1960 exercised admirable restraint in its postevent dealings with the press. Of course the absence of follow-up programming by the TV networks erased the need for on-air spinners. The debate reaction story belonged to newspapers, which focused on matters other than how campaign aides felt their candidates had fared. For the most part the journalists and the handlers maintained a respectful distance from each other.

In the *New York Times*'s morning-after account of the first debate, an unusual sidebar story on page 30 did deal with reactions from the Kennedy and Nixon camps. JFK's brother and campaign manager, Robert F. Kennedy, said that the Kennedy team had been "tremendously pleased," and Nixon press secretary Klein allowed that the vice president "presented the issues, and when he does that he always comes out very well." The story went on to note, "Some Kennedy aides, asking not to be quoted, said they felt their candidate had scored more points and over-all had made the best impression."[20] The air of modesty conveyed in this sentence would soon become a relic of the past.

The candidates themselves offered virtually no comment in the press about their debate performances, leaving behind a woefully slim record for historians. After the first debate Kennedy was quoted only as saying that the exchange had been "very useful." Nixon told reporters, "A debater never knows who wins. That will be decided by the people November eighth. I thought he presented his case very well."[21] Later debates in the 1960 series produced similarly tepid candidate reactions in the media or no reactions at all.

Over the years the public has come to expect its presidential debaters to deliver a pithy postevent sound bite, either at a rally that evening or the next day on the campaign trail. At the end of the first 1996 debate NBC's Tim Russert conducted the fastest postdebate interview in history by nabbing Bill and Hillary Clinton just seconds after the program concluded. Materializing at the apron of the stage, Russert stuck a microphone in the president's face and asked for a self-assessment. "I did the best I could," said the grinning Clinton. Russert then asked the First Lady how the next day's headlines would read. "President outlines his vision for America in the twenty-first century," Mrs. Clinton replied. A few minutes later, Russert returned with quick sound bites from Bob and Elizabeth Dole, though only Elizabeth's made it on the air.[22]

Russert's postdebate floor interviews touched off an angry protest from campaign representatives and competing journalists, who complained that NBC had violated the ground rules—as, in fact, they had. Without permission from the sponsors, technicians had strung an audio cable from backstage to the front of the house, where Russert was seated. Just as the debate went off the air, a crew member hooked up the microphone and handed it to Russert. "In the annals of spin," wrote media critic Howard Kurtz, "this was a new indoor record."[23]

In 1976, when the Ford-Carter audio breakdown prematurely initiated the practice of organized spin, the two campaigns were well positioned to supply representatives to plug the silence. As part of their press strategies, both operations had assigned key individuals to appear on the networks' postdebate specials with the goal of creating a positive buzz. According to Ford press secretary Ron Nessen, Republican aides held a conference call before the debate ended to agree on a "line" they would follow in talking to reporters. "We decided to declare flatly that the president was the clear winner—decisive, specific, in control of the situation and in command of the facts. Our theory was that our own enthusiasm would sway the judgments of voters and press commentators trying to decide who won."[24]

Larry Speakes, press secretary to 1976 Republican vice presidential candidate Bob Dole, deployed a trio of spinners to go on the networks immediately after the Dole-Mondale debate: the candidate's wife, Elizabeth; Texas governor John Connally; and Vice President Nelson Rockefeller. "As the debate ended they were to get out of their front-row seats, go straight to an assigned camera, beating the Mondale aides to the airwaves," Speakes wrote. "Each one claimed debate victory for Dole on each of the three networks, so we had nine at-bats."[25]

Speakes and his team also contrived a made-for-TV telephone call in which President Ford publicly congratulated Bob Dole on his performance. Dole took the call in his backstage holding room, where network cameras had been set up. Ford's side of this staged-managed conversation, heard but not seen by television viewers, is a classic of transparent postdebate spin:

FORD: Bob?

DOLE: Yes, Mr. President?

FORD: You did great. And Betty and I on our anniversary are very,
very grateful for the anniversary present because your performance was superb and we all are applauding and very, very proud of
your accomplishments.

DOLE: Well, I'm very proud of you, Mr. President. I hope I did a good
job. I had a bad cold, but I guess my voice held out long enough.

FORD: You were confident, you hit hard but hit fairly and you differ-
entiated the issues, I think very effectively between their platform
and ours, between our promises and theirs, where we have consistently said that taxes ought to be reduced and they have, as we all
know, played both sides of the street. You've done a fine job in
showing that they're the big spenders and we're the ones that think
we should spend responsibly and effectively.

As Walter Cronkite reported at the end of the exchange, "President Ford,
in congratulating him, got in some more campaign licks of his own
tonight."[26] Meanwhile ABC's Hal Bruno was among the reporters present in
Dole's green room during the call. "They hung up," Bruno recalled, "and
Dole turned to me and said, 'I wonder what *he* was watching.' "[27]

By contemporary standards the spinning in 1976 seems measured, bal-
anced, and lacking in the desperation that makes later political reaction so
excruciating to sit through. Audiences today are accustomed to shameless
ballyhooing by everyone from running mates and spouses to the lowliest
aides. But spinners did not burst onto the scene fully formed; instead,
their profile as players in the postdebate drama has advanced incrementally. "We had three or four people who'd go out and talk to the media
afterward," said Michael Deaver of the campaigns of 1980 and 1984, in
which he served as an aide to Ronald Reagan, "but it was nothing like it is
now."[28]

As early as the Reagan-Mondale debates of 1984 network analysts had
begun to openly disparage spinning, even as they gave it a thorough airing.
NBC's postevent coverage of the 1984 Bush-Ferraro vice presidential debate
featured a three-way interview between Roger Mudd and a handler from
each of the two campaigns that began with Mudd asking his guests to "raise
your right hands and swear to tell the truth, the whole truth, and nothing
but the truth." After dutifully complying, the predictable propaganda kicked
in. At the end of the chat, Mudd said, "I'm going to get indictments of per-
jury on you two guys," and the three shared a laugh, united in appreciation

of the fatuousness of postdebate gamesmanship, yet unable to break themselves of the habit.[29]

THE RISE AND FALL OF THE SPIN DOCTOR

Although the word *spin* appears to have come into common use around 1984, the Bush-Dukakis election of 1988 is generally considered the "year of the spin doctor." Media researcher James Lemert and colleagues found a threefold increase in spin doctor references between 1984 and 1988, the year partisan endorsements reached the level of an art.[30] As Tom Brokaw said on NBC after the 1988 vice presidential debate, "There was so much spinning going on here tonight it's a wonder that the Omaha Civic Auditorium didn't lift off into orbit."[31]

Michael Oreskes, analyzing the trend in the *New York Times*, wrote, after the first 1988 match, that the campaigns "spent almost as much time and effort trying to influence what was said after the debate as they spent deciding what [the candidates] should say in the debate." Oreskes likened the spinners' arrival in the press facility at the end of the program to an "invasion landing force," and added: "A decade ago campaign staff members were evicted from press rooms on occasion for interfering with reporters at work on debate stories. But tonight they were quickly surrounded by reporters, cameramen and photographers recording their views."[32] As Oreskes's comment suggests, the collusionary aspect of postdebate spin is what makes the whole custom so creepy.

Listen to what the journalists themselves have to say: "I think it's a format that we ought to kill off" (Tom Brokaw of NBC); "it's an embarrassing, horrible zoo" (Richard Berke of the *New York Times*); "the spinning has become a self-parody" (CNN political director Tom Hannon); "it's useless, preposterous" (CBS's Bob Schieffer);[33] and so on. Almost to a person, reporters profess disgust at postdebate spin, but in fact the press has allowed the practice to thrive. According to political journalist Roger Simon: "Spin fulfills two essential purposes: It fills stories with official "react," and it is an excuse for reporters to leave home. Consider: Reporters fly hundreds of miles, staying in expensive hotels, eating expense account meals, to watch an event on TV that they could just as easily watch from their newsrooms or at home."[34]

On some level, members of the media regard postdebate spinning as a show staged for their own amusement. The external audience, the public, gets almost nothing out of the spectacle except, perhaps, a perverse strain of secondary entertainment. But postdebate spin is not about the television viewers of America, it is about the cast of characters—the journalists and politicos—who inhabit Spin Alley. "I've never known anybody who in any way was influenced by the spinning," says ABC's Hal Bruno. "It's sort of a ritual that we all do together—it's kind of fun if you don't take it seriously."[35] Unfortunately for viewers, some of the most amusing spin never makes the air waves: In 1988 a Dukakis operative told Jeff Greenfield that Bernard Shaw's "raped and murdered" question had allowed the candidate to "humanize himself" because he had not flinched at the query.[36]

With every election cycle Spin Alley undergoes a population explosion. For the first debate in 1960, 200 reporters were expected at WBBM; 380 showed up, and a second press room had to be installed in an adjacent studio. By the 1980s each presidential debate could expect to draw as many as fifteen hundred accredited journalists. In 1996 that figure topped two thousand. The more reporters, the more spinners; like an arms race, the numbers escalate as each side piles on. "It's always been bad," says Bill Nichols, White House correspondent for *USA Today*, "but I think now it's almost a separate event from the debate itself, with its own separate set of rules and expectations and cliches."[37]

In recent years Spin Alley has gotten so big it has moved out of the debate hall and into an off-site facility. "It's an amazing scene," says Richard Berke of the *New York Times*. "You see five people sitting side by side on stools, each talking to different affiliates and saying the same thing. It's like a factory."[38] With factory expansion has come a stepped-up production timetable. In 1996 Clinton operatives handed journalists in the press center a six-page set of talking points called "Prebuttal: Dole versus the Facts" twenty minutes *before* the first debate began.[39]

To its credit, the elite national press, especially the written press, has largely backed away from covering spinners. According to David Broder of the *Washington Post*: "It's been a problem for us, in fact, to the point that we generally take a copy aide or somebody out just to stand guard and keep people away from the reporters who are writing the debate on the scene. Because the spinners are very aggressive."[40] Some of the TV networks have also banned live political interviews after presidential debates, offering viewers a "spin-free zone" that is long on reporter commentary and short on partisan cheerleading.

As network and print journalists grow more wary of the practice, spin-ners have successfully sought to ply their wares to regional news organiza-tions. "In an era when the national media have become more skeptical in their attitude toward the candidates, technology and the growing appetite of local news is allowing the presidential campaigns to simply bypass them," wrote Thomas Rosenstiel in the *Los Angeles Times* during the 1992 cam-paign.[41] Much of the action has moved to local television newscasts, which remain fertile ground for political spin, particularly from a hometown celebrity like a governor or senator. Before the 1996 San Diego debate Clinton press secretary Mike McCurry had this advice for his troupe of spinners: "The national press, talk to them, but as quickly as you can, get to regional press—that's where you are likely to get more coverage."[42]

In rare instances, when it is used to undo damage incurred during the live broadcast, postdebate spin may actually qualify as news. In the wake of Gerald Ford's verbal slip about Eastern Europe, campaigns learned that a candidate's misstatements must be rectified as hastily as possible. During the first debate of 1988 George Bush implied that women who obtained ille-gal abortions might be considered criminals; the next day campaign man-ager James Baker appeared on the morning news shows to announce that, after reconsidering, Bush did not believe that a woman seeking an abortion should be deemed a criminal. As Brit Hume said on ABC, "This was fast action to head off political trouble, something this campaign is good at."[43]

Handlers face a more daunting hurdle when the task requires putting a good face on a bad performance. In the wake of Ronald Reagan's stumbling loss in the first 1984 debate against Walter Mondale, Baker did a live inter-view with Roger Mudd on NBC in which Mudd suggested that "the presi-dent was off his form . . . At times he seemed to get lost and he was not as sharp as past debate experience would have led us to believe." Baker, with-out missing a beat, replied, "All of us felt unanimously that he was relaxed, confident, in command both of the issues and the debate." Four years later Dan Quayle's abysmal showing in the 1988 vice presidential debate was too much even for the silver-tongued Baker. "When you think about what could have happened," Baker said on CNN, in a remarkably unguarded comment, "we have to be pretty happy."[44]

The campaign documentary *The War Room*, by D. A. Pennebaker and Chris Hegedus, offers a rare behind-the-scenes journey into one of the most impressive of all spin machines, the 1992 Clinton operation. In the film Clinton aide George Stephanopoulos is seen sprinting toward Spin Alley to take part in the postevent feeding frenzy just as one of the TV debates is wrapping up. Poking his head into a backstage staff room, he energetically exhorts aides to remember the party line: "Bush was on the defensive. Keep repeating, 'Bush was on the defensive.' " When Stephanopoulos finally makes his way onto the set and goes on air, the first words out of his mouth are, "Bush was on the defensive all night long."[45]

Shortly after the 1992 election, at a debate postmortem at Harvard University, Stephanopoulos admitted that "one of the lessons we learned from this campaign is that spin after debate doesn't matter because of the preponderance of polling and focus groups." According to Stephanopoulos, the networks' postdebate poll results have impeded campaign efforts to shape the media agenda. In the future, he said, spin "may not matter at all."[46] Even so, given its entrenchment, the custom does not appear likely to go down without a fight.

POSTDEBATE POLLING

The morning after the first Kennedy-Nixon debate the *New York Times* contacted a Mr. and Mrs. John F. Kennedy of Stuyvesant Town, New York City, for their comment on the big event. "What show you talking about?" asked Mrs. Kennedy. "Oh, the television show. We didn't get around to it. We were out visiting."[47] This quote, included in a larger roundup of viewer opinion, typifies the down-home nature of audience-reaction coverage in 1960. Individual reactions counted more than either aggregate numbers or professional pundits.

Press emphasis was not so much on who had won the debate but on whether people had changed their minds. In a *Times* survey of several hundred Americans after the first debate, only one viewer reported shifting his allegiance, a "Negro janitor" in Topeka, Kansas, who went from Nixon to Kennedy. A "Baptist housewife" from Tallahassee, Florida, said, "I just can't bring myself to vote for a Catholic," and a Republican Party worker in Austin, Texas, complained that Nixon had looked "too grim" and that he had been "trying to be too liberal."[48]

In the 1990s audience-reaction stories have come to rely less on quirky individual opinions than on broadly collected scientific data. Like so much in modern politics, viewer response to presidential debates is now a matter for polling. "These instant polls, which have all manner of flaws to them, are very important," says Democratic debate strategist Tom Donilon. Donilon describes the surveys as "pernicious" because of their tendency to create a bandwagon effect among debate analysts. "Watch the postdebate coverage some night," Donilon said. "The commentators will come on and they'll be a little leery about who won. With the instant poll results, the commentators all go the way of the poll. Lock-cinch pattern."[49]

Polls give reporters an opportunity to render win-loss judgments that rise above personal opinion. "Quantifying an ambiguous situation imparts a greater sense of objectivity," explains political scholar Christopher Arterton. Arterton has written that polls serve not the public but "the media's need to reduce uncertainty by using numbers. The goal of debates, after all, is to present a discussion of the issues and the men themselves, not to provoke a discussion of how to win a debate."[50]

The most egregious example of debate polling by the media happened in 1980, when ABC commissioned a telephone survey that immediately became mired in controversy. Viewers were invited to call in and vote for their favorite candidate at fifty cents a pop. Some seven hundred thousand did so, naming Reagan the winner over Carter by a two-to-one margin. Even as ABC disclaimed the poll as "strictly unscientific," results were projected on a map of the United States whose graphics resembled election-night returns.[51]

The next day newspapers reported that the system set up to tally the votes had not properly functioned. As Robert G. Kaiser said in the *Washington Post*, "The lines jammed and clogged, tens or hundreds of thousands of Americans never got through, and some who thought they were registering a pro-Carter sentiment apparently got counted in the Reagan column." Kaiser dismissed the poll as a "nonfunctioning nonsample of nonrepresentative Americans," a sentiment widely shared.[52]

John J. O'Connor, in the *New York Times*, wrote that ABC tellingly opened its postevent coverage not from the debate site "but with a remote pick-up from Bell Laboratories in New Jersey. This above all in electronic coverage: technology marches on."[53] Indeed, ABC's analysis, presented in the *Nightline* time slot and anchored by Ted Koppel, is a singularly silly demonstration of media gimmickry. Throughout the program, in a series of eight updates, Koppel returned to the AT&T operations center in New Jersey where reporter Ron Miller would pull the latest numbers off a machine and announce them on the air. At one point Koppel informed viewers that people in urban areas were having difficulty getting through, adding, "There is the possibility that some of you are trying to stack the deck." The results were being disavowed even as they were being reported.[54]

Hal Bruno, then political director of ABC News, recalled arriving at LaGuardia Airport in New York the morning after the 1980 debate with Barbara Walters, who had moderated the program. When Bruno saw the pack of reporters waiting at the gate, he assumed they wanted to interview Walters. Instead, they were there for Bruno; the phone-in poll had become big news. Looking back on the episode, Bruno admitted, "Sometimes you think you have a good idea, and you don't know what the unforeseen consequences are."[55]

After the pounding ABC took in the press for its 1980 experiment, media polling became more efficient, if only somewhat less whimsical. Among other innovations, news organizations borrowed a survey technique from the campaigns that allowed viewers to indicate their ongoing, real-time debate reactions by pressing buttons on a handheld measuring device. For the second debate of 1988, local station KHQ in Spokane, Washington, pioneered the technique on television, gathering a studio audience of ninety voters and displaying their live reaction by way of a superimposed graph.

CNN adopted the gimmick for its 1992 debate coverage, creating a "living graph" that showed the unfolding responses of uncommitted voters on a moment-to-moment basis. Howard Rosenberg, in the *Los Angeles Times*, called the poll "goofy," and said, "If you thought Perot was sidesplitting, then you should have caught CNN commentator William Schneider trying to explain what it all meant." Four years later NBC carried its own moment-to-moment graph, which *Washington Post* critic Howard Kurtz termed "incomprehensible."[56]

However clumsy, these efforts at postdebate polling at least give the public a voice in the national reaction. To the press's further credit, journalists in recent elections have attempted to go beyond the faceless numbers-crunching of audience surveys and cover presidential debates in a more personal way. The *Washington Post* is one of several news organizations that assembles small groups of debate watchers and sends its reporters to write about them. Still, media accounts of citizen reaction to presidential debates often feel perfunctory, added to the mix in order to mute the louder, more insistent voices of the pundits and the spinners.

Not all audience-reaction stories have been unimaginative. After the first Ford-Carter debate in 1976 NBC reporter Jack Perkins filed an unusual person-on-the-street piece that started at one end of the country and ended at the other. Perkins began his report on the campus of UCLA, where he interviewed a series of students, two of whom confessed to being more confused after the debate than they were before. The crew then hopped a midnight flight heading east from California, recording mid-air debate reactions from fellow passengers and a flight attendant. In Arlington Heights, Illinois, Perkins boarded the 6:42 A.M. commuter train for downtown Chicago, collecting more responses before proceeding to the bluegrass country of Kentucky for interviews with a farmer in his field and a woman in her garden. Perkins ended his cross-country trek soliciting opinions in the New York City subway.[57] If not the most methodologically advanced of audience survey stories, this certainly ranks among the most creative.

KEEPING THE STORY ALIVE: THE EASTERN EUROPE GAFFE

Reporters covering presidential debates pray to the news gods that the encounter will produce a follow-up story that extends into the days beyond. The shelf life of most debates is less than twenty-four hours: recaps later that night in local news programs and network specials, and again on the next day's morning shows and newscasts. Debates then vanish into the mists of history, memorable only if they contain a transcendent clip for the "greatest hits" reel. As with so many big-ticket TV events, like lackluster Super Bowls and long-winded Oscar shows, presidential debates often deliver less than they promise.

In 1960, and again in the first debate of 1976, production problems—Richard Nixon's appearance, the audio gap—dominated postdebate coverage. The first major *performance* story to break from a televised presidential debate was Gerald Ford's Eastern Europe gaffe, committed in the second program of 1976 and kept alive by a combination of Ford's stubborn refusal to retract the misstatement and media insistence on an apology.

In the initial postdebate television coverage, commentators were slow to recognize the error. On CBS, Walter Cronkite's first summation of the event failed to note what *Time* magazine would call "the blooper heard round the world."[58] Harry Reasoner also ignored the issue in his close-of-program remarks on ABC. Only during the later news specials did the subject crop up. CBS diplomatic correspondent Marvin Kalb held that the president's comment would "come as a great surprise to the people in Eastern Europe," and Bob Schieffer called it "a major blunder." David Brinkley of NBC speculated that Ford's "rather curious statement . . . may have been a slip of the tongue. We think he may have meant Western Europe."[59] As Brinkley's line suggests, reporters at this point were more baffled than derisive.

In the next morning's newspapers the story evolved from curiosity to folly. The *New York Times* devoted a front-page sidebar exclusively to Ford's slip of the tongue. The *Boston Globe* quoted exultant Carter aides, one of whom described it as an "incredible statement." A *Washington Post* account included a prescient observation from Hamilton Jordan, Carter's campaign manager, who said of the error, "You will hear a great deal about that in the next few days."[60]

Just as Jordan forecast, within twenty-four hours the story had exploded. The gaffe dominated network newscasts the evening after the debate, leading all three networks. Coverage was extensive, including reaction stories from Eastern European ethnic communities in the United States, as well as response from around the world. Jimmy Carter used the occasion to say his opponent had "disgraced our country," and vice presidential candidate Walter Mondale joked that after the telecast he had gone looking for a Polish bar, certain that drinks would be on the house for Democrats.[61]

The day after the San Francisco debate, Ford embarked on an ill-fated odyssey of clarification that for the better part of a week effectively brought his campaign to a standstill. At an event at the University of Southern California the president offered a lukewarm amendment to his original declaration. "Last night in the debate I spoke of America's firm support for the aspirations for independence of the nations of Eastern Europe," Ford stated, then added that the United States "has never conceded and will never concede their domination by the Soviet Union." As Marilyn Berger said on NBC, "It was a stab at correcting a costly impression."[62]

For the news media, it was also insufficient. Again the next day Ford labored to explain himself, first at a breakfast appearance before business supporters in Los Angeles. Recalling a 1975 trip to Poland, the president said that Polish citizens "don't believe they are going to be forever dominated— if they are—by the Soviet Union. They believe in the independence of that great country and so do I. We're going to make certain, to the best of our ability, that any allegation of dominance is not a fact."

Things got even fuzzier in an impromptu statement to the press a few hours later, just after a midday rally in Glendale. Bizarrely Ford read his explanation into a walkie-talkie, sound from which was transmitted to the press buses via the handlers' walkie-talkies. Speaking in the third person, Ford said, "President Ford does not believe that the Polish people over the long run—whether they are in Poland or whether they are Polish-Americans here—will ever condone domination by a foreign force."[63]

Finally, on October 12, six days after the debate, a chastened Ford flatly admitted, albeit off-camera, that he had made a mistake. In a meeting with ethnic leaders at the White House, the president finally spoke the words the news media had been waiting to hear. "Let me be blunt," he said. "I did not express myself clearly when this question came up in the debate. The countries of Eastern Europe are, of course, dominated by the Soviet Union."[64] The apology was duly reported, and the press moved on to greener pastures.

Why did Ford take so long to perform his ritual act of contrition? According to press secretary Ron Nessen, advisers urged the president the morning after the debate to acknowledge that he had misspoken, but he refused. "I can be very stubborn when I think I'm right," Ford wrote in his memoirs, "and I just didn't want to apologize for something that was a minor mistake."[65]

On the same day he issued his final apology Ford took the press to task in a meeting with New York newspaper and broadcasting executives, lamenting that 90 percent of reporting on the San Francisco debate involved the single remark about Soviet domination. "There was such a concentration on that one point, ignoring virtually everything else, that I think the news media didn't give a full and accurate picture of the substance in many of the questions and many of the answers," Ford said.[66]

What may at first appear to be an effort to shift blame is, on closer inspection, a legitimate complaint. Why should journalists have fixated on Ford's mistake to the exclusion of almost everything else? Why was the president of the United States hounded into issuing an apology when he felt none was required? Is it the proper function of the news media to demand atonement from public figures? As political scientist Thomas Patterson notes: "The candidate usually has no choice but to respond to the press's demands for a mea culpa. The price of silence is crippling news coverage for days on end." Ford aide Richard Cheney described the 1976 incident as a case of reporters extracting their "pound of flesh."[67]

Media coverage of the Ford gaffe offers a case study in the power of the press to alter perceptions. Right after the debate, between eleven at night and one o'clock the next morning, Republican pollster Robert Teeter conducted a poll of viewers who named Ford the winner by a percentage point.

After news reports of the mistake appeared the next day, the surveys began to reflect a downward trend; Teeter's poll showed that 62 percent of those queried between 5:00 P.M. and midnight the day after the debate thought Carter had done the better job, compared to 17 percent for Ford. "Reports of the debate had reemphasized the president as a mistake prone, inept bumbler, exactly what we had spent six or seven weeks trying to get away from," Teeter said.[68]

"The volunteered descriptions of the debate by voters surveyed immediately after the debate included no mentions of Ford's statement on Eastern Europe," wrote researcher Fred Steeper of the Republican study. "Not until the afternoon of the next day did such references appear, and by Thursday night they were the most frequent criticism given of Ford's performance." A voter who participated in a different research study said: "I thought that Ford had won. But the papers say it was Carter. So it must be Carter." As Ford press secretary Ron Nessen put it, "The average guy in his living room watching the debate didn't see the Eastern European comment as a monumental mistake. But after twenty-four hours of being told how bad a mistake it was, people changed their minds."[69]

OTHER POSTDEBATE STORY LINES: THE "AGE ISSUE" AND BEYOND

The first presidential debate of 1984 ignited perhaps the biggest follow-up story in debate history: Was Ronald Reagan competent to lead the country? Like the Ford gaffe, the matter did not fully surface in the program's immediate aftermath. Bruce Morton, on CBS, hinted at a problem, saying that Reagan "floundered" more than usual and appeared "ill at ease." John Chancellor, on NBC, asserted that "the president got very tired at the end and seemed quite disorganized in his closing statements."[70] But none of the analysts came close to questioning Reagan's fitness for office.

Morning-after newspaper accounts also noted President Reagan's tentative delivery without linking the debate to a discussion of jobworthiness. "Mr. Reagan appeared less confident than he customarily does on television," wrote Howell Raines in the *New York Times*, in a typically subdued comment, and Tom Shales in the *Washington Post* joked, "Obviously, it's back to the old briefing books for the Reagan team."[71]

Ronald Reagan's inferior performance did not morph into the "age issue" until two mornings after the debate, when the *Wall Street Journal* ran a story with the headline, "New Question in Race: Is Oldest U.S. President Now Showing His Age?" The article, by Rich Jaroslovsky and James M. Perry, got to the point in its fourth paragraph: "Until Sunday night's debate, age hadn't been much of an issue in the election campaign. That may now be changing. The president's rambling responses and occasional apparent confusion injected an unpredictable new element into the race."

The story went on to quote from a psychologist and Reagan supporter who said: "I'd be concerned to put him into a corporate presidency. I'd be all the more concerned to put him into the U.S. presidency." Democratic congressman Tony Coelho of California told the *Journal*: "He created an issue that has not yet come in this campaign—age. He looked old and acted old." The piece ended with thoughts on how other presidents had aged in office, interviews about the warning signs of senility, and a reminder that candidate Reagan in 1980 had pledged to undergo regular tests for senility if he became president.[72]

The same day the story by Jaroslovsky and Perry ran, the *Washington Post* carried an op-ed column by influential political writer David Broder. Broder also candidly addressed the broader implications of Reagan's performance:

He let the age issue emerge as it had not done in any of his previous campaigns. On the big screen in the press room where I watched the debate, the contrast in physical appearance between Mondale and Reagan was at least as great as the seventeen-year difference in their ages—probably the most startling contrast since that between the healthy John F. Kennedy and the infection-weakened, underweight Richard M. Nixon in the first 1960 debate.[73]

The combination of the *Journal* article and Broder's column seemed to unleash pent-up energy in the press, legitimizing the age issue as fair game for media scrutiny. "It was as if the men and women of the press felt they needed permission before they could truthfully describe what they had seen the night before," wrote media critic Mark Hertsgaard. Hertsgaard castigated journalists for "poaching" off the *Journal* story instead of undertaking their own investigations into Reagan's health.[74]

The same day the newspaper pieces ran, the networks scrambled to air TV versions of the story. "This was one of those rare days in schizophrenic Washington when the whole town seemed to focus on one thing—Ronald

Reagan's age," said Jim Wooten on ABC. Wooten's piece included a series of unflattering shots: a debate sound bite in which Reagan sputtered and stumbled, a clip that showed the president nodding off during an audience with the pope, and an excerpt in which First Lady Nancy Reagan appeared to be prompting her husband in response to a reporter's question.[75]

CBS ran a similar montage, a "worst-of" collection of Reagan bloopers that included some of the same moments ABC had used. As Thomas Rosenstiel wrote in the *Los Angeles Times*: "The abbreviated tape clips had an impact far beyond what they had in their original context. Reagan's debate fumbles in clip form seemed more drastic than they did live during the debate."[76] The networks also brought on doctors and psychiatrists to speak about the effects of aging on mental acuity.

At first the president's vaunted team of public relations experts appeared caught off-guard by the barrage of bad press. "I'll challenge him to an arm-wrestle any time," Reagan told reporters on the day the *Journal* and Broder stories ran, but for once the joke rang hollow.[77] The White House came back the next day with a statement about the president's physical health that said, "Mr. Reagan is a mentally alert, robust man who appears younger that his stated age." Reagan's personal physician, Dr. Donald Ruge, was trotted out to describe his patient as being in "excellent" health, though when asked if Reagan had lost any of his stamina over the past four years, the doctor replied, "I don't know, you have to ask him."[78]

"I wasn't tired," Reagan informed the press corps, and to underscore the point Republican strategists made sure that their candidate was photographed getting out of his limousine at a campaign stop and taking an "impromptu" on-camera stroll. "The White House today did everything but put a Superman cape on President Reagan as it wrestled with questions about his age and fitness," said Tom Brokaw on NBC.[79]

The relentless coverage took an obvious personal toll on Reagan. Displaying an uncharacteristic testiness, the president grumbled about his opponent, "If I had as much makeup on as he did, I'd have looked younger, too." Reagan insisted to reporters that he never wore makeup, even as an actor. This claim prompted a *Los Angeles Times* story that quoted one Hollywood makeup artist as saying Reagan had used cosmetics on TV's *General Electric Theater*, and another from the Warner Brothers film studio who said Reagan avoided makeup in the movies. Mondale himself joined the dialogue, telling a crowd in Pittsburgh, "Mr. President, the problem isn't makeup on the face, it's the makeup on those answers that gave you a problem."[80]

Just as media reaction upended voter opinion after Gerald Ford's Eastern Europe gaffe, so did coverage of the "age issue" realign public thinking about the first 1984 debate. "The initial public response was that Reagan had won; with the passage of time and news media spin, his early victory turned into something approaching a historic defeat," wrote political scientist Austin Ranney. The first poll on ABC, taken during the final minutes of the telecast, had Reagan in the lead by three points. An hour later, after negative reviews came in for the president, the lead had shifted to Mondale by a point. Two days after the debate a CBS News–*New York Times* poll showed an edge for Mondale of forty-nine points. The unceasing media focus on the "age issue" had completely reversed public opinion about who won the match.[81]

The unprecedented drubbing of Dan Quayle in the 1988 debate with Lloyd Bentsen sparked a narrative line that would sustain several days of lively coverage. The specific impetus for the story was Bentsen's "You're no Jack Kennedy" sound bite, an irresistible snippet of videotape that was like catnip to television news producers. As Bob Schieffer predicted on CBS immediately after the broadcast, this was the bite the whole country would see, even those who had not watched the debate. When ABC's *Nightline* came on the air half an hour after the debate, the program opened with the clip. The next day NBC aired the exchange four times on its morning show, and all three major networks repeated it in their evening newscasts.[82]

Intentionally or not, George Bush exacerbated Quayle's problems by not appearing in public with his running mate the day after the debate, as Michael Dukakis did with Lloyd Bentsen. Damage control instead fell to President Reagan, who called Bentsen's line a "cheap shot and unbecoming to a senator of the United States." Quayle himself attempted a belated response to the question about his qualifications for office. "There is no doubt I would maintain and build on the excellent policies of President George Bush," Quayle forcefully declaimed at a rally the next day in Joplin, Missouri.[83]

Meanwhile, in half a dozen postdebate appearances, Bush failed even to mention his running mate, a fact that did not go unnoticed by the press. Two days after the event, reporters were still waiting for Bush to endorse Quayle's performance. Finally the vice president had little choice but to issue a statement of support. Maureen Dowd of the *New York Times* sketched the scene, which took place outside Bush's official Washington residence just after an unrelated press event:

Vice President Bush was walking back up the steps of his home . . . when someone called out a question about Senator Dan Quayle's much-debated performance as his running mate.

Mr. Bush, whose carefully managed campaign avoids press conferences for weeks at a time, spun on his heels and returned to the microphone to defend Senator Quayle in what seemed to be a planned expression of outrage.

"The concept that I see in some of these reports that I am not supportive of Dan Quayle are absolutely ludicrous," he said. "They are ridiculous. He did well in that debate, he has my full support, and he is getting strong support since the debate and before around this country."[84]

The postdebate journey of Dan Quayle then veered off in a new direction. Angry at what he perceived as a lack of support from Bush insiders, Quayle made a display in the press of taking charge of his own fate—and, not coincidentally, seizing control of the narrative. "I got tired of all the publicity," Quayle told ABC's Jackie Judd on board his campaign bus. "I figured it couldn't get any worse, and I was going to take over." Quayle declared that from now on "I'm the person that's going to do the spinning." Bob Schieffer, in a report on CBS, questioned this new tactic: "It was all so unexpected, some wondered if Bush aides had planned the whole thing to show Quayle was his own man."[85]

In a strange way the negative aftermath of the debate seemed to liberate Dan Quayle. As B. Drummond Ayres wrote in the *New York Times*, "Something happened to Dan Quayle in Omaha, or shortly thereafter, something besides that 'You're no Jack Kennedy' verbal leveling administered by Senator Bentsen. Mr. Quayle came away a changed campaigner."[86] At the very least the news media *perceived* him as a changed campaigner. Once he had acted out his little role in the drama and obliged reporters by offering up a fresh angle on the story, Dan Quayle started getting better press.

One week after Quayle's devastation in the 1988 vice presidential debate, Michael Dukakis suffered a mortal blow of his own at the hands of Bernard Shaw. Just as Dan Quayle continued to address the bungled question about qualifications in his postdebate appearances, so did Dukakis take to the air waves to recast his response to Shaw's hypothetical about capital punishment. As both candidates proved, a debater's second crack at a question cannot always undo the original answer.

Several days before Election Day 1988 Dukakis appeared in a CNN interview with Shaw, arranged at the request of Democratic handlers. Early in the exchange, before the anchorman had a chance to mention it, Dukakis brought up the notorious opening volley. Assuring Shaw that the question had been fair and reasonable, Dukakis added that he had been thinking about his response and how he might better have stated it.

DUKAKIS: Let me just say this: Kitty is probably the most—*is* the most—precious thing, she and my family, that I have in this world. And obviously, if what happened to her was the kind of thing that you described, I would have the same feelings as any loving husband and father.

SHAW: Would you kill him?

DUKAKIS: I think I would have that kind of emotion. On the other hand, this is not a country where we glorify vengeance.[87]

As journalist Roger Simon observed, "This is what campaigning had come down to. Anyone who wanted to be the leader of a great nation and do great things . . . had to show emotion. And in order to be likable, he had to tell people that, yes, he would want to take a human life."[88]

We conclude our survey of postdebate media coverage with two tempest-in-a-teapot incidents that spawned a flurry of tongue-in-cheek reporting: President Carter's reference during the 1980 debate to his daughter, Amy, and Vice President Bush's assertion after the 1984 Ferraro match that he had "kicked a little ass."

The so-called Amy gaffe, in which Carter recounted a conversation with his daughter on the topic of nuclear weapons, provoked an immediate wave of ridicule in the media. In ABC's postdebate special Barbara Walters, who had moderated the debate, named Amy the winner of the match, and said, "I'm going home to my child, who's the same age as Amy, and if she doesn't tell me that nuclear proliferation is the major concern on her mind, she's going to hear it from her mother." Former secretary of state Henry Kissinger told a reporter, "I gag at that kind of stuff in general, although I like Amy."[89]

The next day ABC reporter Bettina Gregory turned up at Amy's school in Washington and conducted an ambush interview with the thirteen-year-old First Daughter. Amy confirmed to Gregory and several other reporters that she and her father had discussed nuclear war. From there, the conversation degenerated:

REPORTER: Does he talk to you often about your opinions?
AMY: Yeah.
REPORTER: What else is important?
AMY: I don't know.
REPORTER: Were you surprised to hear him mention that he had talked to you about it in the speech?
AMY: Yeah, kind of.[90]

Four years later, in the George Bush episode, it was an indiscreet remark to a group of New Jersey longshoremen that got the media clucking. "We tried to kick a little ass last night," Bush told the dockworkers the morning after the 1984 vice presidential debate, just in time to notice that a sound man from a local TV station was standing nearby with a boom microphone. "Whoops—oh, God, he heard me!" Bush cried, then implored the news crew to "turn that thing off." As the *Washington Post* pointed out, "Minutes earlier, Bush had described Ferraro to reporters as 'gracious' and declined to declare himself the winner."

After videotape of the putdown was made available to journalists, Bush called a news conference to extinguish the media brush fire. The vice president defended his comment as an "old Texas football expression," adding that he had no intention of apologizing. "I stand behind it, I use it all the time," he said. "My kids use it, everybody who competes in sports uses it. I just don't like to use it in public." The story led two of the network newscasts and ran prominently in the next morning's newspapers, though the *New York Times* primly identified the phrase only as a "locker room vulgarity." In an interview on NBC, Ferraro told Tom Brokaw, "I think Mr. Bush was about as accurate in his assessment of the result of the debate as he was in the facts and figures he put forth during the debate."[91]

Bush never did apologize, but in the context of other anti-Ferraro rumblings from the Republican camp, the slur seemed curiously ill-advised. *Time* magazine called it "one of the silliest blunders of the campaign,"[92] as it most certainly was. What *Time* failed to add is that for the news media silly blunders are manna from heaven.

Chapter Eight

THE AUDIENCE

*T*he one undisputed fact about presidential debates is their popularity. From the outset the public has shown a willingness, even an eagerness, to sit up and pay attention to these programs. The 70 million Americans who watched the first Kennedy-Nixon broadcast inaugurated a tradition of high viewership that continues today.[1] In the face of declining voter turnout at the polls, audiences for debates between presidential candidates have remained enormous.

The single meeting between President Jimmy Carter and challenger Ronald Reagan in 1980 drew more than 100 million people, making this the most-watched presidential debate—and one of the most-watched television shows—of all time. The second highest-rated debate, the final match between Clinton, Bush, and Perot in 1992, attracted at least 90 million. More typically debate viewership ranges in size from 60 to 80 million for appearances between presidential candidates, 30 to 50 million for vice presidential nominees.[2]

By any standard the ratings are extraordinary. To understand the significance of these numbers, it is useful to compare debates to other productions on the list of top-ranked TV programs. Traditionally the two highest-rated shows of any year are the Super Bowl and the Academy Awards. Super Bowl audiences regularly surpass the 100-million mark, and Oscar telecasts pull in 70 to 80 million, roughly the same number who see a presidential debate.[3]

Debate viewership correlates to another type of programming on the most-watched list: special episodes of TV series and miniseries. In this category, the final broadcast of *M*A*S*H** (1983) holds the ratings record of 125 million people, followed by 99 million for the two-hour conclusion of *Roots* (1977), and 83 million for the "Who Shot J.R.?" installment of *Dallas* (1980).[4] More recently the farewell episode of NBC's *Seinfeld* (1998) reached 76 million people, slightly fewer than the 80 million who saw the finale of *Cheers* (1993).[5]

This roster of television's highest-rated shows spans a wide range of programming, and viewers may be attracted for any number of reasons. But particularly among the live telecasts, common bonds exist: big stars, high stakes, competition, spontaneity, and hype. To one degree or another, presidential debates borrow these ingredients from the sports spectaculars and entertainment extravaganzas and refashion them into a political program that is sui generis. In this unique hybrid of show biz and civics, audiences find a TV genre that effectively mixes entertainment with information.

To what can we attribute the staggering popularity of presidential debates? Why, in an age of apathy and cynicism toward politics, do viewers continue to tune in? What are the benefits and limitations of these programs? And what influence, if any, do they have on voter decision making? Let us explore the relationship of debates to the people who watch them.

THE DRAMATIC APPEAL OF TV DEBATES

Presidential debates represent a highly personal transaction between candidates and voters—or, to view it another way, between stars and an audience. A debate is human drama at its rawest: the obvious drama between the participants onstage but also the more subtle and complex drama that unfolds between presidential contenders and the citizens passing judgment on them. *New York Times* columnist William Safire has called presidential debates "political-emotional events . . . great moments in American life when the nation comes together to share an experience neither frightening nor artificial."[6]

It is the visceral nature of these programs that sets them apart from other highly watched television shows. Debates, says Walter Mondale, "go to this mysterious, primal question of who's ready to be president, who's presidential, who's got stature. That is not a technical question; it's a deep, emotional issue." Mondale believes that debates appeal to the public because they exist in a "kind of environment that people remember: combat. It's not giving a speech. This was real war, and people find it credible."[7]

Live televised debates teem with dramatic conflict: interpersonal conflict between candidates; intrapersonal conflict within a debater's psyche; the conflicts between expectation and performance, preparation and spontaneity. These juxtapositions make irresistible TV, for conflict is the engine that propels all narrative, be it political, journalistic, dramatic, or athletic. Television, with its hunger for personalities and its compulsion to reduce abstractions to particularities, is especially well suited to the mano-a-mano clash of presidential debates.

"Straight exposition in any form is always the most difficult way to engage and hold the attention of anyone," wrote CBS's Frank Stanton after the Kennedy-Nixon debates. "Conflict, on the other hand, in ideas as in action, is intriguing and engrossing to great numbers of people. Drama has always got more attention than essays."[8] As Stanton's comment suggests, debates entice audiences because they are formatted as duels. No other televised political encounter presents such a strong structural incentive to watch.

Conflict that is live and unedited further compels viewership, for, by definition, live events are fragile events. In this sense, presidential debates parallel other high-power "event programming" like the Super Bowl or the Academy Awards or the Miss America Pageant: All are shows whose ending cannot be scripted in advance. In each case, audiences watch in the knowledge that vast stretches of boredom await; still, right up until the final second, some unforeseen plot twist could come rocketing off the screen to justify the investment of time.

As live television, presidential debates are a good example of the contradiction being contained within itself: These are simultaneously the most unpredictable and most ritualized of events. No matter what protective measures the campaigns take, a televised debate cannot be completely domesticated. At a time when the race for the White House has become ever more sanitized and risk-averse, presidential debates represent a rare walk on the wild side.

Before the 1992 joint appearances, *New York Times* TV critic Walter Goodman wrote, "In a season of set pieces, a television debate could offer one of the few hopes of unprogrammed revelation."[9] If we accept the analogy of presidential debates as job interviews, the question of the "unprogrammed revelation" becomes all the more significant. As in any job interview, what is most interesting is not the applicant's carefully practiced facade but the reality lurking behind the mask.

Beginning with the first Kennedy-Nixon broadcast in 1960, debates have had a way of delivering inadvertent messages to the audience, providing viewers with insights both large and small. As *Saturday Review* editor Norman Cousins observed after the 1976 forums,

> No amount of TV makeup can change the way a man's eyes move, or the way his lips are drawn under surges of animus or temper. When the camera burrows into a man's face, the fact that some wrinkles may be covered up by pancake makeup is not so important as the visibility of the emotions that come to the surface. The strength of the TV debates derives less from what is hidden than from what is impossible to conceal.[10]

Richard Nixon could not conceal the fact that he was uncomfortable in his own skin. Jimmy Carter and Gerald Ford could not conceal their inflexibility when faced with an unexpected turn of events. Ronald Reagan could not conceal his befuddlement in the Louisville debate with Walter Mondale. George Bush could not conceal his patronizing attitude toward Geraldine Ferraro. Michael Dukakis could not conceal his lack of empathy. Dan Quayle could not conceal an inferior intellect. The list goes on. In each situation the inadvertent message shines through, contributing to our understanding of the debaters as human beings.

Do such unplanned episodes give voters legitimate reasons to accept or reject a particular candidate as president? Generally not, though the most sobering instance—Reagan's addled performance in the opening match of 1984—presents a possible exception. That debate, remarkable for the degree to which it diverged from the preordained script, alerted the public to an issue the Washington press corps had neglected to report. If only momentarily, the significance of this data caused voters to question Reagan's fitness for the job.

In retrospect, one wonders if the message of the first 1984 debate ought not to have been more closely heeded, by both the media and the public. Charles P. Pierce, a journalist who began writing about Alzheimer's disease when it struck his father, is one of many observers who see evidence in Reagan's performance of the illness that would not be officially acknowledged until 1994. Early Alzheimer's patients, Pierce said, "can waver between clarity and startling blankness," remembering events from the distant past, but not what happened yesterday. "That night in Louisville, Reagan passed in and out of himself, like a broadcast signal filtered through mountains," Pierce wrote in an essay for the *Boston Globe* fifteen years after the debate. "He was lucky none of the panelists asked him where he was."[11]

If the images emanating from the screen in 1984 were trying to tell the audience that its leader was in an early stage of mental decline, then TV debates were doing their job, even if the news did not fully sink in. Although it is important not to overconclude from presidential debates, inadvertent signals deserve to be listened to, particularly in a campaign environment dominated by manufactured messages and masked realities. At their best, debates reflect what Walter Lippmann called television's capacity to serve as a "truth machine";[12] viewers who pay close attention are bound to spot the chinks in a candidate's armor.

Reagan's performance in the first 1984 appearance with Mondale is history's most stunning example of debates as purveyors of unintended truths. But a less-pronounced television moment also stands out from that same program. At the end of closing statements, as soon as the moderator adjourned, Joan Mondale and her children swarmed onstage to offer their husband and father some obviously affectionate support. The shot also illustrated that not a single one of the Reagan children had bothered to show up.

In this instance, live television vividly communicated a subtle but significant difference between Mondale and Reagan, one that overrode weeks of meticulous planning. The visual message at the end of that first debate gave contrasting glimpses into the private lives of the two candidates, and the observant voter gained a nugget of information about Reagan that his handlers would just as soon have kept under wraps. Four days later, in the Bush-Ferraro debate, campaign officials made sure that the family of George Bush was on hand to strike an appropriately domestic tableau. When Reagan and Mondale returned for their follow-up encounter, the president's son and daughter-in-law performed a similar function, Ron Junior locking his father in a conspicuous postdebate hug.

The best-known inadvertent message in recent years came during the Richmond town hall meeting of 1992, when George Bush got caught stealing a glance at his wristwatch. To many viewers Bush appeared bored, eager for the ordeal to be over. Jeff Greenfield, in ABC's postdebate analysis, said the president looked "as though he had some place more important to go."[13] On the next day's newscasts, shots of Bush peeking at his watch were "replayed like debate sound bites," in the words of CBS reporter Mark Phillips, whose own story made use of the images.[14] Republican handlers attempted to contain the damage by explaining that Bush had been checking to see if his opponents were running past their allotted time. But viewers and the media had perceived something else.

Moments like this bust through the veneer of campaign control much as Toto pulls back the curtain to reveal the Wizard of Oz. In a live debate, no matter how the deck has been stacked, little arrows of verisimilitude manage to shoot out of the screen and into the living rooms of America. Lawrence E. Spivak, the creator and for many years host of NBC's *Meet the Press*, came to honor TV's ability to act as a magnifying glass. "Television has an awesome facility for showing up sincerity as well as insincerity," Spivak said. "So if a man is honest and knows his stuff, he'll emerge with his proper stature. By the same token, so will a phony."[15] Apply this scrutiny to candidates over the length of a ninety-minute debate, and audiences cannot help but acquire valuable information.

Another, less high-minded explanation for the high ratings of presidential debates merits passing mention. Viewers may tune in for voyeuristic reasons; there is, after all, a certain sadistic pleasure to be taken from watching fellow human beings, politicians in particular, operating under the gun. Journalist Valerie Helmbreck, who has regularly covered the Miss America pageant, makes a connection between beauty pageants and debates. "What both things are about," she says, "is seeing how poised people can look in a ridiculous situation."[16] Helmbreck's analogy stands to reason: The sheer audacity of debates, their high-wire daring, virtually defies the public not to tune in.

BENEFITS OF PRESIDENTIAL DEBATES

An underappreciated attribute of televised debates is their insulation from the financial machinery that drives most contemporary electoral politics. Debates are the only event on the presidential campaign schedule untainted by money. They exist outside the whirl of fund-raising and paid political announcements that characterizes the day-to-day pursuit of the White House. No infusion of cash can upgrade a candidate's performance; no deep-pocket donation can buy a more favorable set of ground rules. By any index, presidential debates are financially incorruptible.

In this sense they pose a striking contrast to campaign commercials. With political advertising a candidate is able to raise his profile only by spending more; debates are a meritocracy in which each participant has an equal opportunity to reach the audience and present a case. Messages in campaign ads must be stated in less than thirty seconds and are selected by the political pros; debates allow for a more thorough discourse on topics chosen by voters and the press. Most important, disembodied advertisements encourage negative campaigning, while face-to-face debates raise accountability among office seekers. A candidate making a claim against his opponent in a presidential debate must do so personally, as the entire nation looks on. Inevitably the dynamic is more tempered than the nasty tone that prevails in political commercials.

For the networks, too, presidential debates represent an uncommon departure from the usual bottom-line mentality—"television's best chance to make up for its many failed opportunities," in the view of critic Walter Goodman.[17] Unlike other "event programming"—athletic contests, entertainment specials, and awards shows—debates are not given over to advertising. Far from generating revenue, they cut into profits, especially for the pool network that must absorb the expense of putting the telecast on the air.

Consciously or not, these distinctions enhance the standing of presidential debates with the public. Alone among television spectaculars, debates carry an aura of civic virtue. Without the participation of the citizenry these events are meaningless, which distinguishes them from football games, where professional athletes determine the outcome, or the Oscars, which are voted on exclusively by members of the motion picture industry. In a presidential debate the folks at home decide who takes home the prize. As an Arizona man said in a focus group study, "I think debates are one of the good old American ways to do it."[18]

Communications scholar Robert G. Meadow has written that debates "offer the viewers a chance to observe 'history,' be it the event itself as history or the possibility that a candidate will make a verbal error, stumble, or otherwise appear less than presidential."[19] To pass up such an occasion is to deprive oneself of both entertainment and duty. Debates provide a sense of connectedness, granting individual viewers a voice in the collective discourse. In contemporary America, to miss a presidential debate is a violation of the societal norm.

In a discussion on PBS's *News Hour* during the 1996 campaign, political scientist Thomas Patterson spoke of the meaning of presidential debates to the American public. By getting people interested in the election, he said, debates extend their influence well beyond the ninety minutes in which they take place. According to Patterson,

> I think you could even argue that the '92 debates saved the campaign. In September Americans were very soured on the campaign, and Perot's reentry into the race perked the campaign up a bit—and then the four debates in October. By the end of October people were into the campaign and we had a 5 percent increase in voter turnout. I think in terms of connecting the American public to the campaign, the debates are probably the central event.[20]

For most Americans debates are also informative. Political scientist Doris Graber says that presidential debates serve as a "last-minute cram session for preparing the voting public,"[21] a point reinforced by other researchers. Whereas journalists may scrutinize debates for headlines, vast numbers of citizens are getting their first exposure to the candidates' stands on the issues. "The ability of viewers to comment sensibly on the candidates and their stands on issues increases with debates," wrote communication scholars Jamieson and Birdsell. The professors describe the educational impact of debates as "surprisingly wide," cutting across differences of class, race, income, and educational level.[22]

When a debate series is exceptionally audience-friendly, like the Bush-Clinton-Perot programs of 1992, learning seems to increase. In a survey by the Times-Mirror Center for the People and the Press, 70 percent of respondents said that the 1992 debates had been helpful in deciding who to vote for. Four years earlier, in a similar poll taken the weekend of the election, only 48 percent rated the debates as helpful. Furthermore, said Center director Andy Kohut, "While the public credits the debates as being helpful in making a choice among candidates, the polling also suggests that the debates served to focus public attention on a number of important national issues."[23]

Debates provide the electorate with another benefit: they preview how a candidate is likely to communicate with the nation on television. The morning of the first Clinton-Dole debate in 1996, ABC's Cokie Roberts pointed out the importance of TV skills in a would-be chief executive: "This man might be called upon to ask us to send our children to war. He certainly will ask you to send our dollars to Washington. He will do it through the medium of television and we have to be able to believe him there and respond to him there."[24] In other words, at the same time they elect a chief executive, Americans are also electing a chief television personality. For the next four to eight years one of the individuals occupying the debate stage will lead the national colloquy. Although a debate may not foreshadow precisely how a president will talk to the people, it is among the best guides they have.

The public seems to appreciate this chance to examine candidates with the usual filters removed. At least for the duration of the live event, viewers can apply their own criteria and reach their own decisions about the individuals seeking office. The protective layers in which presidential contenders so carefully wrap themselves fall away, if only fleetingly. Handlers and journalists step aside, and the conversation becomes what it ought to be: a dialogue between candidates and the voters.

According to Diana Carlin, a University of Kansas professor who has conducted extensive research on debate audiences, joint appearances between presidential nominees offer several key advantages to viewers. First, debates present an opportunity for voters to measure the candidates side by side. Second, because debaters answer the same set of questions, comparisons on positions can be easily drawn. Third, viewers can assess the candidates' statements in an overall context, not as a disparate collection of media-selected sound bites.[25] On all these points, the body politic exhibits its understanding of presidential debates as programming that requires the audience's active engagement.

"One thing the debates do is put the candidates on an equal plane," a Texas woman told one of Carlin's 1992 focus groups. "They are right there. Both of them together at the same time, same situation, with the same questions."[26] In the absence of face-to-face contact between candidates and voters, TV debates serve as a substitute mechanism for rendering judgments. They allow the audience to evaluate not just statements but also non-verbal signals—the facial expressions and body language that lawyers call "demeanor evidence."

As communication professor Goodwin Berquist has observed: "What Americans feel confident in doing, what each of us does day-in and day-out, in both face-to-face and televised encounters, is to size up the quality of a stranger. . . . The miracle of television makes it possible for each of us to draw our own conclusions in the privacy of our living rooms."[27]

LIMITATIONS OF PRESIDENTIAL DEBATES

Do presidential debates make a valuable contribution to voter enlightenment, or do they reduce the campaign to a political beauty contest? From 1960 on, observers have criticized TV debates for putting image before issues, style ahead of substance. The genre has been dismissed as contrived, counterfeit, even countereducational.

The objections coalesce around several points. After the Kennedy-Nixon telecasts historians derided debates on conceptual grounds, defining them as fundamentally flawed both in structure and objective. Henry Steele Commager, in a widely circulated magazine piece that ran just before the 1960 election, argued that America's greatest presidents—George Washington, Thomas Jefferson, Abraham Lincoln, and Woodrow Wilson— would all have lost TV debates. Commager condemned the programs for prizing "the glib, the evasive, the dogmatic, the melodramatic" over "the sincere, the judicious, the sober, the honest in political discussion."

Like other critics, Commager feared that the institutional strictures of television made political debates not just ineffective but downright disinformational. The process, he wrote, "encourages the American public to believe that there are no questions, no issues before us that are so difficult that they cannot be disposed of in two or three minutes of off-the-cuff comment." Television itself was not to blame for this failing, Commager wrote. "It would be imbecility not to take full advantage of television in this and future campaigns. The trouble is that we are not taking advantage of it at all, but permitting it to take advantage of us."[28]

In his 1962 classic, *The Image*, historian Daniel Boorstin stepped up the reproach, calling the Kennedy-Nixon debates "remarkably successful in reducing great national issues to trivial dimensions." Boorstin cited presidential debates as a "clinical example" of his new coinage, the "pseudo-event":

Pseudo-events thus lead to emphasis on pseudo-qualifications. Again the self-fulfilling prophecy. If we test presidential candidates by their talents on TV quiz performances, we will, of course, choose presidents for precisely these qualifications. In a democracy, reality tends to conform to the pseudo-event. Nature imitates art.[29]

To some extent, the damning of presidential debates by both Commager and Boorstin reflects the fears of an era now passed. Television in 1960 was far less a medium of information than a medium of entertainment; much of the early trepidation stems from the very real concern that the values of commercial TV would infect those of electoral politics. This is, of course, exactly what has happened, and presidential debates had a hand in facilitating the shift.

Harvey Wheeler, another critic of the 1960 debates, worried that John Kennedy's physical attractiveness—his resemblance to "a composite picture of all the good stereotypes television has created"—may have unduly influenced audience reaction. Wheeler cautioned that a potentially dangerous dynamic could develop in presidential debates, with television viewers swayed by "invisible visual values" that preempted their conscious desires. "It seems likely that in the future one of the tests of a candidate's 'availability' for political nomination will be his correspondence with the then current image of the good guy," Wheeler wrote.[30]

After four decades Wheeler's prophecy has not come to pass; nonetheless the warning merits consideration. By substituting televisual talent for facial attractiveness, we can argue that debate audiences may indeed be responding to a set of "invisible values," imposed by the institution of television and bearing more on stylistic fluency than intellect. Don Hewitt of CBS, who produced and directed history's first debate, began almost immediately to question the value of the matches, wondering if too much emphasis had been placed on performing ability. "When it was over, I remember thinking there's something wrong here," Hewitt recalled. "We may have made the right choice, but it worried me that it might have been for the wrong reasons. We were electing a matinee idol."[31]

Critics of presidential debates have long bemoaned TV's weakness for glittering personalities. Not surprisingly Richard Nixon added his voice to this chorus, writing, after the Ford-Carter debates in 1976, "I doubt that they can ever serve a responsible role in defining the issues of a presidential campaign. Because of the nature of the medium, there will inevitably be a greater premium on showmanship than on statesmanship."[32] Nixon might have agreed with the assessment of Sidney Kraus, one of the first communication scholars to study presidential debates seriously, who concluded that "Americans are fans who want to be entertained."[33]

Undoubtedly candidates who play well on TV hold an advantage in the high-performance world of live televised debates. Kennedy proved this, as did Reagan and Clinton. In each case, superior performing skills strongly accrued to the individual's benefit. But telegenic gifts in themselves may not be enough to satisfy a debate audience.

An interesting case study in this regard is Ross Perot, who in 1992 demonstrated the pros and cons of coming across as a colorful character. Perot's initial appearance in the three-way debates with Clinton and Bush brought something revolutionary to presidential debates: an endearing, and genuine, sense of humor. But audience surveys found that even as viewers responded favorably to the comic relief, they also dismissed Perot as shallow. It is possible, in other words, for a debater to be entertaining and unpersuasive at the same time.

Still, one wonders how a charismatic candidate without Perot's negative baggage might fare in a presidential debate. Could a more polished practitioner of the television arts, someone who better understood the principles of pacing and novelty and drama, use these skills to win a debate on superficial criteria? In a close election, could the scales tip in favor of the candidate who puts on the more convincing show? Might a candidate who is trailing in the polls misappropriate the innate instability of a live debate to advance his cause?

Among the skeptics who have raised doubts about debates is veteran Washington journalist Elizabeth Drew. During the campaign of 1992, Drew wrote:

Debates are of mixed value to the process of picking a president. While they do give the country a sustained look at the candidates, debates—and the media's interpretations of them afterward—tend to reward wrong, or irrelevant, qualifications. A gaffe can decide the presidency. The talents called forth—being quick on one's feet, memorizing the better responses, hiring the better writer of one-liners—have little to do with what we need in a president. The media tend to turn the things into sports events—stressing who won or who threw the most potent punch (which is often the best one-liner). The debates are measured by their entertainment value.[34]

Drew calls debates a "false test" for the presidency,[35] an opinion widely shared by critics. As academic researcher Stephen Mills noted, "Debating requires brevity, consistency, extensive briefing, and constant rebuttal of the opponent. Governing requires more time, perhaps some inconsistency, improvisation, and compromise with opponents." Mills is one of a number of analysts to point out the mistaken emphasis that debates place on *individual* performance, a structure at odds with the collegial functioning of the executive branch. "Governing requires skillful management of a team of advisers," he wrote. "Debating, in contrast, focuses on the presidential candidates in isolation."[36]

The argument that debates have limited relevance to the presidency has not been lost on the political professionals. After Ronald Reagan's debacle in the first debate of 1984, Republican strategist Lee Atwater devised a preemptive plan in case Reagan went on to a second flop. In an internal memo known as "The Great American Fog Machine," Atwater proposed a series of alibis to be repeated to the media in the event of another Reagan disaster: "TV debates are artificially contrived 'pressure cookers' which do not coincide with the actual pressures that confront a president"; "there is something fundamentally degrading about the entire process"; "most if not all civilized nations managed to select their leaders without subjecting them to this bizarre ritual";[37] and so on.

Because the age joke put Reagan back on track in the second debate, Atwater's strategy never saw the light of day. As long as the "bizarre ritual" of presidential debates did not harm the candidate, it would be allowed to endure.

THE INFLUENCE OF DEBATES ON VOTING

"Debates are to elections what treaties are to wars," says political scientist and Democratic debate adviser Samuel Popkin. "They ratify what has already been accomplished on the battlefield."[38] After forty years of analysis experts agree that joint candidate appearances move perceptions more than votes. Evidence from countless academic studies and political surveys indicates that, despite their high profile, presidential debates are but one of many factors considered at the ballot box. To further muddy the question, it is virtually impossible to isolate debates from other influences on voters' decisions.

The mythos of presidential debates would have us believe that Kennedy won the 1960 election because he looked better on TV than Nixon; that Ford's Eastern Europe gaffe cost him the White House in 1976; that Reagan's "there you go again" was the coup de grace that finished the Carter presidency. As with most legends, these assertions reflect at least a kernel of truth. But contrary examples make the opposite case.

In 1984 an exceptionally bad debate did not stop Ronald Reagan's electoral landslide, while an exceptionally good one did not help Walter Mondale. If debates were determinative, Reagan's wobbly performance in Louisville ought to have inflicted more damage. Vice presidential debates appear to have even less of an effect. According to Dukakis campaign manager Susan Estrich, Lloyd Bentsen's victory over Dan Quayle, as conclusive a triumph as general election debates have ever known, bestowed only a slight, temporary bump in the polls. "Quayle's performance that night was nothing you would want to show in his library," Estrich said, "but it didn't hurt George Bush very much."[39]

Debate scholars Lanoue and Schrott have observed that the scheduling of presidential debates relatively late in the campaign means that most members of the viewing audience come to the programs predisposed in their preferences:

> Clearly a majority of those watching any given presidential debate have already decided how they are going to vote in November. It is quite possible, therefore, that they tune in to political debates for the drama of the live confrontation between two celebrities rather than for education or guidance.[40]

It speaks well of the audience's common sense that although debates have been highly watched, they have not been excessively influential. Voters regard live TV debates as only one device for evaluating candidates—and an imperfect one at that. After nearly forty years' experience watching presidential debates, Americans seem to have reached a fairly sophisticated understanding of what the programs can and cannot do.

With each new series of presidential debates, the electorate's frame of reference expands. Increasingly viewers recognize the coaching, the planted one-liners, the jockeying for position, and the expectations-setting that color the televised encounters. Audiences for the Kennedy-Nixon broadcasts approached the "Great Debates" with few preconceptions; today's public watches with a more solid understanding of the tactical considerations at play.

Researcher Diana Carlin has found recent audiences to be "incredibly" aware of the artifice of debates, and equally quick to dismiss it. "We often misjudge what the general public does and doesn't understand, or why they are or aren't interested, and we often attribute motives that are very different from reality," Carlin said. "They're on to the sound bites, they're on to when candidates are avoiding, they're on to strategies."[41]

Amid so many mixed signals, one solid conclusion can be drawn about debate viewers: They are as unpredictable as the programs themselves. To the chagrin of political strategists, conventional wisdom formed in one debate season cannot accurately foretell what will happen in the next. It used to be believed that the first debate of a series generated the highest ratings, but the 1992 programs proved that theory wrong. Image was once thought to carry more weight with viewers than issues, but contradictory research has indicated otherwise. Audience effects are difficult to establish with any certainty because public reaction is not fixed; at best, the lessons lack definition.

"Perhaps we have not yet witnessed enough presidential debates to determine which are the rules and which are the exceptions," wrote Lanoue and Schrott in the wake of the 1988 election, and, after two additional debate series, the statement remains valid. "Perhaps viewers' reactions to each individual encounter are more idiosyncratic than we would like to think."[42] If so, the audience may once again be demonstrating its wisdom. For an idiosyncratic response keeps candidates on their toes—and vests the power of presidential debates with the people.

Conclusion

THE FUTURE OF PRESIDENTIAL DEBATES

*I*n a study of the 1960 and 1976 debates, political communication researchers Marilyn Jackson-Beeck and Robert G. Meadow identified the "triple agenda" of presidential debates: the conflicting constituencies of campaigns, journalists, and the public that these programs are called on to serve. "It is possible for all three parties to the debates to be concerned with entirely different issues," the professors wrote, "while engaging in what would seem to be trialogue." Jackson-Beeck and Meadow concluded that in this three-way division of interests, it was candidates who derived the greatest benefit.[1]

Today, after a nearly forty-year tradition of presidential debates, candidates still hold the upper hand. By controlling every important aspect of debates, the political pros exercise their muscle in ways that run contrary to the ideals of participatory democracy. "Whose campaign is it?" asked David Broder at a 1990 symposium on presidential debates. "We have accepted, I think, far too passively the notion that it is up to the candidates and their advisers to determine what takes place and what's talked about and how it's talked about in a presidential campaign. This campaign belongs to the public."[2]

From Kennedy-Nixon to Clinton-Dole, political handlers have staked out debates as their exclusive territory—and have protected their interests accordingly. This has been a defining characteristic, perhaps *the* defining characteristic, of the staging of televised presidential debates. But as the institution matures, changes are at hand. With debates gaining status as a public entitlement, and with media technologies promising greater audience interactivity, the power equation of the triple agenda may be due for a realignment.

Let us close our analysis of presidential debates by looking at each of the three constituencies and examining how the role of these debates is evolving as they enter their fifth decade.

THE CANDIDATES

After so many years in the driver's seat, is it unrealistic to expect the politicos to loosen their grip on the wheel? On some level they may have no alternative. Already the critical question of candidate participation in presidential debates appears to have slipped from the jurisdiction of the campaigns. A strong case can be made that voters and journalists consider themselves "owed" joint appearances, that taking part is no longer a candidate's option. Although debates may not be 100 percent institutionalized, demand by the public and the media seems likely to ensure their longevity.

Another hopeful sign, one underreported in the press, came in June 1992 when the Clinton campaign broke precedent and accepted the debate commission's proposal for that year's candidate forums several months in advance. No previous presidential contender had ever seen fit to entrust debate arrangements to a third party ahead of schedule. "We thought [the recommendation] was fair and rational," chief Democratic negotiator Mickey Kantor explained, "and we didn't want to quibble over details or go into a lengthy negotiation. We didn't think that was in the public interest or in our interest politically."[3]

Had the proposal been agreed to by both sides, 1992 would have been the first election to lack a predebate debate; at last the essential planning decisions would have been removed from the candidates' hands. But because President Bush's team refused to cooperate, that year's debate arrangements played out with the usual down-to-the-wire gamesmanship and posturing. As Republicans learned, toying with the debates carried a substantial political cost. If the "Chicken George" phenomenon makes future candidates think twice about shirking a co-appearance, then Bush will have performed a backhanded service to the institution.

Unfortunately the promise of 1992 did not carry over into the next round of debates. The 1996 debates brought a return to business as usual, with the Clinton and Dole camps conducting their own negotiations, largely divorced from the debate commission's recommendations. The Democrats, who had so eagerly signed the 1992 agreement, now saw no reason to jinx their huge lead by acceding to any outside agent's terms. This move may have made tactical sense, but it poorly served presidential debates. Advance endorsement by a pro-debate incumbent like Bill Clinton might have helped persuade subsequent candidates, especially those in the lead, to follow suit.

For the race of 2000 the Commission on Presidential Debates unveiled its fall debate package at the beginning of the year, several weeks before the opening primaries of the season. Sites, dates, and formats were announced in January, and nominees will be asked to sign on well ahead of the fall campaign. As before, the commission's hope is to kill off once and for all the debilitating practice of predebate negotiations. The organization is banking on several factors: an untarnished track record of sponsorship that includes all ten presidential and vice presidential debates since 1988; the lack of an incumbent president in the race; and increased media pressure on the candidates to end their let's-make-a-deal shenanigans.

We have seen that, on occasion, campaigns can show a willingness to be flexible, not just in empowering outside sponsors but in accepting format innovations. With an assist from Bill Clinton, presidential debates in the 1990s began to experiment with structures that have made the programs more interesting as television. Now that audiences have experienced the town hall and single-moderator formats, it seems difficult to conceive that debates could return to the rigid press conference setup of the past or that candidates would want them to.

It is interesting to note that the looser structures used in the last two series have moved presidential debates closer to the original concept proposed by network planners back in 1960. Until negotiators for Kennedy and Nixon balked, the broadcasters lobbied for a so-called direct confrontation, or "Oxford" debate, in which participants would question one another directly with minimal input from a moderator. This remains the holy grail of debate formats, the one regularly promoted by sponsors, scholars, and journalists, and just as regularly swept off the bargaining table by cautious candidates.

It may be too much to hope that campaigns will voluntarily cede their longstanding control over key issues regarding the structure, scheduling, and production of presidential debates. But incrementally, hard-line attitudes can be softened, and recent developments suggest that handlers are capable of giving ground when the time is right. Even more important, as debates become further rooted as a public expectation, politicos may have no choice but to accept rules not of their own making.

THE PRESS

Are the media losing influence in leading the national conversation about presidential debates? In a general sense, probably not; if anything, the collective power of the various news outlets, electronic and otherwise, appears to be intensifying. But within the chorus, individual voices may be waning. As audiences fragment beyond the traditional over-the-air networks and national publications, the media giants find themselves competing for thinner slices of the public's attention.

Regrettably the growing hubbub that surrounds presidential debates has failed to produce a higher grade of journalism. Both before and after the fact, debate news centers almost exclusively on the horse race: Who got the edge on whom and why? Obviously strategy and performance are valid topics of inquiry for reporters covering presidential debates. But when these issues draw disproportionate attention, the opportunity to educate the public on more substantive points gets crowded out.

Consider, for example, how journalists cover the predebate haggling that determines the shape of the programs. As former Democratic Party chairman Paul Kirk says, "The first round of the debate is who the press thinks won the negotiations."[4] Kirk's comment properly pinpoints the problem: Reporters frame debate negotiations as a high-stakes poker game among Washington insiders, an end unto themselves. From the audience's point of view, the talks represent something altogether different: a set of preproduction decisions that will define how the debates play out as television events. Journalistic coverage of negotiations, so preoccupied with the political angle, tends to overlook the viewers' perspective.

Improving press coverage of debates will require reporters to rethink their overly collusive relationship with the campaigns. Although we cannot expect a return to the media innocence of the first Kennedy-Nixon debate, a sensible middle ground can be found between the circumspection of 1960 and the incestuous clamor of more recent debate journalism. Reporting that functions as an internal dialogue among members of the Washington press corps may satisfy the principal players, but it ill serves the millions who tune in for electoral enlightenment.

Both before and after the fact, debate coverage should be of practical value to the audience. Anthony Corrado, a political communication specialist who has extensively studied these programs, offers several suggestions for improvements in the predebate period. Although Corrado's recommendations refer specifically to the time slot immediately preceding the telecast, they might also apply to advance reporting in general. Corrado proposes that news anchors open the debate with information about the candidates' positions; provide a general summary of the campaign to date; then outline the major issues in the race. "This approach," he says, "would give the audience a better and more informative context for viewing the debates, and would offer voters more than the current fare of pundits and reporters talking about what 'we might expect to see' in the debate or what each candidate has to do to win."[5]

Building on these suggestions, coverage after the debate might expand beyond the usual tactical discussions and win-loss declarations. "At the minimum," wrote Jamieson and Birdsell, "the possibility that both candidates have won should be considered."[6] As a number of observers have pointed out, the proper analogy for journalistic evaluation of debates ought not to be a heavyweight boxing match, with one party getting knocked cold and the other left standing. More logically a presidential debate resembles a job interview in which the applicants' pluses and minuses are weighed against each another. Using this standard, reporters could assess the substance of the participants' responses, in addition to critiquing along presentational lines—who looked more like a leader, who made a mistake, who got off the best one-liner.

News coverage that fails to serve the public interest runs the risk of being ignored on the grounds of irrelevance. Today's debate watchers have more control than ever over how and where they view the program. For most of the history of debates, the only option was to experience the candidates within a mediated context, as part of regular network coverage. Now viewers can pick and choose.

C-Span, for example, offers a "video verite" version of the debates that lets audiences dispense with journalists altogether. While the broadcast networks fill the pre- and postdebate screen with pundits and spinners, C-Span cameras and microphones transmit raw pictures and sound from the hall, putting viewers in the position of flies on the wall. The C-Span audience gets to sample the live warm-up, observe the candidates as they come onstage, study their faces as the countdown gets under way. When the debate ends, C-Span stays with its location coverage, showing the candidates as they interact with each other, with the questioners, and with spectators in the theater. On a number of levels, this makes for more compelling television than the predictable chatter of well-paid talking heads.

Some viewers have chosen to supplant postdebate media reactions with discussions of their own. In 1992 and 1996 a commission-sponsored project called DebateWatch brought together thousands of citizens around the country to screen and then talk about the programs. Many of these groups, in turn, generated local and national press coverage.

The latest media twist is the Internet, which in 1996 gave citizens another avenue into presidential debates. The populist nature of interactive computer technology coincides neatly with the propensity of debates to stimulate conversation. According to Mark Kuhn, who ran the DebateWatch '96 on-line discussion groups, "The Internet has taken power away from media analysts and pundits and told people they, too, can look and analyze for themselves."[7] Although this electronic experiment got off to a modest start, with only about fifty on-line participants in each of the 1996 discussions, future presidential debates hold out the potential for widespread citizen engagement.

As media structures change, it is probable that the gatekeeping function of the press will continue to be challenged by alternative, grass-roots approaches, in debates as in other news events. To too great a degree, journalists have regarded presidential debates as a private preserve held in partnership with the campaigns. If the press is to maintain its centrality in this story, the reporting will need to connect less to the political establishment and more to the people.

THE PUBLIC

Throughout the history of presidential debates voters have played a paradoxical role in the proceedings. On the one hand, they are the raison d'être, and the final arbiters, of debates. On the other, they have been woefully underrepresented in the programs' planning and execution, and either ignored or patronized in much of the postevent reaction.

An encouraging departure from this dynamic occurred in 1992, when the combination of experimental formats, multiple candidates, and a compressed timetable repackaged presidential debates into an eminently watchable miniseries. For the first time, the broadcasts became something other than politicians standing at lecterns giving serial responses to a panel of reporters. Most radically, the groundbreaking "people's debate" in Richmond placed citizens directly into the mix and proved that, when average Americans ask the questions, the focus moves away from the character assaults so beloved by journalists.

The introduction of the town hall format marks a turning point in the power structure of presidential debates. Still, the challenge for voters is to gain even greater influence. As long as these events remain the privileged turf of campaign and media elites, citizens will be relegated to the stands as onlookers. That debates are television programs should not doom the audience to the passivity that is customary in the viewing transaction; after all, these are not just any TV shows.

"One of the things that kept coming out of our 1992 focus groups," said audience researcher Diana Carlin, "is the statement that the public should own the debates. The media has chances to ask these candidates questions for years. Now there has to be a way for public input. What they're saying is, it has to be our agenda." This assertiveness bodes well for televised debates; as voters take a more proprietary interest, politicians and journalists will come under increasing pressure to include the audience in all phases of the process.

It is only fair that the wishes of the people be heeded, given the loyalty viewers have consistently accorded this programming genre. Beginning with that first night in Chicago, the public has responded enthusiastically to the authenticity and drama that presidential debates convey. From Kennedy-Nixon to Clinton-Dole, audiences have awarded these programs the highest of accolades: vast viewership. Because debates happen so rarely, their exalted status as "must-see TV" seems likely to hold firm for many years to come.

For all their faults—manipulation by the campaigns, oversaturation by the media, institutional strictures—televised presidential debates are the best vehicle voters have to personally judge candidates for the White House.

After forty years' experience, the electorate has learned to decode the incongruities of live TV debates, watching with a combination of skepticism, amusement, and respect. We are ready to be educated but not to be sold a bill of goods; we are eager to be entertained but willing to honor the seriousness of the occasion.

What was true of the first Kennedy-Nixon encounter remains true for audiences today. Within their limitations, presidential debates work. They work because they speak to the nation in a language that is every American's second tongue: the language of television.

Notes

INTRODUCTION

1. David Halberstam, "President Video," *Esquire*, June 1976, 130.

2. On 26 September 1985 the Chicago Museum of Broadcast Communications held a "Twenty-Fifth Anniversary Gala," which brought together many of the surviving principals involved in the first Kennedy-Nixon debate. The event took place in Studio One at WBBM, the site of the debate.

3. Rogers was interviewed on the *Lee Phillip Show*, WBBM, Chicago, 22 September 1985.

4. Jules Witcover, "The Bottom Line Is Style," *Washington Post*, 19 September 76, A4.

5. Howard K. Smith, *Events Leading up to My Death* (New York: St. Martin's, 1996), 263; and *Lee Phillip Show*.

6. Rogers was interviewed on the PBS documentary *Nixon*, produced by Elizabeth Deane for the *American Experience* series, 1990.

7. Christopher Matthews, *Kennedy and Nixon: The Rivalry That Shaped Postwar America* (New York: Simon & Schuster, 1996), 145.

8. Ibid., 149.

9. Sig Mickelson, *From Whistle Stop to Sound Bite: Four Decades of Politics and Television* (New York: Praeger, 1989), 123.

10. Mary Cremmen, "Listening Party," *Boston Globe*, 27 September 1960, 1, 9.

11. Earl Mazo et al., *The Great Debates* (Santa Barbara: Center for the Study of Democratic Institutions, 1962), 4; and J. Leonard Reinsch, *Getting Elected: From Radio and Roosevelt to Television and Reagan* (New York: Hippocrene Books, 1988), 143.

12. Halberstam, "President Video," 132.

13. Theodore White, *The Making of the President 1960* (New York: Atheneum, 1961), 288–89.

14. Eric Barnouw, *The Image Empire: A History of Broadcasting in the United States from 1953* (New York: Oxford University Press, 1970), 164.

15. Terry Turner, "What 'Debate' Didn't Show," *Chicago Daily News*, 27 September 1960, 35.

16. Mickelson, *From Whistle Stop to Sound Bite*, 122.

17. White, *The Making of the President 1960*, 285.

18. Debate transcriptions used throughout this book were prepared by the Commission on Presidential Debates. They are available on the commission's website (www.debates.org).

19. Fawn Brodie, *Richard Nixon: The Shaping of His Character* (New York: Norton, 1981), 427.

20. Kenneth P. O'Donnell and David F. Powers, with Joe McCarthy, *Johnny, We Hardly Knew Ye: Memories of John Fitzgerald Kennedy* (Boston: Little, Brown, 1972), 213.

21. William Braden, "Some Tidbits for Posterity," *Chicago Sun-Times*, 27 September 1960, 18.

22. Hewitt made this remark at the "Twenty-fifth Anniversary Gala."

23. Cremmen, "Listening Party," 9.

24. Emilie Tavel, "Back at Hyannis Port . . .," *Christian Science Monitor*, 27 September 1960, 6.

25. Richard Nixon, *Six Crises* (Garden City, N.Y.: Doubleday, 1962), 340.

26. "Pat Sees Nixon 1st Time on TV: 'Looked Great,' " *Boston Evening Globe*, 27 September 1960, 9; and Richard T. Stout, "Nixon Aides Admit Makeup Job," *Chicago Daily News*, 30 September 1960, 4.

27. White, *The Making of the President 1960*, 291; and "The Campaign: Candid Camera," *Time*, 10 October 1960, 20.

28. Todd Gitlin, "Bites and Blips: Chunk News, Savvy Talk, and the Bifurcation

of American Politics," in *Communication and Citizenship: Journalism and the Public Sphere in the New Media Age* (London: Routledge, 1991), 132.

29. George J. Church, "Debating the Debates," *Time*, 29 October 1984, 31.

30. James B. Lemert et. al., *News Verdicts, the Debates, and Presidential Campaigns* (New York: Praeger, 1991), 85.

CHAPTER ONE

1. Halberstam, "President Video," 134.

2. Ibid., 94.

3. Transcript of "Debating the Debates: Defining Moments in Presidential Campaigns," a symposium presented by the Ronald Reagan Center for Public Affairs, 15 October 1996, 31; and Herbert G. Klein, *Making It Perfectly Clear: An Inside Account of Nixon's Love-Hate Relationship with the Media* (Garden City, N.Y.: Doubleday, 1980), 103.

4. Earl Mazo, "The Great Debates," in Mazo et al., *The Great Debates*, 3.

5. Walter Lippman, "Today and Tomorrow; the TV Debate," *Washington Post*, 29 September 1960, A23; and Mickelson, *From Whistle Stop to Sound Bite*, 134.

6. Goldwater's quote was replayed in an obituary of the Arizona senator that aired on *The News Hour with Jim Lehrer*, PBS, 28 May 1998. See also two autobiographical books by Goldwater: *The Conscience of a Majority* (Englewood Cliffs, N.J.: Prentice-Hall, 1970), 37; and *With No Apologies: The Personal and Political Memoirs of United States Senator Barry M. Goldwater* (New York: Morrow, 1979), 156.

7. Newton Minow, J. B. Martin, and Lee Mitchell, *Presidential Television* (New York: Basic Books, 1973), 54.

8. Edward Walsh, "Ford Picks Dole for No. 2 Spot, Challenges Carter to a Debate," *Washington Post*, 20 August 1976, 1.

9. Jonathan Moore and Janet Fraser, eds., *Campaign for President: The Managers Look at '76* (Cambridge, Mass.: Ballinger, 1977), 122.

10. Anthony Corrado, "Background Paper," in *Let America Decide* (New York: Twentieth Century Fund, 1995), 117.

11. Walter Fisher, "Soap Box Derby," *University of Southern California Chronicle*, October 1980, 3.

12. Pat Oliphant, *Washington Star*, 11 September 1980, A-17; Robert G. Kaiser, "Carter Winning Gamble on Debates," *Washington Post*, 18 September 1980, A1.

13. Godfrey Sperling Jr., "The 2/3 Debate: Whose Risks Are Greatest?" *Christian Science Monitor*, 19 September 1980, 3.

14. Jimmy Carter, *Keeping Faith: Memoirs of a President* (New York: Bantam, 1982), 543.

15. Hamilton Jordan, *Crisis: The Last Year of the Carter Presidency* (New York: Putnam's Sons, 1982), 353; and Elizabeth Drew, *Portrait of an Election: The 1980 Presidential Campaign* (New York: Simon & Schuster, 1981), 410. Patrick Caddell's "Debate Strategy Memorandum," reprinted in its entirety (410–39) offers an interesting insight into the Carter camp's strategic thinking before the 1980 debate.

16. Michael Deaver, interview by author, 17 June 1998.

17. Richard Wirthlin, interview by author, 2 September 1998.

18. Rowland Evans and Robert Novak, "The Decision to Debate," *Washington Post*, 20 October 1980, A21.

19. Myles Martel, *Political Campaign Communication: Images, Strategies, and Tactics* (New York: Longman, 1983), 18.

20. NBC News, "Postscript," 28 October 1980.

21. William F. Buckley, "When I Debated Reagan," *New York Times*, 11 September 1984, A23.

22. Deaver, interview.

23. Michael Kelly, "Those Chicken Georges And What They Mean," *New York Times*, 30 September 1992, A21.

24. Ibid. Bush's draft reference was to Bill Clinton's military inexperience; "Arkansas River" apparently had to do with water pollution caused by the chicken-processing industry in Clinton's home state.

25. Dan Routman, interview by author, 31 August 1998.

26. James Brooke, "Perot Assails His Exclusion from Debates," *New York Times*, 19 September 1996, 1, B12.

27. James A. Baker 3d, interview by author, 4 September 1998.

28. Mickey Kantor, interview by author, 20 July 1998.

29. Charles T. Royer, ed., *Campaign for President: The Managers Look at '92* (Hollis, N.H.: Hollis Publishing, 1994), 236.

30. "Twenty-Fifth Anniversary Gala," Chicago Museum of Broadcast Communications, 26 September 1985.

31. Herbert A. Seltz and Richard D. Yoakam, "Production Diary of the Debates," in Sidney Kraus, ed., *The Great Debates: Background, Perspective, Effects* (Bloomington: Indiana University Press, 1962), 122.

32. Memorandum, Stephen M. Travis to Stuart E. Eizenstat and Al Stern, 27 August 1976, Domestic Policy Staff: Stern Box 1, Folder "Debates—Carter/Ford," Jimmy Carter Library.

33. James Karayn, "Debate '88: Political Pillow Fight," *Washington Post*, 25 September 1988, C2.

34. Sidney Kraus, *Televised Presidential Debates and Public Policy* (Hillsdale, N.J.: Erlbaum, 1988), 48.

35. Jody Powell, "When We Organized the Debates," *New York Times*, 11 September 1984, A23.

36. Janet Brown, interview by author, 11 March 1998.

37. Robert Goodwin, interview by author, 15 January 1999.

38. Clay Mulford, interview by author, 28 August 1998.

39. 1992 Memorandum of Understanding, 5, 31.

40. Baker, interview.

41. Lou Cannon, *Reagan* (New York: Putnam's Sons, 1982), 295.

42. Jack W. Germond and Jules Witcover, *Blue Smoke and Mirrors: How Reagan Won and Why Carter Lost the Election of 1980* (New York: Viking, 1981), 276.

43. Terence Smith, "Presidential Debate Format Set; Camps Differ on Time and Place," *New York Times*, 21 October 1980, A1.

44. David Hoffman, "At Least One Debate by Reagan, Mondale Agreed to by Aides," *Washington Post*, 1 September 1984, A4.

45. Elizabeth Drew, *Election Journal: Political Events of 1987–1988* (New York: Morrow, 1989), 283.

46. Richard L. Berke, "If Big Guys Ever Agree, Perot Is Welcome, Too," *New York Times*, 2 October 1992, A18.

47. Robert Goodwin, Memorandum of Conversation, written after the negotiating meeting on 1 October 1992 and provided to the author by Goodwin.

48. David Von Drehle, "Punditocracy Faces Dizzying Spin Cycle," *Washington Post*, 3 October 1992, A1.

49. Roger Simon, *Show Time* (New York: Times Books, 1998), 278.

50. Joan Quigley, *What Does Joan Say? My Seven Years as White House Astrologer to Nancy and Ronald Reagan* (Secaucus, N.J.: Birch Lane, 1990), 92.

51. Deaver, interview.

52. Klein, *Making It Perfectly Clear*, 103.

53. Richard M. Nixon, *Six Crises* (Garden City, N.Y.: Doubleday, 1962), 324.

54. Richard C. Leone, interview by author, 6 April 1998.

55. Robert W. Sarnoff, "An NBC View," in Kraus, *The Great Debates: Background, Perspective, Effects*, 61.

56. Nancy Reagan, *My Turn: The Memoirs of Nancy Reagan* (New York: Random House, 1989), 266.

57. Elizabeth Drew, *Campaign Journal: The Political Events of 1983–1983* (New York: Macmillan, 1985), 691–92.

58. Douglass Cater, "Notes from Backstage," in Kraus, *The Great Debates: Background, Perspective, Effects*, 129.

59. B. Drummond Ayres, "Bush Rejects Panel's Plan for 3 Debates," *New York Times*, 4 September 1992, A13.

60. Kantor, interview; and Royer, *Campaign for President*, 254.

61. Edward M. Fouhy, "The Debates: A Winning Miniseries," *Washington Journalism Review*, December 1992; Baker, interview.

62. Fouhy, "The Debates," 28.

63. Richard L. Berke, "Debating the Debates: John Q. Defeats Reporters," *New York Times*, 21 October 1992, A19.

64. David M. Alpern, "The Debates," *Newsweek*, 27 September 1976, 28.

65. Baker, interview.

66. J. Leonard Reinsch, *Getting Elected: From Radio and Roosevelt to Television and Reagan* (New York: Hippocrene, 1988), 137.

67. Sidney Kraus, ed., *The Great Debates: Carter vs. Ford, 1976* (Bloomington: Indiana University Press, 1979), 98.

68. Transcript of "Debating the Debates: Defining Moments in Presidential Campaigns," 76.

69. Memorandum from Robert Goodwin, 1 September 1988, provided to the author by Goodwin.

70. Robert Ajemian, "Jostling for the Edge," *Time*, 27 September 1976, 11.

71. Memorandum, Greg Schneiders to Jerry Rafshoon, August 1980, Press Powell, Box 8, Folder "Debate Invitations, 8/25/80–9/24/80," Jimmy Carter Library.

72. Bill Keller, "League Irate as Campaigns Select 3 Panelists," *New York Times*, 7 October 1984, 33.

73. Victoria Harian Strella, interview by author, 2 April 1998; and Dorothy Ridings, interview by author, 2 April 1998.

74. Eleanor Randolph, "Journalists Deplore 'Blackballing' of Prospective Debate Panelists," *Washington Post*, 8 October 1984, A16.

75. Ridings, interview.

76. Baker, interview.

77. 1988 Memorandum of Understanding, 7.

78. Paul Taylor, "Democrats Pledge Aggressive Debate," *Washington Post*, 6 October 1984, A3.

CHAPTER TWO

1. Kathleen Hall Jamieson, *Eloquence in an Electronic Age: The Challenge of Creating an Informed Electorate* (New York: Oxford University Press, 1988), 51.

2. Transcript of "Debates '92: A Symposium," presented by the Commission on Presidential Debates, 9 May 1990, 38.

3. Lou Cannon, *Reagan* (New York: Putnam, 1982), 297.

4. Myles Martel, "Debate Preparations in the Reagan Camp: An Insider's View," *Speaker and Gavel* 18 (winter 1981): 44.

5. Ronald Reagan, *An American Life* (New York: Simon & Schuster, 1990), 221.

6. Ibid., 329.

7. Richard Wirthlin, interview by author, 2 September 1988.

8. David S. Broder, "Encounter Leaves Reagan on Course," *Washington Post*, 22 October 1984, A1.

9. Roger Simon, *Roadshow* (New York: Farrar, Straus, Giroux, 1990), 271.

10. Richard Stengel, "Ninety Long Minutes in Omaha," *Time*, 17 October 1988, 21.

11. *This Week with David Brinkley*, ABC, 6 October 1996.

12. Jonathan Moore, ed., *Campaign for President: The Managers Look at '84* (Dover, Mass.: Auburn House, 1986), 217–18.

13. *Newsweek* Election Issue, November/December 1992, 88.

14. Ibid., 89.

15. Transcript of "Debates '92: A Symposium," 35.

16. Jack W. Germond and Jules Witcover, *Mad as Hell: Revolt at the Ballot Box 1992* (New York: Warner, 1993), 478.

17. Robert V. Friedenberg, "Patterns and Trends in National Political Debates: 1960–1992," in Robert V. Friedenberg, ed., *Rhetorical Studies of National Political Debates, 1960–1992,* 2d ed. (Westport, Conn.: Praeger, 1994), 243.

18. Wirthlin, interview.

19. Austin Ranney, *The American Elections of 1984* (New York: AEI, 1985), 197.

20. Elizabeth Drew, *Portrait of an Election: The 1980 Presidential Campaign* (New York: Simon & Schuster, 1981), 411–12.

21. Jules Witcover, *Marathon: The Pursuit of the Presidency, 1972–1976* (New York: Viking, 1977), 572.

22. Ron Nessen, *It Sure Looks Different from the Inside* (Chicago: Playboy, 1978), 261–62.

23. Drew, *Portrait of an Election*, 426.

24. Wirthlin, interview.

25. Germond and Witcover, *Mad as Hell*, 465.

26. David S. Broder and Edward Walsh, "Sharp Exchange Marks Democratic Debate," *Washington Post*, 16 March 1992, A1, A11; and Gwen Ifill, "Clinton's 4-Point Plan to Win the First Debate," *New York Times*, 9 October 1992, A21.

27. Jack W. Germond and Jules Witcover, *Wake Us When It's Over: Presidential Politics of 1984* (New York: Macmillan, 1985), 519.

28. Dayle Hardy-Short, "An Insider's View of the Constraints Affecting Geraldine Ferraro's Preparation for the 1984 Vice Presidential Debate," *Speaker and Gavel* 24 (1986): 18.

29. Judith S. Trent, "The 1984 Bush-Ferraro Vice Presidential Debate," in Friedenberg, *Rhetorical Studies of National Political Debates*, 128.

30. Germond and Witcover, *Wake Us When It's Over*, 520.

31. Michael J. Robinson, "The Potential of Presidential Debates," *Washington Post*, 11 September 1976, A15.

32. Diana Carlin, interview by author, 1 September 1998.

33. James A. Baker 3d, interview by author, 4 September 1998.

34. Jack Hilton, "10 Guidelines for Scoring the Debate," *Washington Post*, 26 October 1980, C2.

35. Christine M. Black and Thomas Oliphant, *All by Myself: The Unmaking of a Presidential Campaign* (Chester, Conn.: Globe Pequot, 1989), 269.

36. Kathleen Hall Jamieson and David S. Birdsell, *Presidential Debates: The Challenge of Creating an Informed Electorate* (New York: Oxford University Press, 1988), 218.

37. Memorandum, Ted Sorensen to Stu Eizenstat, 27 August 1976, Domestic Policy Staff: Stern Box 1, Folder "Debates—Carter/Ford," Jimmy Carter Library.

38. Myles Martel, "Debate Preparations in the Reagan Camp: An Insider's View," *Speaker and Gavel* 18 (winter 1981): 42.

39. Germond and Witcover, *Wake Us When It's Over*, 497.

40. Elizabeth Drew, *Campaign Journal: The Political Events of 1983–1984* (New York: Macmillan, 1985), 688–89.

41. Peter Goldman and Tony Fuller, *The Quest for the Presidency 1984* (New York: Bantam Books, 1985), 332.

42. Richard C. Leone, interview by author, 12 May 1998.

43. Jack W. Germond and Jules Witcover, *Whose Broad Stripes and Bright Stars? The Trivial Pursuit of the Presidency, 1988* (New York: Warner, 1989), 10.

44. David R. Runkel, ed., *Campaign for President: The Managers Look at '88* (Dover, Mass.: Auburn House, 1989), 68.

45. Royer, *Campaign for President*, 251.

46. Charles McCarry, "The Unasked Question," *U.S. News and World Report*, 28 October 1996, 7.

47. Carlin, interview.

48. Katharine Q. Seelye, "Searing Images from Debates Past Are Continuing to Haunt Dole," *New York Times*, 17 October 1996, B11.

49. Joe Klein, "Learning to Run," *The New Yorker*, 8 December 1997, 53.

50. Michael Deaver, interview by author, 17 June 1998.

51. Leone, interview; and Runkel, *Campaign for President*, 221.

52. Nessen, *It Sure Looks Different from the Inside*, 262–63.

53. Stephen R. Brydon, "The Two Faces of Jimmy Carter: The Transformation of a Presidential Debater, 1976 and 1980," *Central States Speech Journal* 16 (fall 1985): 150–51.

54. Drew, *Portrait of an Election*, 435.

55. Cannon, *Reagan*, 295.

56. Leone, interview.

57. Roger Ailes, *You Are the Message: Secrets of the Master Communicators* (Homewood, Ill.: Dow Jones–Irwin, 1988), 22.

58. Craig Allen Smith and Kathy B. Smith, "The 1984 Reagan-Mondale Presidential Debates," in Friedenberg, *Rhetorical Studies of National Political Debates*, 110.

59. Carlin, interview.

60. Stanley A. Renshon, *High Hopes: The Clinton Presidency and the Politics of Ambition* (New York: New York University Press, 1996), 106–7.

61. Jonathan Alter, "The Expectations Game," *Newsweek*, 26 September 1988, 17.

62. Samuel Popkin, "Incumbency and Debates in 1996," provided to the author by Popkin.

63. Kevin Sauter, "The 1976 Mondale-Dole Vice Presidential Debate," in Friedenberg, *Rhetorical Studies of National Political Debates*, 59.

64. James Hoge, interview by author, 27 March 1998.

65. "Debate Lines," OA/ID 08130, Curt Smith File, White House Office of Speechwriting, Bush Presidential Records, George Bush Presidential Library.

66. Robert Goodwin, interview by author, 15 January 1999.

67. Dan F. Hahn, "The 1992 Carter-Bush-Perot Presidential Debates," in Friedenberg, *Rhetorical Studies of National Political Debates*, 194.

68. Mari Boor Tonn, "Flirting with Perot: Voter Ambivalence about the Third Candidate," in Diana B. Carlin and Mitchell S. McKinney, *The 1992 Presidential Debates in Focus* (Westport, Conn.: Praeger, 1994), 119.

69. James J. Pinkerton, "Instead of Whatever, Dole Needs a Slogan," *Newsday*, 18 October 1996, A55.

70. ABC Postdebate Coverage, 9 October 1996; and *Today Show*, NBC, 10 October 1996.

71. Christopher Matthews, *Kennedy and Nixon: The Rivalry That Shaped Postwar America* (New York: Simon & Schuster, 1996), 147.

72. David M. Alpern, "The Debates," *Newsweek*, 27 September 1976, 25, 27.

73. Fay S. Joyce and Joseph Albright, "Carter, Ford Cram for First TV Exam," *Atlanta Constitution*, 19 September 1976, 1.

74. Gerald Ford, *A Time to Heal: The Autobiography of Gerald Ford* (New York: Harper & Row, 1979), 415.

75. Joyce and Albright, "Carter, Ford Cram for First TV Exam," 12A.

76. Samuel Popkin, interview by author, 7 October 1998.

77. Hamilton Jordan, *Crisis: The Last Year of the Carter Presidency* (New York: Putnam's Sons, 1982), 356; and Popkin, interview.

78. David Stockman, *The Triumph of Politics: The Inside Story of the Reagan Revolution* (New York: Harper & Row, 1986), 50.

79. Deaver, interview.

80. Reagan, *An American Life*, 328.

81. N. Reagan, *My Turn*, 266.

82. *ABC World News Tonight*, 11 October 1984.

83. Lou Cannon, *President Reagan: The Role of a Lifetime* (New York: Simon & Schuster, 1991), 547.

84. Ailes, *You Are the Message*, 22–23.

85. Unedited videotape of the Reagan pep rally can be viewed in the archives of the Ronald Reagan Presidential Library in Simi Valley, California.

86. Deaver, interview.

87. Geraldine Ferraro, *Ferraro: My Story* (New York: Bantam, 1985), 247.

88. Ibid., 250.

89. Ibid, 252–53.

90. Ibid., 248.

91. Dan Quayle, *Standing Firm* (New York: HarperCollins, 1994), 61–62.

92. Maureen Dowd, "Quayle Gives Up Chance to Study for Bentsen Debate to Discuss It," *New York Times*, 1 October 1988, 8.

93. Quayle, *Standing Firm*, 63.

94. Transcript of "Debating the Debates: Defining Moments in Presidential Campaigns," a symposium presented by the Ronald Reagan Center for Public Affairs, 15 October 1996, 17.

95. Roger Simon, *Show Time* (New York: Times Books, 1998), 269.

96. Tom Donilon, interview by author, 14 July 1998.

97. Simon, *Show Time*, 252.

98. Clay Mulford, interview by author, 28 August 1998.

99. *NBC Nightly News*, 5 October 1996.

100. Transcript of "Debating the Debates: Defining Moments in Presidential Campaigns," 51–52.

CHAPTER THREE

1. "Century-Apart Rivals Similar," *Chicago Tribune*, 25 September 1960, 9.

2. John Harris, "Jack, Dick Tense as They Clear Decks for Historic TV Encounter Tomorrow," *Boston Globe*, 25 September 1960, 1.

3. Austin C. Wehrwein, "Nominees Agreed on Debate's Value," *New York Times*, 25 September 1960, 52.

4. *New York Times*, 26 September 1960, 66.

5. Marie Torre, " 'Great Debate' of 1960 Won't Be One After All," *New York Herald Tribune*, 16 September 1960, 8.

6. *Tonight Show*, NBC, 25 August 1960.

7. "Castro Considers Closing Down U.S. Base by 'International Law,' " *Washington Post*, 27 September 1960, A1.

8. Thomas Patterson, *Out of Order* (New York: Knopf, 1993), 82.

9. CBS Radio and MBS Radio, 26 September 1960.

10. Roscoe Drummond, "Studio Brinksmanship," *Boston Globe*, 24 September 1960, 6.

11. Robert J. Donovan, "Nixon, Kennedy to Meet in 2nd Debate Tonight," *Washington Post*, 7 October 1960.

12. Joseph Lelyveld, "Kennedy-Nixon Debates a Key to What '76 Clashes May Hold," *New York Times*, 30 August 1976, 11.

13. Jules Witcover, "The Bottom Line Is Style," *Washington Post*, 19 September 1976, A1.

14. *NBC Nightly News*, 22 September 1976.

15. Elizabeth Drew, "A Reporter in Washington, D.C.," *The New Yorker*, 10 January 1977, 54.

16. Jack Kelly, interview by author, 26 March 1998.

17. *NBC Nightly News*, 6 October 1976.

18. *ABC World News Tonight*, 6 October 1976.

19. David S. Broder, "The Final, Crucial Debate," *Washington Post*, 22 October 1976, 1; *ABC World News Tonight*, 22 October 1976; and *NBC Nightly News*, 22 October 1976.

20. *This Week*, ABC, 21 October 1984; and Howard Rosenberg, "Which Skills Will Win Debate?" *Los Angeles Times*, 5 October 1984, VI-1.

21. Steven Strasser, "And Now, Debate II," *Newsweek*, 22 October 1984, 31.

22. James T. Wooten, "Carter's Aides Expecting Debate to Put People 'Closer to Jimmy,' " *New York Times*, 23 September 1976, 37.

23. Lou Cannon, "Carter Sees Debate 'Tie' as Victory," *Washington Post*, 4 September 1976, 1.

24. *ABC World News Tonight*, 5 October 1976.

25. *CBS Evening News*, 20 September 1980.

26. Lou Cannon and Edward Walsh, "The Debate: A Single Roll of the Dice with White House at Stake," *Washington Post*, 19 October 1980, A5.

27. *ABC World News Tonight*, 17 October 1980.

28. Germond and Witcover, *Whose Broad Stripes and Bright Stars?*, 430.

29. Gerald M. Boyd, "Bush Discounts Rise in Jobless Rate," *New York Times*, 4 September 1988, 30.

30. Andrew J. Finke and Todd J. Gillman, "Leading the News: Television Strategies in the 1988 Presidential Campaign," John F. Kennedy School of Government, April 1989, 59.

31. *Good Morning America*, ABC, 5 October 1988.

32. *Inside Politics*, CNN, 13 October 1992.

33. Robin Toner, "2 Campaigns Begin Direct Discussion on Debate Format," *New York Times*, 1 October 1992, A1, A18.

34. *Today*, NBC, 30 September 1996; *Inside Politics*, CNN, 26 September 1996; and Adam Nagourney, "Dole Stages a Dress Rehearsal for the Debates," *New York Times*, 2 October 1996, A16.

35. William Goldschlag, "Pardon Bill if He's Ready for Bob Salvo," *New York Daily News*, 5 October 1996, 2; *Live with Regis and Kathie Lee*, 1 October 1996; and Gene Gibbons, "Clinton Begins Debate Prep "Slightly Apprehensive," Reuters North American Wire, 3 October 1996.

36. Margot Hornblower, "Major Debate Impact Held Unlikely," *Washington Post*, 15 October 1976, A7; and *NBC Nightly News*, 15 October 1976.

37. *ABC World News Tonight*, 11 October 1984.

38. "Bush's Wife Assails Ferraro, but Apologizes," *New York Times*, 9 October 1984, A29; and Juan Williams and Dale Russakoff, "Bush Sticks to Duties as Debate Approaches," *Washington Post*, 10 October 1984, A4.

39. Ferraro, *My Story*, 249.

40. David Shribman and Laurie McGinley, "Bush, Ferraro to Air Differences," *Wall Street Journal*, 11 October 1984, 64; and "Ferraro Called 'Too Bitchy,'" *Washington Post*, 12 October 1984, A20.

41. *ABC World News Tonight*, 22 September 1976.

42. Nessen, *It Sure Looks Different from the Inside*, 263.

43. Richard L. Berke, interview by author, 5 September 1988.

44. Robert G. Kaiser, "Carter Winning Gamble on Debates," *Washington Post*, 18 September 1980, A1.

45. Terence Smith, "Presidential Debate Format Set; Camps Differ on Time and Place," *New York Times*, 21 October 1980, A1.

46. *ABC World News Tonight*, 20 October 1980.

47. *Inside Politics*, CNN, 18 September 1996.

48. Interview by author, 5 August 1998. The interviewee, a Clinton negotiator, wishes to remain anonymous.

49. Judy Woodruff, interview by author, 8 March 1998.

50. *This Week with David Brinkley*, ABC, 11 October 1992.

51. Patterson, *Out of Order*, 81.

52. Godfrey Sperling Jr., "The Debate—What Carter, Reagan Want to Get from It," *Christian Science Monitor*, 20 October 1980, 12; Cannon and Walsh, "The Debate," A5; CBS Debate Coverage, 28 October 1980.

53. Jeff Greenfield, *The Real Campaign: How the Media Missed the Story of the 1980 Campaign* (New York: Summit, 1982), 232.

54. Jimmy Carter, *Keeping Faith: Memoirs of a President* (New York: Bantam, 1982), 561.

55. Caddell's 1980 memorandum is quoted in Elizabeth Drew, *Portrait of an Election: The 1980 Presidential Campaign* (New York: Simon & Schuster, 1981), 436–37.

56. Germond and Witcover, *Wake Us When It's Over*, 497.

57. *NBC Nightly News*, 5 October 1984.

58. E. J. Dionne Jr., "Poll Shows U.S. Voter Optimism Is Helping Bush in the Campaign," *New York Times*, 13 October 1988, 1; and Bernard Weinraub, "No Warming Trend, Dukakis Aides Insist," *New York Times*, 13 October 1988, B10.

59. *ABC World News Tonight*, 11 October 1984.

60. Jonathan Alter and Eleanor Clift, "The Veep Showdown," *Newsweek*, 10 October 1984, 40.

61. Gerald M. Boyd, "Quayle Getting His Big Chance to Clear Doubts," *New York Times*, 5 October 1988, A30.

62. *Inside Politics*, CNN, 13 October 1992; Kevin Sack, "Quayle Speaks Just Fine (With a Script, That Is)," *New York Times*, 7 October 1992, A17; and Tad Devine, "Quayle Can't Lose Tonight," *Washington Post*, 13 October 1992, A21.

63. David Von Drehle, "Punditocracy Faces Dizzying Spin Cycle," *Washington Post*, 3 October 1992, A1.

64. CNN Predebate Special, 11 October 1992.

65. *This Week with David Brinkley*, ABC, 11 October 1992.

66. Ibid.

67. *Inside Politics*, CNN, 19 October 1992.

68. Ibid., 13 October 1992; and *Good Morning America*, ABC, 13 October 1992.

69. *CBS Evening News*, 23 September 1976.

70. Royer, *Campaign for President*, 252.

71. E. J. Dionne Jr., "Clinton Gets Testy in TV Exchange with Donahue," *Washington Post*, 7 October 1992, A1; and Cathleen Decker, "Clinton Returns to Donahue Show—for a Replay of Feisty Exchanges," *Los Angeles Times*, 7 October 1992, A12.

72. Charles Babington and Paul Duggan, "Gore-Kemp Debate Could Preview Race for White House in 2000," *Washington Post*, 9 October 1996, A16; *ABC World News Tonight*, 9 October 1996; and *Inside Politics*, CNN, 9 October 1996.

73. *Meet the Press*, NBC, 29 September 1996.

74. *CBS Evening News*, 16 October 1996.

75. Howard Fineman, "At Close Range," *Newsweek*, 7 October 1996, 38–39.

76. Michael Kramer, "What Dole Must Say," *Time*, 7 October 1996, 50–51.

77. *ABC World News Tonight*, 22 October 1976.

78. Myles Martel, *Political Campaign Debates: Images, Strategies, and Tactics* (New York: Longman, 1983), 13.

79. *ABC World News Tonight* and *NBC Nightly News*, 28 October 1980.

80. *CBS Evening News*, 28 October 1980.

81. CBS Debate Coverage, 7 October 1984, 21 October 1984.

82. *ABC World News Tonight*, 5 October 1988.

83. *McNeil-Lehrer News Hour*, PBS, 5 October 1988.

84. *ABC World News Tonight*, 5 October 1988.

85. *Face the Nation*, CBS, 16 October 1988.

86. *CBS Evening News* and *ABC World News Tonight*, 13 October 1988.

87. *ABC World News Tonight*, 16 October 1996.

CHAPTER FOUR

1. Walter Mondale, interview by Kevin Sauter, 31 March 1989.

2. *News Hour with Jim Lehrer*, PBS, 4 October 1996.

3. Eric Barnouw, *The Image Empire: A History of Broadcasting in the United States from 1953* (New York: Oxford University Press, 1970), 160.

4. Harvey Wheeler, "The Great Debates," in Mazo et al., *The Great Debates*, 18.

5. "Memorandum on Television Debate with Vice President Nixon September 26th," Clark M. Clifford to Senator John F. Kennedy, 27 September 1960, Personal Papers of Robert F. Kennedy, Pre-Administration Political Files 1952–1960, Kennedy-Nixon Debate Folder, Box 36, John F. Kennedy Library.

6. Seymour M. Hersh, *The Dark Side of Camelot* (Boston: Little, Brown, 1997), 89.

7. Eric Barnouw, *Tube of Plenty: The Evolution of American Television* (New York: Oxford University Press, 1975), 277.

8. Kathleen Hall Jamieson, *Eloquence in an Electronic Age: The Transformation of Political Speechmaking* (New York: Oxford University Press, 1988), 50.

9. Wheeler, "The Great Debates," in Mazo et al., *The Great Debates*, 11.

10. Eugene Patterson, "Kennedy Owes a Debt to TV," *Atlanta Constitution*, 8 October 1960, 4.

11. Wallace Westfeldt, interview by author, 3 March 1998.

12. Gerald Gardner, *All the President's Wits: The Power of Presidential Humor* (New York: Beech Tree, 1986), 157.

13. Elizabeth Drew, "A Reporter in Washington, D.C.," *The New Yorker*, 10 January 1977, 56; Memorandum, Mike Duval to President Gerald Ford, 18 October 1976, White House Special Files Unit: Presidential Files, Folder "Third Debate: Memos from Duval," Box 3, Gerald R. Ford Library; and Lloyd Bitzer and Theodore Reuter, *Carter vs. Ford: The Counterfeit Debates of 1976* (Madison: University of Wisconsin Press, 1980), 132.

14. James Gannon, "Our Man Survives the Great Debate, Is Glad It's All Over," *Wall Street Journal*, 27 September 1976, 1; and Jules Witcover, *Marathon: The Pursuit of the Presidency, 1972–1976* (New York: Viking, 1977), 578.

15. Nessen, *It Sure Looks Different from the Inside*, 267.

16. Memorandum, Bill Carruthers to Mike Duval, 20 September 1976,

Michael Raoul-Duval Papers, Folder "Input—Bill Carruthers," Box 29, Gerald R. Ford Library.

17. Memorandum, Dorrance Smith to Mike Duval, 3 September 1976, Michael Raoul-Duval Papers, Folder "Carter Primary Forums," Box 25, Gerald R. Ford Library.

18. *CBS Evening News*, 24 September 1976.

19. Richard Steele, "Round Two to Carter," *Newsweek*, 18 October 1976, 21.

20. William Greider, "Last Debate: Substance over Bumbles," *Washington Post*, 23 October 1976, 1.

21. "Words, and Music, in the Debate," *New York Times*, 30 October 1980, A26; and Elizabeth Drew, *Portrait of an Election: The 1980 Presidential Campaign* (New York: Simon & Schuster, 1981), 323.

22. David S. Broder, "Carter on Points, but No KO," *Washington Post*, 29 October 1980, A1, A10; and Tom Brokaw, interview by author, 14 April 1998.

23. Germond and Witcover, *Blue Smoke and Mirrors*, 284.

24. Broder, interview by author, 12 May 1998.

25. Carter, *Keeping Faith*, 564–65.

26. William A. Henry III, *Visions of America: How We Saw the 1984 Election* (Boston: Atlantic Monthly Press, 1985), 242.

27. Hugh Sidey, "The Big Fight Syndrome," *Time*, 29 October 1984, 32; and John Corry, "A Look at Debate Between Reagan and Mondale," *New York Times*, 9 October 1984, C18.

28. *ABC World News Tonight*, 8 October 1984.

29. Germond and Witcover, *Wake Us When It's Over*, 535.

30. Transcript of "Debating the Debates: Defining Moments in Presidential Campaigns," a symposium presented by the Ronald Reagan Center for Public Affairs, 15 October 1996, 41.

31. Bernard Weinraub, "Mondale Farewell," *New York Times*, 8 November 1984, A24.

32. Richard Ben Cramer, *What It Takes: The Way to the White House* (New York: Random House, 1992), 759.

33. William Greider, "Mondale and Dole Better TV Debaters," *Washington Post*, 16 October 1976, A6.

34. Tom Shales, "Round 1: No Big Winner to Speak Of," *Washington Post*, 7 October 1996, C1; and ABC Postdebate Coverage, 6 October 1996.

35. *Today*, NBC, 17 October 1996.

36. Michael Deaver, interview by author, 17 June 1998.

37. Broder, interview.

38. F. Richard Ciccone and Jon Margolis, "Taxes, Energy Focus of Debate," *Chicago Tribune*, 22 September 1980, 1, 5.

39. Gil Troy, *See How They Ran: The Changing Role of the Presidential Candidate* (New York: Free Press, 1991), 244.

40. Broder, "Carter on Points, but No KO," A1, A10; and John Stacks, "Anatomy of a Landslide," *Time*, 17 November 1980, 31.

41. Germond and Witcover, *Wake Us When It's Over*, 510; and Mary McGrory, "A Ghost of His 1980 Self," *Washington Post*, 9 October 1984, A2.

42. Henry, *Visions of America*, 26.

43. Hedrick Smith, "Reagan, Anderson Disagree in Debate on Most Key Issues," *New York Times*, 22 September 1980, 1.

44. *CBS Evening News*, 20 September 1980.

45. Drew, *Portrait of an Election*, 412.

46. Royer, *Campaign for President*, 258.

47. Ellen Goodman, "A Debate between Candidates, Not Genders," *Boston Globe*, 13 October 1984, 15.

48. David Hoffman, "Bush Applying Lessons of '84 Ferraro Bout," *Washington Post*, 24 September 1988, A10.

49. George Will, "A National Embarrassment," *Washington Post*, 27 September 1988, A21.

50. "Lectern to Lectern," *Newsweek* Election Issue, 21 November 1988, 140.

51. Michael Kelly, "Clinton Basks in Glow of Easy Lead in Race," *New York Times*, 13 October 1992, A16.

52. *Newsweek* Election Issue, November/December 1992, 91.

53. Monica Crowley, *Nixon Off the Record* (New York: Random House, 1996), 125.

54. Brit Hume, interview by author, 21 May 1998.

55. *CNN Crossfire*, 9 October 1996.

56. Elizabeth Drew, *Campaign Journal: The Political Events of 1983–1984* (New York: Macmillan, 1985), 697.

57. *CNN Crossfire*, 9 October 1996.

58. Robert Healy, "Ferraro Seemed a Natural on TV," *Boston Globe*, 12 October 1984, 1.

59. Peter Goldman and Tony Fuller, *The Quest for the Presidency 1984* (New York: Bantam, 1985), 330–31; and William R. Doerner, "Co-Stars on Center Stage," *Time*, 22 October 1984, 30–31.

60. Ferraro, *My Story*, 265–66.

61. "Lectern to Lectern," *Newsweek*, 21 November 1988, 124; and Christine M. Black and Thomas Oliphant, *All by Myself: The Unmaking of a Presidential Campaign* (Chester, Conn.: Globe Pequot, 1989), 269.

62. David Nyhan, "How Dukakis Is Self-Destructing," *Boston Globe*, 16 October 1988, A31.

63. Kitty Dukakis, *Now You Know* (New York: Simon & Schuster, 1990), 220.

64. Runkel, *Campaign for President*, 253–54.

65. Michael Dukakis, interview by author, 11 June 1998.

66. David S. Broder, "JFK's Ghost and the 'Quayle Factor,' " *Washington Post*, 6 October 1988, A1, A32.

67. Warren Weaver, "Bentsen Faces Dual Job in TV Debate Tonight," *New York Times*, 5 October 1988, A30; Jonathan Alter and Eleanor Clift, "The Veep Showdown," *Newsweek*, 10 October 1984, 40; and *Today*, NBC, 5 October 1988.

68. NBC Postdebate Coverage, 5 October 1988.

69. Germond and Witcover, *Whose Broad Stripes and Bright Stars?*, 43.

70. Elizabeth Drew, *Election Journal: Political Events of 1987–1988* (New York: Morrow, 1989), 302.

71. Dan Quayle, *Standing Firm* (New York: HarperCollins, 1994), 65; Tom Shales, "Bentsen and Quayle: A Single Point of Light," *Washington Post*, 6 October 1988, C1; Dukakis, interview.

72. Broder, "JFK's Ghost and the 'Quayle Factor,' " A1, A32; Drew, *Election Journal*, 298.

73. George Will, "Never Give a Child a Sword," *Washington Post*, 6 October 1988, A23.

74. Quayle, *Standing Firm*, 65.

75. *This Week with David Brinkley*, ABC, 6 October 1996.

76. Tad Devine, "Quayle Can't Lose Tonight," *Washington Post*, 13 October 1992, A21.

77. R. W. Apple Jr., "Quayle on the Attack," *New York Times*, 14 October 1992, 1.

78. William Safire, "Humans Confront Android," *New York Times*, 15 October 1992, A15.

79. Tom Shales, "The Veep Follies: A Heartbeat Away," *Washington Post*, 14 October 1992, C1.

80. Crowley, *Nixon Off the Record*, 121.

81. Germond and Witcover, *Mad As Hell*, 13–14.

82. Richard L. Berke, "Candidates Cram for First Debate," *New York Times*, 11 October 1992, 1.

83. *Today*, NBC, 7 October 1996.

84. Thomas Oliphant, "Another Wipeout," *Boston Globe*, 17 October 96, A17.

85. Jeffrey Rosen, "Washington Diarist," *The New Republic*, 11 November 1996, 62.

86. Joe Klein, "Learning to Run," *The New Yorker*, 8 December 1997, 53–54.

87. Elizabeth Kolbert, "Standing Toe to Toe and Slugging It Out on the Air," *New York Times*, 15 October 1992, A11.

88. Tom Shales, "The Veep Follies," C1; ABC Postdebate Coverage, 13 October 1992; and William Safire, "Humans Confront Android," *New York Times*, 15 October 1992, A15.

89. ABC Postdebate Coverage, 13 October 1992; "Reaction: Viewers Comment," *Boston Globe*, 10 October 1996, A34; Broder, interview; and Robert Goodwin, interview by author, 15 January 1999.

90. Hume, interview.

91. Crowley, *Nixon Off the Record*, 120.

92. ABC Postdebate Coverage, 11 October 1992; and Michael Kelly, "Clinton Basks in Glow of Easy Lead in Race," *New York Times*, 13 October 1992, A16.

93. Brokaw, interview; and Tom Shales, "The Debate Goes On . . . and On and On," *Washington Post*, 16 October 1992, D1.

94. John Mashek, interview by author, 31 March 1998; and Clay Mulford, interview by author, 28 August 1998.

95. Brokaw, interview.

96. *Newsweek* Election Issue, November/December 1992, 90; Shales, "The Veep Follies," C1, C2; and Germond and Witcover, *Mad as Hell*, 477.

97. Kolbert, "Standing Toe to Toe," A11.

98. James Bond Stockdale 2d, "Why Was He There?" *New York Times*, 17 October 1992, A21.

99. *Inside Politics*, CNN, 14 October 1992.

100. Mary McGrory, " 'No Surprises' School of Debate," *Washington Post*, 20 October 1992, A2.

101. Broder, interview.

102. Dan Goodgame, "From Savior to Scapegoat," *Time*, 21 October 1996, 37; and *Nightline*, ABC, 13 October 1996.

103. *This Week with David Brinkley*, ABC, 13 October 1996.

104. Martin F. Nolan, "Civility Reigns," *Boston Globe*, 10 October 1996, A27; Christopher Buckley, "No Bark, No Bites," *New York Times*, 11 October 1996, A39; and ABC Postdebate Coverage, 9 October 1996.

CHAPTER FIVE

1. David S. Broder, *Behind the Front Page: A Candid Look at How the News Is Made* (New York: Simon & Schuster), 267–68; and "Real Presidential Debates," *Washington Post*, 5 September 1984, A19.

2. Tom Brokaw, interview by author, 14 April 1998.

3. Jon Margolis, interview by author, 4 March 1998.

4. Peter Jennings, interview by author, 5 May 1998.

5. Jim Lehrer, interview by author, 11 May 1998.

6. Norma Quarles, interview by author, 23 February 1998.

7. Jack White, interview by author, 24 February 1998.

8. Jeff Greenfield, "There's No Debate: The Format Works," *New York Times*, 13 October 1988, A27.

9. Ibid.

10. Mary McGrory, "Politics Without Punditry," *Washington Post*, 20 September 1992, C1.

11. "TV Debate Backstage: Did the Cameras Lie?" *Newsweek*, 10 October 1960, 25.

12. James P. Gannon, "Our Man Survives the Great Debate, Is Glad It's All Over," *Wall Street Journal*, 27 September 1976, 1; Annie Groer, interview by author, 3 March 1998; and Andrea Mitchell, interview by author, 25 March 1998.

13. John Mashek, interview by author, 31 March 1998.

14. Elizabeth Drew, interview by author, 3 March 1998.

15. Jennings, interview; and Mitchell, interview.

16. Henry Trewhitt, interview by author, 16 March 1998.

17. Nixon, *Six Crises*, 339.

18. *CNN Evening News*, 6 October 1988; and Brit Hume, interview by author, 21 May 1998.

19. Brokaw, interview.

20. Jennings, interview.

21. Max Frankel, interview by author, 25 February 1998.

22. Harris Ellis, interview by author, 25 February 1998.

23. Sander Vanocur, interview by author, 2 March 1998.

24. Hal Bruno, interview by author, 10 March 1998.

25. Walter Mears, "A View from the Inside," *Columbia Journalism Review*, January/February 1977, 24.

26. Jack Nelson, interview by author, 23 February 1998.

27. Brokaw, interview.

28. Hume, interview.

29. Brokaw, interview.

30. Walter Mears, interview by author, 23 February 1998.

31. Robert Boyd, interview by author, 23 February 1998.

32. Jane Bryant Quinn, "A Reporter's Complaint," *Newsweek*, 3 October 1980, 42.

33. Mitchell, interview.

34. Simon, *Roadshow*, 280–98.

35. Robin Toner, "Dukakis Returns to Stump as Aides Paint Rosy Picture," *New York Times*, 15 October 1988, 9; Walter Shapiro, "Bush Scores a Warm Win," *Time*, 24 October 1988, 18; and Bruno, interview.

36. Judy Woodruff, interview by author, 8 March 1998.

37. James Hoge, interview by author, 27 March 1998.

38. Dorothy Ridings, interview by author, 2 April 1998.

39. James A. Baker 3d, interview by author, 4 September 1998; and Richard C. Leone, interview by author, 6 April 1998.

40. Tom Shales, "The Debates, Round 1," *Washington Post*, 8 October 1984, D1, D4.

41. Eleanor Randolph, "Three Journalists, Also on the Line," *Washington Post*, 24 September 1988, C1.

42. Jennings, interview.

43. Lehrer, interview.

44. Ibid.

45. Simon, *Roadshow*, 283.

46. Walter Goodman, "A Cool Head at the Eye of the Calm," *New York Times*, 3 November 1996, H37.

47. Lehrer, interview. Other quotes in this section also come from the author's interview with Lehrer.

48. Bruno, interview. Other quotes in this section also come from the author's interview with Bruno.

49. Carole Simpson, interview by author, 25 October 1994. Other quotes in this section also come from the author's interview with Simpson.

50. Royer, *Campaign for President*, 255.

51. Ibid., 254.

52. *Spin*, documentary film by Brian Springer, 1995.

53. "Oprah Loses out to Lehrer," *Broadcasting and Cable*, 7 October 1996, 28.

54. Paul Kirk Jr., interview by author, 4 May 1998.

55. David S. Broder, interview by author, 12 May 1998.

56. Janet Brown, interview by author, 11 March 1998.

57. ABC News and NBC News Postdebate Coverage, 15 October 1992; and "Citizens' Arrest," *Christian Science Monitor*, 19 October 1996, 20.

58. Crowley, *Nixon Off the Record*, 122.

59. Robert Goodwin, interview by author, 15 January 1999.

60. Simpson, interview.

61. Elizabeth Kolbert, "Bypassing the Press Helps Candidates; Does It Also Service the Public Interest?" *New York Times*, 8 November 1992, E2.

62. Simpson, interview.

63. Lehrer, interview.

64. Frank Fahrenkopf Jr., interview by author, 12 May 1998.

CHAPTER SIX

1. ABC News Debate Coverage, 23 September 1976.

2. Transcript of "Debating the Debates: Defining Moments in Presidential Campaigns," 50.

3. Transcript of "Debates '92: A Symposium," 13.

4. Joseph Lelyveld, "Focus in the Hall and on the TV Set Differed," *New York Times*, 25 September 1976, 8.

5. *NBC Nightly News*, 24 September 1976.

6. Seltz and Yoakam, "Production Diary of the Debates," in Kraus, *The Great Debates: Carter vs. Ford, 1976*, 136.

7. Jack Kelly, interview by author, 26 March 1998.

8. Edward M. Fouhy, interview by author, 27 February 1998.

9. Annie Groer, interview by author, 3 March 1998.

10. Edward M. Fouhy, "The Debates: A Winning Miniseries," *Washington Journalism Review* (December 1992): 29.

11. Richard L. Berke, "A Few Tense Moments in the Control Room," *New York Times*, 15 October 1992, A11.

12. Janet Brown, interview by author, 11 March 1998. Other quotes in this chapter also come from the author's interview with Brown.

13. Fouhy, interview.

14. Transcript of "Debates '92: A Symposium," 34–35.

15. 1992 Memorandum of Understanding, 32–33.

16. Frank Fahrenkopf Jr., interview by author, 12 May 1998.

17. Mark Sauer, "USD Audience on Its Best Sunday Behavior," *San Diego Union-Tribune*, 17 October 1996, A21.

18. James T. Wooten, "Feeling of Victory Is Sensed by Each Side," *New York Times*, 7 October 1976, 38.

19. Seltz and Yoakam, "Production Diary of the Debates," in Kraus, *The Great Debates: Carter vs. Ford, 1976*, 139.

20. Brady Williamson, interview by author, 14 November 1998.

21. Ibid.

22. Seltz and Yoakam, "Production Diary of the Debates," in Kraus, *The Great Debates: Carter vs. Ford, 1976*, 131.

23. Tom Donilon, interview by author, 14 July 1998.

24. Victoria Harian Strella, interview by author, 2 April 1998.

25. Rich Hood and Celeste Hadrick, "Pre-Debate Debate: Candidates' Aides Battle over Lights," *Kansas City Star*, 21 October 1984, 1, 21A.

26. Michael Deaver, interview by author, 17 June 1998.

27. Dudley Clendinen, "Debate Battle Moves to News Shows," *New York Times*, 23 October 1984, A24.

28. Beverly Lindsey, interview by author, 8 December 1998.

29. Maureen Dowd, "Mean and Meaner," *New York Times*, 20 October 1996, IV-5.

30. Robert Goodwin, interview by author, 15 January 1999.

31. Williamson, interview.

32. Goodwin, interview.

33. Williamson, interview.

34. Ibid.

35. Donilon, interview.

36. Harian Strella, interview.

37. Merriman Smith, "Most Hectic Debate Was Off Camera," *New York World-Telegram*, 8 October 1960, 2.

38. Seltz and Yoakam, "Production Diary of the Debates," in Kraus, *The Great Debates: Background, Perspective, Effects*, 103.

39. J. Leonard Reinsch, *Getting Elected: From Radio and Roosevelt to Television and Reagan* (New York: Hippocrene Books, 1988), 145.

40. W. H. Lawrence, "Nixon Is 'Shocked' by Kennedy Notes," *New York Times*, 14 October 1960, 22.

41. 1996 Memorandum of Understanding, 7.

42. Seltz and Yoakam, "Production Diary of the Debates," in Kraus, *The Great Debates: Carter vs. Ford, 1976*, 131.

43. John LiBretto, interview by author, 17 March 1994.

44. Robert Asman, interview by author, 11 March 1998.

45. Goodwin, interview.

46. Seltz and Yoakam, "Production Diary of the Debates," in Kraus, *The Great Debates: Carter vs. Ford, 1976*, 144.

47. Lawrence Laurent, "ABC Facilities Tonight Just as 'Equal' as Can Be," *Washington Post*, 13 October 1960, B6.

48. John P. Shanley, "Studios on Both Coasts Set Up to Handle Third in TV Debates," *New York Times*, 14 October 1960, 22.

49. David M. Alpern, "The Debates," *Newsweek*, 27 September 1976, 31.

50. Memorandum, William Carruthers to Michael Duval, 30 August 1976, Michael Raoul-Duval Papers, Folder "Input—Bill Carruthers," Box 29, Gerald R. Ford Library.

51. Alpern, "The Debates," 31.

52. Seltz and Yoakam, "Production Diary of the Debates," in Kraus, *The Great Debates: Carter vs. Ford, 1976*, 151.

53. 1988 Memorandum of Understanding, 10.

54. LiBretto, interview.

55. Asman, interview.

56. Williamson, interview.

57. John J. O'Connor, "TV: Instant Poll Steals Post-Debate Scene," *New York Times*, 30 October 1984, C26.

58. Jim Lehrer, interview by author, 11 May 1998.

59. Berke, "A Few Tense Moments in the Control Room," A11.

60. Asman, interview.

61. LiBretto, interview.

CHAPTER SEVEN

1. *Douglas Edwards with the News*, CBS, 27 September 1960.

2. Richard L. Strout, "Not One Slip on Banana Peel!" *Christian Science Monitor*, 27 September 1960, 1; Peter Lisagor, "How Candidates Did in the Big Debate," *Chicago Daily News*, 27 September 1960, 1; Percy Shain, "Candidates Today Must Know Facts, TV Is Too Discerning for Bluffing," *Boston Globe*, 27 September 1960, 9.

3. Richard T. Stout, "Nixon Aides Admit Makeup Job," *Chicago Daily News*, 30 September 1960, 4; "Nixon Says Lost Weight Shows in Face," *Boston Globe*, evening edition, 27 September 1960, 9.

4. Richard T. Stout, "Was Nixon Sabotaged by TV Makeup Artist?" *Chicago Daily News*, 29 September 1960, 1.

5. "TV Debate Backstage: Did the Cameras Lie?" *Newsweek*, 10 October 1960, 25.

6. "Nixon Laments Make-Up in Chat With TV Actor," *New York Times*, 13 October 1960, 27.

7. Russell Baker, *The Good Times* (New York: Morrow, 1989), 326.

8. "How the Battle Shapes Up Now," *U.S. News and World Report*, 17 October 1960, 42.

9. Ralph McGill, "TV vs. Radio in the Great Debate," *Washington Evening Star*, 1 October 1960, A-5.

10. "Los Angeles Watches and Listens to the Great Debate," *Los Angeles Times*, 27 September 1960, 3.

11. NBC Debate Coverage, 23 September 1976.

12. Mudd and Cronkite both took part in CBS's postdebate coverage, 23 September 1976.

13. David S. Broder, interview by author, 12 May 1998.

14. David S. Broder, *Behind the Front Page: A Candid Look at How the News Is Made* (New York: Simon & Schuster, 1987), 293.

15. Diana Carlin, interview by author, 1 September 1998.

16. Bob Schieffer, interview by author, 18 November 1998.

17. James B. Lemert et al., *News Verdicts, the Debates, and Presidential Campaigns* (New York: Praeger, 1991), 43, 59.

18. *Nightline*, ABC News, 28 October 1980; and Eric Alterman, *Sound and Fury: The Washington Punditocracy and the Collapse of American Politics* (New York: HarperCollins, 1992), 101.

19. Herbert G. Klein, *Making It Perfectly Clear: An Inside Account of Nixon's Love-Hate Relationship with the Media* (Garden City, N.Y.: Doubleday, 1980), 106.

20. W. H. Lawrence, "Neither Nominee Claims a Triumph," *New York Times*, 27 September 1960, 30.

21. Ibid.

22. NBC News Postdebate Coverage, 6 October 1996.

23. Howard Kurtz, "The New Spin on Spin: Instant Interviews, Polls; Respondents Tended to Side with Their Favorites," *Washington Post*, 8 October 1996, A7.

24. Nessen, *It Sure Looks Different from the Inside*, 266.

25. Larry Speakes, *Speaking Out: Inside the Reagan White House* (New York: Scribner's, 1980), 55.

26. CBS Postdebate Coverage, 15 October 1976.

27. Hal Bruno, interview by author, 10 March 1998.

28. Michael Deaver, interview by author, 17 June 1998.

29. NBC Postdebate Coverage, 11 October 1984.

30. Lemert et al., *News Verdicts, the Debates, and Presidential Campaigns*, 69.

31. NBC News Postdebate Coverage, 5 October 1988.

32. Michael Oreskes, "Both Parties Offer a Spin to the Event," *New York Times*, 26 September 1988, A1, A20.

33. Interviews by author: Brokaw, 14 April 1998; Berke, 5 September 1998; Hannon, 7 May 1998; and Schieffer, 18 November 1998.

34. Simon, *Show Time*, 267–68.

35. Bruno, interview.

36. Thomas Rosenstiel, "Spin Doctors Now Just Draw Laughs," *Los Angeles Times*, 12 October 1992, A23.

37. Bill Nichols, interview by author, 19 May 1998.

38. Berke, interview.

39. Ken Auletta, "Annals of Communication: Inside Story," *The New Yorker*, 18 November 1996, 58.

40. Broder, interview.

41. Thomas Rosenstiel, "Uplinked and Beamed Out: The Latest Spin in Politics," *Los Angeles Times*, 17 October 1992, A20.

42. Simon, *Show Time*, 277.

43. *ABC World News Tonight*, 26 September 1988.

44. NBC News Postdebate Coverage, 7 October 1984; E. J. Dionne Jr., "The Debates: Revival for Democrats," *New York Times*, 7 October 1988, B4.

45. *The War Room*, documentary film by Pennebaker and Hegedus, 1993.

46. Royer, *Campaign for President*, 239.

47. "Debate Audience Yields Wide Range of Reaction," *New York Times*, 27 September 1960, 1, 29.

48. "TV Debate Switched Few Votes, Nation-Wide Survey Shows," *New York Times*, 28 September 1960, 26.

49. Tom Donilon, interview by author, 14 July 1998.

50. F. Christopher Arterton, *Media Politics: The News Strategies of Presidential Campaigns* (Lexington, Mass.: Lexington Books, 1984), 54.

51. *Nightline*, ABC News, 28 October 1980.

52. Robert G. Kaiser, "Looking for Old Ghosts," *Washington Post*, 30 October 1980, A1, A4.

53. John J. O'Connor, "TV: Instant Poll Steals Post-Debate Scene," *New York Times*, 30 October 1980, C26.

54. *Nightline*, ABC News, 28 October 1980.

55. Bruno, interview.

56. Howard Rosenberg, "Perot Pitches, Bush Swings . . . Oops, That's CBS," *Los Angeles Times*, 12 October 1992, A23; Kurtz, "The New Spin on Spin," A7.

57. *NBC Nightly News*, 24 September 1976.

58. "The Blooper Heard Round the World," *Time*, 18 October 1976, 13.

59. CBS News and NBC News Postdebate Coverage, 6 October 1976.

60. Bernard Gwertzman, "Ford Denies Moscow Dominates East Europe; Carter Rebuts Him," *New York Times*, 7 October 1976, 1; Curtis Wilkie, "Aides Celebrate Carter 'Home Run,'" *Boston Globe*, 7 October 1976, 20; and David S. Broder and Lou Cannon, "A Tense, Highly Charged Atmosphere in San Francisco," *Washington Post*, 7 October 1976, A10.

61. *NBC Nightly News*, 7 October 1976.

62. Charles Mohr, "Ford, Trying to Bind Up Wound, Backs Freedom for East Europe," *New York Times*, 8 October 1976, A18; and *NBC Nightly News*, 7 October 1976.

63. Charles Mohr, "Ford Makes 2 Attempts to Clarify Statement," *New York Times*, 9 October 1976, 1, 7.

64. Curtis Wilkie, "Ford Admits Error on E. Europe," *Boston Globe*, 13 October 1976, 1.

65. Nessen, *It Sure Looks Different from the Inside*, 272; and Gerald Ford, *A Time to Heal: The Autobiography of Gerald R. Ford* (New York: Harper & Row, 1979), 424.

66. Nessen, *It Sure Looks Different from the Inside*, 276.

67. Thomas E. Patterson, *Out of Order* (New York: Knopf, 1993), 156; Nessen, *It Sure Looks Different from the Inside*, 276.

68. Jonathan Moore and Janet Fraser, eds., *Campaign for President: The Managers Look At '76* (Cambridge, Mass.: Ballinger, 1977), 142.

69. Frederick T. Steeper, "Public Response to Gerald Ford's Statements on Eastern Europe in the Second Debate," in George F. Bishop, Robert G. Meadow, and Marilyn Jackson-Beeck, eds., *The Presidential Debates: Media, Electoral, and Policy Perspectives* (New York: Praeger, 1978), 101; Doris Graber, *Processing the News: How People Tame the Information Tide* (New York: Longman, 1984), 264; and David Chagall, *The New Kingmakers: An Inside Look at the Powerful Men*

behind America's Political Campaigns (New York: Harcourt Brace Jovanovich, 1991), 108.

70. CBS News and NBC News Postdebate Coverage, 7 October 1984.

71. Howell Raines, "Reagan and Mondale Debate; Clash on Deficit and Religion," *New York Times*, 8 October 1984, 1; and Tom Shales, "The Debates, Round 1," *Washington Post*, 8 October 1984, D1.

72. Rich Jaroslovsky and James M. Perry, "New Question in Race: Is Oldest U.S. President Now Showing His Age?" *Wall Street Journal*, 9 October 1984, 1.

73. David S. Broder, "Reagan's Late-Inning Letdown," *Washington Post*, 9 October 1984, A19.

74. Mark Hertsgaard, *On Bended Knee: The Press and the Reagan Presidency* (New York: Farrar, Straus, Giroux, 1988), 246–47.

75. *ABC World News Tonight*, 9 October 1984.

76. Thomas Rosenstiel, "Debate Aftermath: Media Alter View of Candidates," *Los Angeles Times*, 14 October 1984, 1.

77. *ABC World News Tonight*, 9 October 1984.

78. *NBC Nightly News*, 10 October 1984.

79. Ibid.

80. Steven R. Weisman, "Reagan Criticizes Comments on Age," *New York Times*, 11 October 1984, 1; George Skelton, "Reagan Called 'Alert' in May 18 Medical Report," *Los Angeles Times*, 11 October 1984, 1; and *CBS Evening News*, 10 October 1984.

81. Austin Ranney, ed., *The American Elections of 1984* (New York: American Enterprise Institute, 1985), 198–99.

82. *CBS Evening News* and ABC News *Nightline*, 5 October 1988; and NBC *Today*, *ABC World News Tonight*, *CBS Evening News*, and *NBC Nightly News*, 6 October 1988.

83. *CBS Evening News*, 6 October 1988; *ABC World News Tonight*, 6 October 1988.

84. Maureen Dowd, "Bush Angrily Insisting He Fully Backs Quayle," *New York Times*, 9 October 1988, 32.

85. *ABC World News Tonight*, 11 October 1988; and *CBS Evening News*, 12 October 1988.

86. B. Drummond Ayres, "Quayle, Free of Handlers, Is Going with His Instincts," *New York Times*, 14 October 1988, B11.

87. CNN, 1 November 1988.

88. Simon, *Roadshow*, 296–97.

89. ABC News Postdebate Coverage, 28 October 1980; "Celebrities Name the Winner according to Own Party Labels," *Cleveland Plain Dealer*, 29 October 1980, 8-A.

90. *ABC World News Tonight*, 29 October 1980.

91. Dale Russakoff, "Bush Boasts of Kicking 'A Little Ass' at Debate," *Washington Post*, 13 October 1984, A8; Fay S. Joyce, "Bush Is Delighted after His Debate," *New York Times*, 13 October 1984, 9; and *NBC Nightly News*, 12 October 1984.

92. George J. Church, "Getting a Second Look," *Time*, 22 October 1984, 26.

CHAPTER EIGHT

1. For a discussion of the 1960 ratings, see Mazo et al., *The Great Debates*, 4. It should be noted that viewership figures for presidential debates, then as now, are notoriously difficult to pinpoint with any precision. As Mazo et al. writes, significant disparities existed between ratings figures cited by the broadcast networks in 1960 and those taken by political pollsters. See also Frank Stanton, "A CBS View," in Kraus, *The Great Debates: Background, Perspective, Effects*, 65–72.

2. "2 Million L.A. Homes View Carter-Reagan Debate," *Los Angeles Times*, 30 October 1980, VI-8. Although network estimates set viewership for the 1980 Carter-Reagan debate at a figure between 105 million and 120 million, the author's figure of "more than 100 million" allows for some inflation. The averages of 60 to 80 million viewers per presidential debate, and 30 to 50 million per vice presidential debates, are general estimates, based on the author's reading of various postdebate ratings data from 1976 to 1996.

3. Steve Coe, "NBC Super Bowl Sets Record," *Broadcasting and Cable*, 5 February 1996, 32; and Bill Carter, "An Oscar Night to Remember," *New York Times*, 25 March 1998, B8.

4. Ratings figures for these special episodes come from *Broadcasting*, 7 March 1983, 35; 1 December 1980, 104.

5. Bill Carter, "Ratings Grazed Super Bowl," *New York Times*, 16 May 1998, A22.

6. William Safire, "Humans Confront Android," *New York Times*, 15 October 1992, A15.

7. Walter Mondale, interview by Kevin Sauter, 31 March 1989.

8. Frank Stanton, "A CBS View," in Kraus, *The Great Debates: Background, Perspective, Effects*, 69.

9. Walter Goodman, "The Presidential Debate That Wasn't," *New York Times*, 22 September 1992, C18.

10. Norman Cousins, "TV and the Presidency," *Saturday Review*, 13 November 1976, 4.

11. Charles P. Pierce, "The Ghost of Alzheimer's," *Boston Globe*, 31 January 1999, C1.

12. Walter Lippmann, "Today and Tomorrow: The TV Debate," *Washington Post*, 29 September 1960, A23.

13. ABC News Postdebate Coverage, 15 October 1992.

14. *CBS Evening News*, 16 October 1992.

15. Richard Severo, "Lawrence E. Spivak, 93, Is Dead; The Originator of 'Meet the Press,'" *New York Times*, 10 March 1994, D21.

16. Henry Allen, "Primate Debate—As the Candidates Face Off, Onlookers Have an Instinctive Reaction," *Washington Post*, 5 October 1996, C1.

17. Goodman, "The Presidential Debate That Wasn't," C18.

18. Elizabeth R. Lamoureux, Heather S. Entrekin, and Mitchell S. McKinney, "Debating the Debates," in Carlin and McKinney, *The 1992 Presidential Debates in Focus*, 58.

19. Robert G. Meadow, "Televised Campaign Debates as Whistle-Stop Speeches," in William C. Adams, *Television Coverage of the 1980 Presidential Campaign* (Norwood, N.J.: Ablex, 1983), 91.

20. *News Hour*, PBS, 4 October 1996.

21. Doris Graber, *Mass Media and American Politics* (Washington, D.C.: CQ, 1997), 257.

22. Kathleen Hall Jamieson and David S. Birdsell, *Presidential Debates: The Challenge of Creating an Informed Electorate* (New York: Oxford University Press, 1988), 127.

23. Transcript of "Hearing before the Subcommittee on Elections of the Committee on House Administration, House of Representatives, 103d Congress, First Session" (Washington, D.C.: 1993), 70–71.

24. *This Week with David Brinkley*, ABC News, 6 October 1996.

25. Carlin, interview.

26. Lamoureux, Entrekin, and McKinney, "Debating the Debates," in Diana B. Carlin and Mitchell S. McKinney, eds., *The 1992 Presidential Debates in Focus*, 57.

27. Goodwin Berquist, "The 1976 Carter-Ford Presidential Debates," in Friedenberg, *Rhetorical Studies of National Political Debates 1960–1992*, 37–38.

28. Henry Steele Commager, "Washington Would Have Lost a TV Debate," *New York Times Magazine*, 30 October 1960, VI-13.

29. Daniel Boorstin, *The Image* (New York: Harper & Row, 1964), 43–44.

30. Wheeler, "The Great Debates," in Mazo et al., *The Great Debates*, 15.

31. Lawrie Mifflin, "An Old Hand's View of TV News: Not Good," *New York Times*, 23 March 1998, AR41.

32. Richard M. Nixon, *RN: The Memoirs of Richard Nixon* (New York: Grossett and Dunlap, 1978), 221.

33. Sidney Kraus, *Televised Presidential Debates and Public Policy* (Hillsdale, N.J.: Erlbaum, 1988), 77.

34. Elizabeth Drew, "High Noon," *The New Yorker*, 19 October 1992, 59.

35. Drew, interview.

36. Stephen Mills, "Rebuilding the Presidential Debates," *Speaker and Gavel* 24 (1986): 48.

37. Germond and Witcover, *Wake Us When It's Over*, 527.

38. Ronald Brownstein, "Pressure Is on Bush for First Debate," *Los Angeles Times*, 11 October 1992, A1.

39. Transcript of "Debating the Debates: Defining Moments in Presidential Campaigns," a symposium presented by the Ronald Reagan Center for Public Affairs, 15 October 1996, 60.

40. David J. Lanoue and Peter R. Schrott, *The Joint Press Conference: The History, Impact, and Prospects of American Presidential Debates* (Westport, Conn.: Greenwood, 1991), 48.

41. Carlin, interview.

42. Lanoue and Schrott, *The Joint Press Conference*, 49.

CONCLUSION

1. Marilyn Jackson-Beeck and Robert G. Meadow, "The Triple Agenda of Presidential Debates," *Public Opinion Quarterly* 5 (1979): 174.

2. Transcript of the proceedings of "Debate '92: A Symposium" (Washington, D.C.: Commission on Presidential Debates, 1990), 19.

3. Mickey Kantor, interview by author, 20 July 1998.

4. Paul G. Kirk Jr., interview by author, 4 May 1998.

5. Anthony Corrado, "Background Paper," in *Let America Decide* (New York: Twentieth Century Fund, 1995), 135.

6. Kathleen Hall Jamieson and David S. Birdsell, *Presidential Debates: The Challenge of Creating an Informed Electorate* (New York: Oxford University Press, 1988), 216.

7. Ric Manning, "In Presidential Campaigns, It's the Year of the Internet—for Voters and Candidates," *Louisville Courier-Journal*, 15 October 1996, 1A.

References

Ailes, Roger, with Jon Kraushar. *You Are the Message: Secrets of the Master Communicators.* Homewood, Ill.: Dow Jones-Irwin, 1988.

Alterman, Eric. *Sound and Fury: The Washington Punditocracy and the Collapse of American Politics.* New York: HarperCollins, 1992.

Arterton, F. Christopher. *Media Politics: The News Strategies of Presidential Campaigns.* Lexington, Mass.: Lexington Books, 1984.

Baker, Russell. *The Good Times.* New York: Morrow, 1989.

Barnouw, Eric. *The Image Empire: A History of Broadcasting in the United States from 1953.* New York: Oxford University Press, 1970.

_____. *Tube of Plenty: The Evolution of American Television.* New York: Oxford University Press, 1975.

Berquist, Goodwin. "The 1976 Carter-Ford Presidential Debates." In *Rhetorical Studies of National Political Debates 1960–1992,* edited by Robert V. Friedenberg. 2d ed. Westport, Conn.: Praeger, 1994.

Bishop, George F., Robert G. Meadow, and Marilyn Jackson-Beeck, eds. *The*

Presidential Debates: Media, Electoral, and Policy Perspectives. New York: Praeger, 1978.

Bitzer, Lloyd, and Theodore Reuter. *Carter vs. Ford: The Counterfeit Debates of 1976.* Madison: University of Wisconsin Press, 1980.

Black, Christine M., and Thomas Oliphant. *All by Myself: The Unmaking of a Presidential Campaign.* Chester, Conn.: Globe Pequot, 1989.

Boorstin, Daniel. *The Image.* New York: Harper & Row, 1964

Broder, David. *Behind the Front Page: A Candid Look at How the News Is Made.* New York: Simon & Schuster, 1987.

Brodie, Fawn M. *Richard Nixon: The Shaping of His Character.* New York: Norton, 1981.

Brydon, Stephen R. "The Two Faces of Jimmy Carter: The Transformation of a Presidential Debater, 1976 and 1980." *Central States Speech Journal* 36 (fall 1985): 138–51.

Cannon, Lou. *Reagan.* New York: Putnam's Sons, 1982.

_____. *President Reagan: The Role of a Lifetime.* New York: Simon & Schuster, 1991.

Carlin, Diana B., and Mitchell S. McKinney, eds. *The 1992 Presidential Debates in Focus.* Westport, Conn.: Praeger, 1994.

Carter, Jimmy. *Keeping Faith: Memoirs of a President.* New York: Bantam Books, 1982.

Chagall, David. *The New Kingmakers: An Inside Look at the Powerful Men Behind America's Political Campaigns.* New York: Harcourt Brace Jovanovich, 1981.

Commager, Henry Steele. "Washington Would Have Lost a TV Debate." *New York Times Magazine,* 30 October 1960, VI-13, 79–80.

Corrado, Anthony. "Background Paper." In *Let America Decide.* New York: Twentieth Century Fund, 1995.

Cousins, Norman. "TV and the Presidency." *Saturday Review,* 13 November 1976, 4.

Cramer, Richard Ben. *What It Takes: The Way to the White House.* New York: Random House, 1992.

Crowley, Monica. *Nixon Off the Record.* New York: Random House, 1996.

Drew, Elizabeth. *Portrait of an Election: The 1980 Presidential Campaign.* New York: Simon & Schuster, 1981.

_____. *Campaign Journal: The Political Events of 1983–1984.* New York: Macmillan, 1985.

_____. *Election Journal: Political Events of 1987–1988.* New York: Morrow, 1989.

Dukakis, Kitty, with Jane Scovell. *Now You Know.* New York: Simon & Schuster, 1990.

Ferraro, Geraldine. *Ferraro: My Story.* New York: Bantam Books, 1985.

Fisher, Walter. "Soap Box Derby," *University of Southern California Chronicle,* October 1980.

Ford, Gerald. *A Time to Heal: The Autobiography of Gerald R. Ford*. New York: Harper & Row, 1979.

Fouhy, Edward M. "The Debates: A Winning Miniseries," *Washington Journalism Review*, December 1992, 27–29.

Friedenberg, Robert V., ed. *Rhetorical Studies of National Political Debates, 1960–1992*. 2d ed. Westport, Conn.: Praeger, 1994.

Gardner, Gerald. *All the President's Wits: The Power of Presidential Humor*. New York: Beech Tree, 1986.

Germond, Jack W., and Jules Witcover. *Blue Smoke and Mirrors: How Reagan Won and Why Carter Lost the Election of 1980*. New York: Viking, 1981.

_____. *Wake Us When It's Over: Presidential Politics of 1984*. New York: Macmillan, 1985.

_____. *Whose Broad Stripes and Bright Stars? The Trivial Pursuit of the Presidency 1988*. New York: Warner Books, 1989.

_____. *Mad as Hell: Revolt at the Ballot Box, 1992*. New York: Warner, 1993.

Gitlin, Todd. "Bites and Blips: Chunk News, Savvy Talk, and the Bifurcation of American Politics." In *Communication and Citizenship: Journalism and the Public Sphere in the New Media Age*, edited by Peter Dahlgren and Colin Sparks. London: Routledge, 1991.

Goldman, Peter, and Tony Fuller. *The Quest for the Presidency 1984*. New York: Bantam Books, 1985.

Goodwin, Richard. *Remembering America: A Voice from the Sixties*. New York: Little, Brown, 1988.

Graber, Doris. *Mass Media and American Politics*. Washington, D.C.: CQ, 1997.

_____. *Processing the News: How People Tame the Information Tide*. New York: Longman, 1984.

Greenfield, Jeff. *The Real Campaign: How the Media Missed the Story of the 1980 Campaign*. New York: Summit Books, 1982.

Hahn, Dan F. "The 1992 Carter-Bush-Perot Presidential Debates." In *Rhetorical Studies of National Political Debates, 1960–1992*, edited by Robert V. Friedenberg. 2d ed. Westport, Conn.: Praeger, 1994.

Halberstam, David. "President Video." *Esquire*, June 1976, 94–97, 130–34.

Hardy-Short, Dayle. "An Insider's View of the Constraints Affecting Geraldine Ferraro's Preparation for the 1984 Vice Presidential Debate." *Speaker and Gavel* 24 (1986): 8–22.

Hellweg, Susan A., Michael Pfau, and Steven R. Brydon. *Televised Presidential Debates. Advocacy in Contemporary America*. New York: Praeger, 1992.

Henry, William A. III. *Visions of America: How We Saw the 1984 Election*. Boston: Atlantic Monthly Press, 1985.

Hersh, Seymour M. *The Dark Side of Camelot*. Boston: Little, Brown, 1997.

Hertsgaard, Mark. *On Bended Knee: The Press and the Reagan Presidency*. New York: Farrar, Straus, Giroux, 1988.

Jackson-Beeck, Marilyn, and Robert G. Meadow. "The Triple Agenda of Presidential Debates." *Public Opinion Quarterly* 5 (1979): 173–80.

Jamieson, Kathleen Hall. *Eloquence in an Electronic Age: The Transformation of Political Speechmaking*. New York: Oxford University Press, 1988.

Jamieson, Kathleen Hall, and David S. Birdsell. *Presidential Debates: The Challenge of Creating an Informed Electorate*. New York: Oxford University Press, 1988.

Jordan, Hamilton. *Crisis: The Last Year of the Carter Presidency*. New York: Putnam's Sons, 1982.

Klein, Herbert G. *Making It Perfectly Clear: An Inside Account of Nixon's Love-Hate Relationship with the Media*. Garden City, N.Y.: Doubleday, 1980.

Kraus, Sidney. *Televised Presidential Debates and Public Policy*. Hillsdale, N.J.: Erlbaum, 1988.

—, ed. *The Great Debates: Background, Perspective, Effects*. Bloomington: Indiana University Press, 1962.

———. *The Great Debates: Carter vs. Ford, 1976*. Bloomington: Indiana University Press, 1979.

Lanoue, David J., and Peter R. Schrott. *The Joint Press Conference: The History, Impact, and Prospects of American Presidential Debates*. Westport, Conn.: Greenwood, 1991.

Lehrer, Jim. *The Last Debate*. New York: Random House, 1995.

Lemert, James B., William R. Elliott, James M. Bernstein, William L. Rosenberg, and Karl J. Nestvold. *News Verdicts, the Debates, and Presidential Campaigns*. New York: Praeger, 1991.

Martel, Myles. "Debate Preparations in the Reagan Camp: An Insider's View." *Speaker and Gavel* 18 (winter 1981): 34–46.

———. *Political Campaign Debates: Images, Strategies, and Tactics*. New York: Longman, 1983.

Matthews, Christopher. *Kennedy and Nixon: The Rivalry That Shaped Postwar America*. New York: Simon & Schuster, 1996.

Mazo, Earl, Malcom Moos, Hallock Hoffman, and Harvey Wheeler. *The Great Debates*. Santa Barbara: Center for the Study of Democratic Institutions, 1962.

Meadow, Robert G. "Televised Campaign Debates as Whistle-Stop Speeches." In *Television Coverage of the 1980 Presidential Campaign*, edited by William C. Adams. Norwood, N.J.: Ablex, 1983.

Mickelson, Sig. *From Whistle Stop to Sound Bite: Four Decades of Politics and Television*. New York: Praeger, 1989.

Mills, Stephen. "Rebuilding the Presidential Debates." *Speaker and Gavel* 24 (1986): 41–51.

Minow, Newton N., J. B. Martin, and Lee M. Mitchell. *Presidential Television.* New York: Basic Books, 1973.

Minow, Newton N., and Clifford M. Sloan. *For Great Debates.* New York: Priority Press, 1987.

Mitchell, Lee M. *With the Nation Watching: Report of the Twentieth Century Fund Task Force.* Lexington, Mass.: Heath, 1979.

Moore, Jonathan, and Janet Fraser, eds. *Campaign for President: The Managers Look At '76.* Cambridge, Mass.: Ballinger, 1977.

Moore, Jonathan, ed. *Campaign for President: The Managers Look at '84.* Dover, Mass.: Auburn House, 1986.

Nessen, Ron. *It Sure Looks Different from the Inside.* Chicago: Playboy, 1978.

Nixon, Richard M. *Six Crises.* Garden City, N.Y.: Doubleday, 1962.

_____. *RN: The Memoirs of Richard Nixon.* New York: Grossett and Dunlap, 1978.

O'Donnell, Kenneth P., and David F. Powers, with Joe McCarthy. *Johnny, We Hardly Knew Ye: Memories of John Fitzgerald Kennedy.* Boston: Little, Brown, 1972.

Patterson, Thomas E. *Out of Order.* New York: Knopf, 1993.

Quayle, Dan. *Standing Firm.* New York: HarperCollins, 1994.

Quigley, Joan. *What Does Joan Say? My Seven Years as White House Astrologer to Nancy and Ronald Reagan.* Secaucus, N.J.: Birch Lane, 1990.

Ranney, Austin, ed. *The Past and Future of Presidential Debates.* Washington, D.C.: American Enterprise Institute, 1979.

_____. *The American Elections of 1984.* New York: American Enterprise Institute, 1985.

Reagan, Nancy. *My Turn: The Memoirs of Nancy Reagan.* New York: Random House, 1989.

Reagan, Ronald. *An American Life.* New York: Simon & Schuster, 1990.

Reinsch, J. Leonard. *Getting Elected: From Radio and Roosevelt to Television and Reagan.* New York: Hippocrene Books, 1988.

Renshon, Stanley A. *High Hopes: The Clinton Presidency and the Politics of Ambition.* New York: New York University Press, 1996.

Royer, Charles T., ed. *Campaign for President: The Managers Look at '92.* Hollis, N.H.: Hollis Publishing, 1994.

Runkel, David R., ed. *Campaign for President: The Managers Look at '88.* Dover, Mass.: Auburn House, 1989.

Sauter, Kevin. "The 1976 Mondale-Dole Vice Presidential Debate." In *Rhetorical Studies of National Political Debates, 1960–1992,* edited by Robert V. Friedenberg. 2d ed. Westport, Conn.: Praeger, 1994.

Seltz, Herbert A., and Richard D. Yoakam, "Production Diary of the Debates." In *The Great Debates: Background, Perspective, Effects,* edited by Sidney Kraus. Bloomington: Indiana University Press, 1962.

_____. "Production Diary of the Debates." In *The Great Debates: Carter vs. Ford, 1976*, edited by Sidney Kraus. Bloomington: Indiana University Press, 1979.

Simon, Roger. *Roadshow*. New York: Farrar, Straus, Giroux, 1990.

_____. *Show Time*. New York: Times Books, 1998.

Smith, Craig Allen, and Kathy B. Smith, "The 1984 Reagan-Mondale Presidential Debates." In *Rhetorical Studies of National Political Debates, 1960–1992*, edited by Robert V. Friedenberg. 2d ed. Westport, Conn.: Praeger, 1994.

Smith, Howard K. *Events Leading Up to My Death*. New York: St. Martin's, 1996.

Speakes, Larry. *Speaking Out: Inside the Reagan White House*. New York: Scribner's, 1980.

Stanton, Frank. "A CBS View." In *The Great Debates: Background, Perspective, Effects*, edited by Sidney Kraus. Bloomington: Indiana University Press, 1962

Swerdlow, Joel L. *Beyond Debate: A Paper on Televised Presidential Debates*. New York: Twentieth Century Fund, 1984.

Swerdlow, Joel L., ed. *Presidential Debates: 1988 and Beyond*. Washington, D.C.: Congressional Quarterly, 1987.

Trent, Judith S., "The 1984 Bush-Ferraro Vice Presidential Debate." In *Rhetorical Studies of National Political Debates, 1960–1992*, edited by Robert V. Friedenberg. 2d ed. Westport, Conn.: Praeger, 1994.

Trent, Judith S., and Robert V. Friedenberg. *Political Campaign Communication: Principles and Practices*. 3d ed. Westport, Conn.: Praeger, 1995.

Troy, Gil. *See How They Ran: The Changing Role of the Presidential Candidate*. New York: Free Press, 1991.

White, Theodore. *The Making of the President 1960*. New York: Atheneum, 1961.

Witcover, Jules. *Marathon: The Pursuit of the Presidency 1972–1976*. New York: Viking, 1977.

Schedule of Televised Presidential and Vice Presidential Debates: 1960–1996

1960

JOHN F. KENNEDY AND RICHARD NIXON

26 September: Chicago
7 October: Washington, D.C.
13 October: Los Angeles (Nixon) and New York City (Kennedy)
21 October: New York City
(Format for all: press panel)

1976

JIMMY CARTER AND GERALD FORD

23 September: Philadelphia
6 October: San Francisco
22 October: Williamsburg, Virginia

WALTER MONDALE AND BOB DOLE

15 October: Houston
(Format for all: press panel)

1980

RONALD REAGAN AND JOHN ANDERSON

21 September: Baltimore

RONALD REAGAN AND JIMMY CARTER

28 October: Cleveland
(Format for both: press panel)

1984

RONALD REAGAN AND WALTER MONDALE

7 October: Louisville
21 October: Kansas City

GEORGE BUSH AND GERALDINE FERRARO

11 October: Philadelphia
(Format for all: press panel)

1988

GEORGE BUSH AND MICHAEL DUKAKIS

25 September: Wake Forest, North Carolina
13 October: Los Angeles

DAN QUAYLE AND LLOYD BENTSEN

5 October: Omaha
(Format for all: press panel)

1992

BILL CLINTON, GEORGE BUSH, AND ROSS PEROT

11 October: St. Louis (Format: press panel)
15 October: Richmond (Format: town hall)
19 October: East Lansing (Format: single moderator, first half;
press panel, second half)

AL GORE, DAN QUAYLE, AND JAMES STOCKDALE

13 October: Atlanta (Format: single moderator)

1996

BILL CLINTON AND BOB DOLE

6 October: Hartford (Format: single moderator)
16 October: San Diego (Format: town hall)

AL GORE AND JACK KEMP

9 October: St. Petersburg (Format: single moderator)

Index

Ailes, Roger, 51, 53, 55, 60, 64, 90
Albright, Madeleine, 61
Allen, Frederic, 129
Alterman, Eric, 180
Anderson, John, 59, 73, 77, 106,
    108–109, 166–167; *see also* Reagan-
    Anderson debate
Apple, R. W. Jr., 115
Arterton, Christopher, 188
"Ask George Bush" forums, 31
Asman, Robert, 163, 166, 169
Atwater, Lee, 50, 212
Audio failure in Ford-Carter debate,
    71, 148–150, 177–178, 182
Ayres, B. Drummond, 197

Bailey, Doug, 45
Bailey, Pearl, 154
Baker, James A. 3d, 21, 23–24, 26–27,
    31, 32, 35–36, 47–48, 74, 126, 136,
    177, 186
Baker, Russell, 175–176
Barnes, Fred, 129
Barnouw, Erik, 6, 96

Begala, Paul, 30
Benefits of presidential debates, 205–
    209
Bentsen, Lloyd, 31, 41–42, 84, 91,
    113–114
Bentsen-Quayle debate (1988),
    113–115, 129–30, 132, 135, 153, 213
Berger, Marilyn, 131, 191
Berke, Richard L., 31, 77, 151, 184, 185
Bernstein, Elliot, 150
Berquist, Goodwin, 208–209
Birdsell, David S., 207, 219
Black, Charles, 21, 43
Black, Christine M., 48, 112
Bode, Ken, 84
Boorstin, Daniel, 209–210
Boyd, Gerald, 83–84
Boyd, Robert, 132–133
Bradley, Bill, 118
Bradley, Ed, 85
Brinkley, David, 85, 149, 177, 191
Broder, David S., 41, 71, 102, 106, 113,
    115, 118, 122, 125, 144, 178–179, 185,
    194, 215–216

Brokaw, Tom, 102, 120, 125, 130, 132, 184, 195, 199

Brountas, Paul, 27

Brown, Janet, 24, 145, 152, 153, 168–169

Brown, Jerry, 46

Brown, Pat, 53

Bruno, Hal, 121, 131, 134, 138, 141–142, 183, 185, 189

Brydon, Stephen R., 52

Buckley, Christopher, 123

Buckley, William F. Jr., 18

Bush, Barbara, 43, 74, 76

Bush, George, 18–20, 42–43, 48, 50, 54–55, 74, 91–92, 113, 124, 126–127, 130, 134–135, 143–144, 159, 196–197, 199, 203; debating Ferraro, 46–47, 75–76, 109–112, 198–199; glancing at watch, 39, 63–64, 110, 165–166, 178, 205; see also "Chicken George"; Clinton-Bush-Perot debates

Bush-Dukakis debates (1988), 110, 112–113, 130, 133–135, 136–137, 153

Bush-Ferraro debate (1984), 46–47, 109–112

Bush, Prescott, 50

Caddell, Patrick, 17, 44, 45, 49, 72, 81, 109

Campbell, Carroll, 79

Cannon, Lou, 26, 40, 53, 60

Carlin, Diana, 47, 51, 53, 179, 208, 214, 221

Carson, Johnny, 16

Carruthers, William, 57, 162, 164

Carter, Amy, 59, 102, 198–199

Carter, Jimmy, 15–17, 26, 31–32, 38–39, 40, 45, 49, 52, 57, 58–59, 69, 71, 72, 80–81, 83, 88, 89, 100–102, 148–150, 154, 161, 198, 203; see also Ford-Carter debates

Carter-Reagan debate (1980), 16–18, 44, 52–53, 101–102, 106–107, 166–167, 180, 200

Carville, James, 42, 110

Castro, Fidel, 67

Cater, Douglass, 30

CBS, 1, 3, 125

Chancellor, John, 114, 145, 193

Cheney, Richard, 192

Chicago Daily News, 175

"Chicken George," 19–20, 27, 217

Chromak, Leon, 160

Ciccone, F. Richard, 106

Clark, Tony, 85

Clifford, Clark, 97

Clinton, Bill, 19–21, 42–43, 44, 46, 50–51, 55–56, 75, 85–86, 92, 105, 116–117, 144, 159, 162–163, 178, 181–182, 211, 217; town hall debates, 30, 46, 53, 63–64, 110, 116–117, 143, 157–158

Clinton-Bush-Perot debates (1992), 50, 63–64, 110, 116–117, 119–120, 138–139, 142–144, 145–146, 200, 205, 207, 211

Clinton-Dole debates (1996), 50–51, 105, 117, 139–140, 146–147, 153, 158

Clinton, Hillary, 46, 75, 92, 181

CNN, 109, 166–167

Coelho, Tony, 47, 194

Commager, Henry Steele, 209, 210

Commission on Presidential Debates, 20, 22, 24, 30, 33, 78, 142, 149, 161, 168, 216–217

Compton, Ann, 133

Control room, 6, 167–168

Corrado, Anthony, 219

Corry, John, 103

Cousins, Norman, 203

Cox, Archibald, 4

Cramer, Richard Ben, 86–87, 104

Cranston, Alan, 90–91
Cronkite, Walter, 80, 173, 178, 183, 190
Crowley, Monica, 146
C-SPAN, 79, 117, 220
Cuomo, Mario, 53

Dale, Billy, 43
Deaver, Michael, 17, 28, 51, 59–60, 61,
    157, 183
Devine, Tad, 84, 115
Diskin, Sonny, 164
Doerner, William R., 112
Dole, Bob, 26, 44, 50–51, 54, 56, 75,
    86–87, 88, 102–103, 104–105, 117,
    122, 123, 140, 158, 163, 182–183;
    "Democrat wars" statement, 39,
    104–105, 132, 135–136; see also
    Clinton-Dole debates
Dole, Elizabeth, 88, 158, 163, 182
Dole-Mondale debate (1976), 47,
    102–103, 104–105, 131, 135–136
Donahue, Phil, 86, 117
Donaldson, Sam, 42, 56, 71, 72, 89, 92,
    123
Donilon, Thomas, 39, 43, 50, 63, 153,
    156, 159–160, 187–188
Donovan, Robert J., 68–69
Dowd, Maureen, 62, 158, 196–197
Drew, Elizabeth, 29, 49, 70, 100,
    101–102, 111, 114, 115, 128, 211–212
Drummond, Roscoe, 68
Dukakis, Kitty, 113, 133–134, 165
Dukakis, Michael, 19, 32, 43, 44, 48,
    50, 53, 62–63, 74, 82–83, 91, 112–113,
    203; "raped and murdered" ques-
    tion, 39, 110, 133–135, 165, 197–198;
    see also Bush-Dukakis debates
Duncan, Dayton, 74
Duval, Michael, 15, 73

Eckart, Dennis, 41–42

Eisenhower, Dwight D., 14, 129
Ellis, Harris, 130
Estrich, Susan, 63, 64, 113, 213
Expectations-setting before presi-
    dential debates, 72–76, 79–87,
    103
Evans, Rowland, 17

Fahrenkopf, Frank J. Jr., 33, 147, 153
Faw, Bob, 108
Federal Communications
    Commission, 15
Ferraro, Geraldine, 32, 46–47, 61–62,
    75–76, 109, 111–112, 199; see also
    Bush-Ferraro debate
Field, Sally, 153
Finch, Bob, 56
Fineman, Howard, 87
Fiorentino, Imero, 156
Fisher, Walter, 15
Fitzwater, Marlin, 75
Fleming, Bob, 129
Flowers, Gennifer, 43
Ford, Betty, 88–89, 154
Ford-Carter debates (1976), 45,
    99–101, 131–132, 148–150, 154,
    177–178, 210
Ford, Gerald, 15, 31–32, 33, 52, 57–58,
    69, 77, 88, 99–101, 153, 162, 182–183,
    203; Eastern Europe statement, 39,
    71, 130, 132, 186, 190–193, 213; see
    also Audio failure
Formats for presidential debates,
    29–31, 33; direct confrontation,
    217–218; reporter panels, 30, 126,
    131–133; single moderator, 31,
    137–143; town hall, 30–31, 142–144,
    145–147, 221
Fouhy, Ed, 30–31, 150, 151, 153, 168
Frankel, Max, 130
Frederick, Pauline, 133

Friedenberg, Robert V., 44
Fuller, Tony, 112

Gannon, James, 100
Gergen, David, 40
Germmond, Jack, 26, 43, 46, 103, 116, 120
Giscard d'Estaing, Valéry, 54
Gitlin, Todd, 9
Goldman, Peter, 112
Goldwater, Barry, 14
Goodwin, Doris Kearns, 96
Goodwin, Robert, 25, 33, 158
Goldenson, Leonard, 2
Goodman, Ellen, 109
Goodman, Walter, 138, 203, 206
Gore, Al, 34, 56, 74, 83, 115, 117–119, 141
Gore-Kemp debate (1996), 86, 118, 122–123, 140
Gore-Perot NAFTA debate, 119
Gore-Quayle-Stockdale debate (1992), 115–116, 118, 120–122, 141–142, 151
Gore, Tipper, 118
Graber, Doris, 207
Greenfield, Jeff, 80, 84, 118, 126–127, 145, 185, 205
Greenfield, Meg, 115
Greer, Frank, 157
Gregory, Bettina, 198–199
Greider, William, 101, 105
Groer, Annie, 126, 127, 137, 150–151

Hahn, Dan F., 55
Hagerty, James, 14
Halberstam, David, 5, 13
Hall, Leonard, 13
Hall, Marisa, 145
Hanna, Lee, 23
Hannon, Tom, 184
Harian, Victoria, 35, 156, 160

Harris, John, 66
Healy, Robert, 111
Hegedus, Chris, 186
Height of presidential debaters, 31–32, 43, 162
Hembreck, Valerie, 205
Henry, William, 103, 107
Hersh, Seymour, 97
Hertsgaard, Mark, 194
Hewitt, Don, 2, 3, 6, 7–8, 67, 210
Higgins, George V., 118
Hilton, Jack, 48
Hoffman, David, 109
Hoge, James, 54, 135–136
Holding rooms, 158–159, 167
Horton, Willie, 43
Hume, Brit, 85, 92, 103, 111, 119, 129–130, 132, 186
Humor in presidential debates, 41, 49, 50, 54–55, 104, 211
Humphrey, Hubert H., 96, 99

Ifill, Gwen, 46
Incumbents, 44–46, 99
Influence of presidential debates on voting, 212–214
Inside Politics, 78–79
Institutionalization of presidential debates, 18, 21, 99, 216–217
Internet, 220

Jackson-Beeck, Marilyn, 215
Jagoda, Barry, 164
Jamieson, Bob, 71
Jamieson, Kathleen Hall, 38, 98, 207, 219
Jaroslovsky, Rich, 194
Jarriel, Tom, 77, 89
Jennings, Peter, 86, 125, 128, 130, 137
Johnson, Lyndon, 14–15, 28, 96, 173
Jones, Phil, 87

Jordan, Hamilton, 59, 191
Judd, Jackie, 90, 197

Kaiser, Robert G., 77, 188
Kalb, Marvin, 190
Kantor, Mickey, 21, 24, 30, 46, 78–79, 216
Karayn, James, 23
Kelly, Jack, 71, 150
Kelly, Michael, 110, 120
Kemp, Jack, 47, 86, 122–123, 140; *see also* Gore-Kemp debate
Kennedy, Jacqueline, 4–5, 8
Kennedy, John F., 1–10, 14, 28, 32, 42, 44, 56, 66–70, 88, 96–98, 101, 111, 127, 129, 211
Kennedy-Nixon debates (1960), 1–10, 65–70, 96–99, 129, 131, 160–161, 163–164, 167, 173–176, 200, 209–210, 222
Kennedy, Robert F., 106, 160, 181
Khrushchev, Nikita, 4, 67, 98
King, Larry, 85, 119, 144
King, Susan, 78
Kirk, Paul G. Jr., 144, 153, 218
Kiker, Douglas, 70, 177–178
Kissinger, Henry, 198
Klein, Herbert G., 8, 14, 28, 174–175, 180–181
Klein, Joe, 51, 117
Kohut, Andy, 207
Kolbert, Elizabeth, 118, 121
Koppel, Ted, 188–189
Kramer, Michael, 87
Kraus, Sidney, 32–33, 210–211
Kristol, William, 122–123
Kuhn, Mark, 220
Kurtz, Howard, 182, 189

Lanoue, David J., 213, 214
Last Debate, The, 137

Laxalt, Paul, 60
"Lazy Shave," 4
League of Women Voters, 16, 22, 34–35, 104, 136, 156, 157, 164
Lecterns, 31–33, 156
Lehrer, Jim, 36, 105, 122, 125–126, 136–137, 138–141, 147, 149, 153, 168
Lehrer, Kate, 139
Lelyveld, Joseph, 69–70, 149
Lemert, James B., 180, 184
Leone, Richard C., 29, 50, 51, 53
Lewis, Fulton, 68
LiBretto, John, 162–163, 165–166, 168, 169
Lighting, 157, 160, 163
Limbaugh, Rush, 143
Limitations of presidential debates, 209–212
Lincoln-Douglas debates, 66, 69
Lindsey, Beverly, 157
Lippmann, Walter, 14, 204
Lisagor, Peter, 174
Lodge, Henry Cabot, 7, 28, 96
Los Angeles Times, 176

Makeup, 3–4, 99, 175, 195
Mankiewicz, Frank, 53
Margolis, Jon, 106, 125, 132
Martel, Myles, 40
Martin, Lynn, 85
Mashek, John, 120, 127, 137
Matalin, Mary, 109
Mazo, Earl, 14
McCarthy, Joseph, 50
McCurry, Mike, 75, 186
McGill, Ralph, 176
McGovern, George, 99
McGrory, Mary, 107, 122, 127
Meadow, Robert G., 206, 215
Meany, George, 54
Mears, Walter, 131, 132

Memorandum of agreement, 24–25, 33, 36, 142, 153, 155, 157, 161, 165, 166, 168

Mickelson, Sig, 4, 6–7, 22

Miklaszewski, Jim, 105

Miller, Ron, 188

Mills, Stephen, 212

Mitchell, Andrea, 127, 128, 133–134

Mitterand, Francois, 54

Mock debates, see Preparation for presidential debates

Moderators of presidential debates: role of, 137–144, selection of, 34, 142, 144

Mondale, Joan, 204

Mondale, Walter, 18, 41, 42, 46, 49–50, 72, 88, 95, 102–104, 107, 129, 135–136, 156, 157, 195–196, 202, 204, 213; see also Dole-Mondale debate; Reagan-Mondale debates

Morris, Dick, 117

Morton, Bruce, 193

Moyers, Bill, 133, 137

Mudd, Roger, 81–82, 90–91, 178, 183–184, 186

Mulford, Clay, 25, 64, 120

Myers, Lisa, 56, 117

NBC, 125, 177–178

Negotiations, 21–37, 154, 216; Bush-Dukakis, 24, 32; Bush-Ferraro, 32; Carter-Reagan, 23, 26–27, 77–78; Clinton-Bush-Perot, 27, 30–31, 216–217; Clinton-Dole, 24, 78–79, 157–158, 217Ford-Carter, 23, 31–32, 33, 156; Kennedy-Nixon, 22, 28, 32; Reagan-Mondale, 23–24, 27, 29, 156–157;

Nelson, Jack, 131–132

Nessen, Ron, 52, 77, 100, 177, 182, 192, 193

Newman, Edwin, 103–104, 148–149

New York Times, 187

Nichols, Bill, 185

Nightline, 188–189

Nixon, Patricia, 8, 175

Nixon, Richard M., 1–10, 13–15, 28, 32, 56–57, 67, 88, 98–99, 110, 116, 119, 129, 146; see also Kennedy-Nixon debates

"Nixopedia," 56

Nolan, Martin F., 123

Novak, Robert, 17

Nyhan, David, 113

O'Connor, John J., 188

Oliphant, Pat, 16

Oliphant, Thomas, 48, 112, 117

Oreskes, Michael, 184

Paar, Jack, 1, 67

Packwood, Robert, 62

Paley, William, 2

Panelists in presidential debates: journalists as panel members, 125–127; 1984 selection controversy, 35, 136; panelists' questions, 126–130; panelists' strategies, 131–133; role of, 124–125; selection of, 34–36

Participation in presidential debates, 13–21; by Bush, 18–20; by Carter, 16–17, 77; by Ford, 15; by Kennedy, 14; by Nixon, 13–15; by Perot, 20–21 by Reagan, 16–18;

Patterson, Eugene, 99

Patterson, Thomas, 67–68, 80, 192, 207

Pennebaker, D. A., 186

Perkins, Jack, 189–190

Perot, Ross, 46, 55, 63–64, 83, 85, 119–120, 121, 139, 159, 162, 211; see also Clinton-Bush-Perot debates

Perry, James M., 194
Pfister, Walter, 164
Phillips, Mark, 205
Pierce, Charles P., 204
Pinkerton, James J., 56
Polling, postdebate, 112, 114, 176,
    187–189, 192–193, 196, 207
Polsby, Nelson, 9
Popkin, Sam, 53–54, 58–59, 212
Powell, Jody, 23, 85, 177–178
Preparation for presidential debates:
    Bentsen, 41–42; Bush, 64; Carter,
    58–59; Clinton, 63–64, 75, 155–156,
    162–163; Dole, 64, 75, 163; Dukakis,
    62–63; Ferraro, 61–62; Ford, 57–58,
    101; Kennedy, 56–57, Quayle, 62;
    Reagan, 59–61
Press coverage of negotiations and
    rehearsals, 76–79, 161–162, 218
Press coverage, postdebate: Bentsen-
    Quayle, 186, 196–197; Bush-
    Dukakis, 184, 185, 186, 197–198;
    Bush-Ferraro, 183–184, 199; Carter-
    Reagan, 180, 198–199; Clinton-
    Bush-Perot, 186–187; Clinton-
    Dole, 181–182, 186Ford-Carter,
    182–183, 190–193; Kennedy-Nixon,
    173–176, 180–181, 187; Reagan-
    Mondale, 183, 186, 193–196
Press coverage, predebate: 79–88, 219;
    Bentsen-Quayle, 74, 83–84; Bush-
    Ferraro, 75–76, 83; Carter-Reagan,
    73, 80–81; Clinton-Bush-Perot,
    84–85, 86; Clinton-Dole, 75, 86–87;
    debate day coverage, 87–92Ford-
    Carter, 69–71, 72–73, 85; Gore-
    Kemp, 86; Gore-Quayle-Stockdale,
    75, 84, 85; Kennedy-Nixon, 65–69;
    Reagan-Anderson, 73; Reagan-
    Mondale, 71–72, 81–82
Primary debates: Clinton, 46, 117;

Gore, 118; Kennedy, 96; Reagan,
    106
Props and notes, use of, 33–34, 160–161

Quarles, Norma, 126
Quayle, Dan, 31, 34, 47, 62, 74, 83–84,
    90–91, 114–116, 118, 124, 129–130,
    135, 141, 186, 196–197, 203, 213;
    "You're no Jack Kennedy," 39,
    41–42, 62, 114–115, 132; see also
    Bentsen-Quayle debate; Gore-
    Quayle-Stockdale debate
Quayle, Marilyn, 74
Quigley, Joan, 28
Quinn, Jane Bryant, 133

Radio audience for presidential
    debates, 5, 176
Radio news coverage of 1960 debates,
    68
Radziwill, Lee, 4
Rafshoon, Gerald, 32
Raines, Howell, 193
Ranney, Austin, 44, 196
Rather, Dan, 89–90, 92
Ratings for presidential debates, 5,
    200–201, 249n1, 249n2
Reaction shots, 6–7, 163–167
Reagan-Anderson debate (1980), 16,
    29, 89, 106, 108–109
Reagan-Mondale debates (1984), 41,
    42, 49–50, 53, 102–104, 107, 136,
    203–204
Reagan, Nancy, 28, 29, 60, 89, 195
Reagan, Ronald, 16–18, 28, 29, 38–39,
    40–41, 44, 45–46, 49–50, 52–53,
    59–61, 72, 82, 83, 89, 101–102, 103,
    105–107, 108, 128, 129, 136, 157, 186,
    211, 213; age issue, 71–72, 107,
    193–196, 203–204, 212, 213; see also
    Carter-Reagan debate

Reagan, Ronald Jr., 204

Reasoner, Harry, 148, 190

Redford, Robert, 57

Reed, Scott, 75

Rehearsal, *see* Preparation for presidential debates

Reinsch, J. Leonard, 32

Renshon, Stanley, 53

Richards, Ann, 114

Ridings, Dorothy, 35, 136

Roberts, Cokie, 119–120, 208

Robinson, Michael, 47, 146–147

Rogers, Ted, 2–4, 6

Rosen, Jeffrey, 117

Rosenberg, Howard, 189

Rosenstiel, Thomas, 186, 195

Routman, Dan, 20

Ruge, Daniel, 195

Rumsfeld, Donald, 78–79

Russert, Tim, 181–182

Sack, Kevin, 84

Safire, William, 115, 118

Sarnoff, Robert, 2, 29

Sauter, Kevin, 54

Sawyer, Diane, 35

Scheduling of presidential debates, 16–17, 20, 26–29

Schieffer, Bob, 92, 179, 184, 191, 196, 197

Schlesinger, Arthur Jr., 4

Schneider, William, 86, 189

Schrott, Peter R., 213, 214

Schwartz, Tony, 48

Scripted moments in presidential debates, 40–41, 52–56; Bentsen's "You're no Jack Kennedy," 41–42, 114–115; Reagan's age joke, 41, 128; Reagan's handshake with Carter, 38–39; Reagan's "There you go again," 38–41, 42, 213

Seltz, Herbert A., 22, 154, 156, 165

Sets for presidential debates, 16, 151, 160, 162; *see also* Lecterns

Shain, Percy, 174

Shales, Tom, 105, 115, 116, 118, 120, 136, 193

Shapiro, Walter, 134

Shaw, Bernard, 30, 39, 63, 110, 113, 124, 133–135, 165, 185, 197–198

Sheehan, Michael, 63

Sherr, Lynn, 83

Sidey, Hugh, 103

Simon, Roger, 27, 63–64, 198

Simpson, Carole, 83, 138, 142–144, 146, 147

Six Crises, 8, 129

Smith, Craig, 19

Smith, Craig Allen, and Kathy B., 53

Smith, Hedrick, 108

Smith, Howard K., 2, 5, 7, 133

Smith, Terence, 77–78

Sorensen, Theodore, 49

Speakes, Larry, 182

Spinners, 85, 176, 180–187

Spivak, Lawrence, 205

Sponsorship of presidential debates, 22, 152, 216–217

Springer, Brian, 144

Squier, Robert, 36–37

Stahl, Lesley, 91, 115, 177–178

Stanton, Frank, 4, 66, 202

Steele, Richard, 101

Steeper, Fred, 144, 193

Stephanopoulos, George, 27, 50, 86

Stockdale, James B., 20, 85, 118, 120–122, 141, 151; *see also* Gore-Quayle-Stockdale debate

Stockdale, James Bond 2d, 121

Stockman, David, 40, 59

Strategic considerations in presidential debates: attitude toward oppo-

nent, 48–51; likability, 48, 82–83; rhetoric, 52–56; surprise maneuvers, 42–43; *see also* Humor in presidential debates
Strauss, Robert, 78, 177
Strout, Richard L., 174

Technical checks, 4, 43, 159–163
Teeley, Peter, 76
Teeter, Robert, 192–193
Third party and independent debaters, 16, 20, 108–109, 119–122, 166–167
Thomas, Lowell, 68
Thomason, Harry, 27, 63
Tillotson, Mary, 84
Town hall debates, *see* Formats for presidential debates
Town hall questioners, 145–147
Trent, Judith S., 47
Trewhitt, Henry, 128
Treyz, Oliver, 2
Troy, Gil, 107
Truman, Harry S., 51, 97
Twentieth Century Fund, 15

Usry, Kimberly, 145

Van Drehle, David, 27, 84
Vanocur, Sander, 129, 131, 133
Venues for presidential debates, 152–154, 157–158
Vice presidential debates, 47–48, 83
Von Fremd, Mike, 85

Voorhis, Jerry, 14

Wallace, George, 99
Wall Street Journal, 125
Walters, Barbara, 71, 131, 133, 136, 189, 198
Walthall, Denton, 145
Warner, Margaret, 48, 133
Warren, Charles, 127
War Room, The, 186
Washington Post, 125, 189
WBBM, 1–7, 151, 185
Weaver, Warren, 113–114
Weinraub, Bernard, 82
Westfeldt, Wallace, 99
Wheeler, Harvey, 97, 98–99, 210
White, Jack, 126
White, Theodore, 5–6, 9
Will, George, 79, 110, 115, 118, 123, 180
Williamson, Brady, 155, 156, 158–159, 166
Wilson, Bill, 6
Winfrey, Oprah, 144
Wirthlin, Richard, 17, 41, 44, 45–46
Witcover, Jules, 26, 43, 45, 46, 70, 100, 103, 116, 120
Woodruff, Judy, 78–79, 89, 132, 133, 135
Woods, Rose Mary, 8
Wooten, James, 154, 194–195

Yankelovich, Daniel, 107
Yoakam, Richard D., 22, 154, 156, 165

Zimbalist, Efrem Jr., 175